SOUTHBURY
THROUGH TIME

Remnants of Our Past

MELINDA K. ELLIOTT

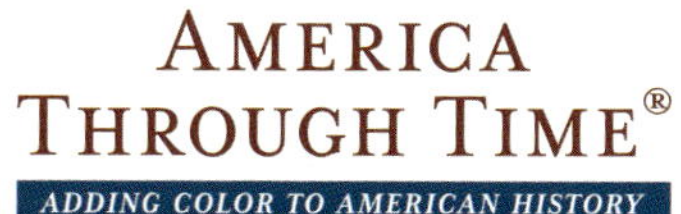

This book is dedicated to all the custodians of Southbury's history, past and present

America Through Time is an imprint of Fonthill Media LLC
www.through-time.com
office@through-time.com

Published by Arcadia Publishing by arrangement with Fonthill Media LLC
For all general information, please contact Arcadia Publishing:
Telephone: 843-853-2070
Fax: 843-853-0044
E-mail: sales@arcadiapublishing.com
For customer service and orders:
Toll-Free 1-888-313-2665

www.arcadiapublishing.com

First published 2019

ISBN 978-1-63500-085-6

Typeset in Mrs Eaves XL Serif Narrow
Printed and bound in England

FOREWORDS

> The world is full of obvious things which nobody by any chance ever observes.
>
> S. Holmes, in *The Hound of the Baskervilles* by Arthur Conan Doyle

You hold in your hand a collection of historic artifacts collected from a local point-of-view. These things have a story to tell of who we are, where we have been, and how we got to be here. When we wish to connect to the past we may do so with varied sentiment: either with nostalgia, aesthetic sentiment, or academic curiosity. But at some time, we all yearn to connect.

However you feel, these objects supply solid evidence of the activities of those who came before us. They describe their lives and tell us what was important to them. Some are quite unique, some are more common, and some are irreplaceable and one-of-a-kind. Hence, it is wise to make a record of them in some form. Here, I trust, that objective is met.

John Dwyer
Southbury Town Historian

I am so very pleased to support this wonderful book. As you will see, Melinda has painstakingly pulled together many of the wonderful pictures which depict life in Southbury. For anyone who is not aware, Southbury has an incredibly rich history. From its pre-Revolutionary war history to the present, Southbury and its residents have played a role in the development of our country. The Hinman family and others had a vital role in the Revolutionary War; Russian expatriates with names like Tolstoy, Sikorsky, and Grebenstchikoff, created Russian Village; and in 1937, the entire town stood up to the German-American Bund (the Nazis) and denied them their pseudo-military camp.

There are so many examples that I would invite you to visit the Southbury Historical Society Museum to learn more. As time has progressed, the unfortunate reality is that many of our tangible historical landmarks have not survived. Nevertheless, it will be through the efforts of our town's historians, including Melinda, that we will maintain our connection to the past. We have a lot to be proud of in Southbury. I know that you will find Melinda's work to be well-researched for sure, but she has gone a step further by bringing our wonderful past to life.

James J. Flaherty, Jr.
President
Southbury Historical Society

Acknowledgments

All books with historical photographs rely on people and organizations from earlier days who had the foresight to take the pictures and preserve them. The Southbury Historical Society has been the repository for a large number of photographs and slides, donated by the residents through the years. Many of the pictures are not labeled with the photographer's name or the person who donated them, but some are in collections attributed to the photographer. Items from the following collections were used in this book: Edward Coer (EC), Dr. William Breg (WB), Katherine Stone Leavensworth (KSL), and Ray Stiles (RS), and will be notated. Unless cited, all other photographs are from the general photograph collections of Southbury Historical Society, or from the author's personal files.

All of the contemporary color photographs were taken by myself or my husband, Ray. As always, Ray has been by my side this whole journey and I could not have completed this book without his help.

One person who was always willing to answer "one more question" is John Dwyer, Town Historian. He has been instrumental in finding elusive answers, and re-checking the facts, in case I missed something.

This Southbury Historical Society board of directors have been a constant encouragement and willing to answer my queries, no matter how silly they seemed to those whose family histories span the whole timeline of Southbury.

Finally, thank you to my husband, children, and grandchildren, who are all exceptionally talented cheerleaders and sales people for my books.

Contents

About the Author

In her second book for America Through Time/Fonthill Media, Melinda K. Elliott has once again matched old photographs with current ones to tell the story. This time she explores the town of Southbury, Connecticut, looking for old and hidden remnants of the town's 350-year-old history in order to learn their tales. Melinda is involved in several historical endeavors, and is always involved with historical research. She wrote a children's book called *Southbury for Young Historians* that was illustrated by a second-grade class. Melinda and her husband have three children and six grandchildren (with another on the way) that they love to spoil. They enjoy historically themed road trips, and are always on the lookout for old grist mills, covered bridges, and one-room schoolhouses.

INTRODUCTION

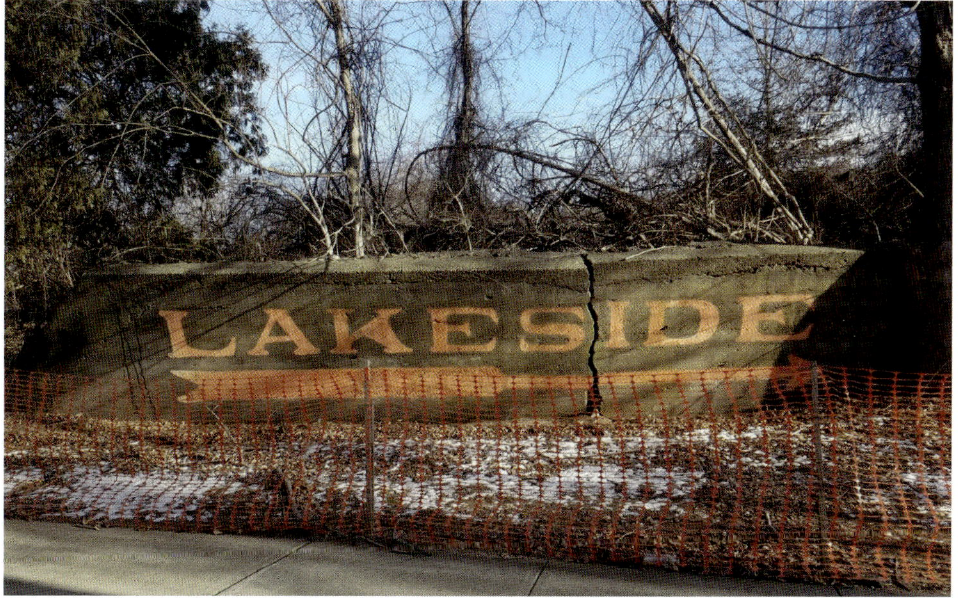

(Photograph courtesy of Charles Rosa.)

In May of 2017, a piece of Southbury's history disappeared. Maybe it wasn't ancient compared to the first houses in the town, but as far as most of us were concerned, it had always been there, standing along the roadside, silently giving direction to those seeking the way. As the town grew and changed to keep up with the times, there was comfort in seeing this remnant of our past.

I started looking around the town to see what else would be missed if it suddenly vanished. With Southbury's rich history spanning 345 years, there were bound to be thousands of remnants and reminders of our earlier existence. Of course, we can point to the beautiful old houses on Main Street North and in South Britain that are still standing, but what is left of everyday life from earlier centuries, the industries, the farmers, and the common man?

My quest was to find things we see in our everyday life as we meander throughout Southbury. That translated into my driving up and down every street, looking for potential remnants. The back roads revealed old stone fences, barns, and foundations, but could the main roads also show us the past? Actually, yes. The town was built following the old route known as the "Indian Path" or "Pomperaug Trail" which is now called Main Street North and is full of historical importance.

The next questions to consider were: "What is history?" and "What is considered historical?" Does an item need to be over 100 years old to be part of our history? Or can something from 1920 fit into that category? My criteria turned out to be: something that baby boomers would say, "It has always been there."

A historical item cannot be measured only by dates and years, but by the lives that were changed or affected by it. Generations of Southbury residents may have heard the story of an artifact from their grandparents; however, the newcomers and the younger generations may not even know of its existence. It is of vital importance that we share these items and stories because they connect us to the past and to help us understand history and the people who came before us.

The goal of this book is to hold a magnifying glass in front of various items, places, and houses of Southbury, to expose the mysteries of the remnants of our past.

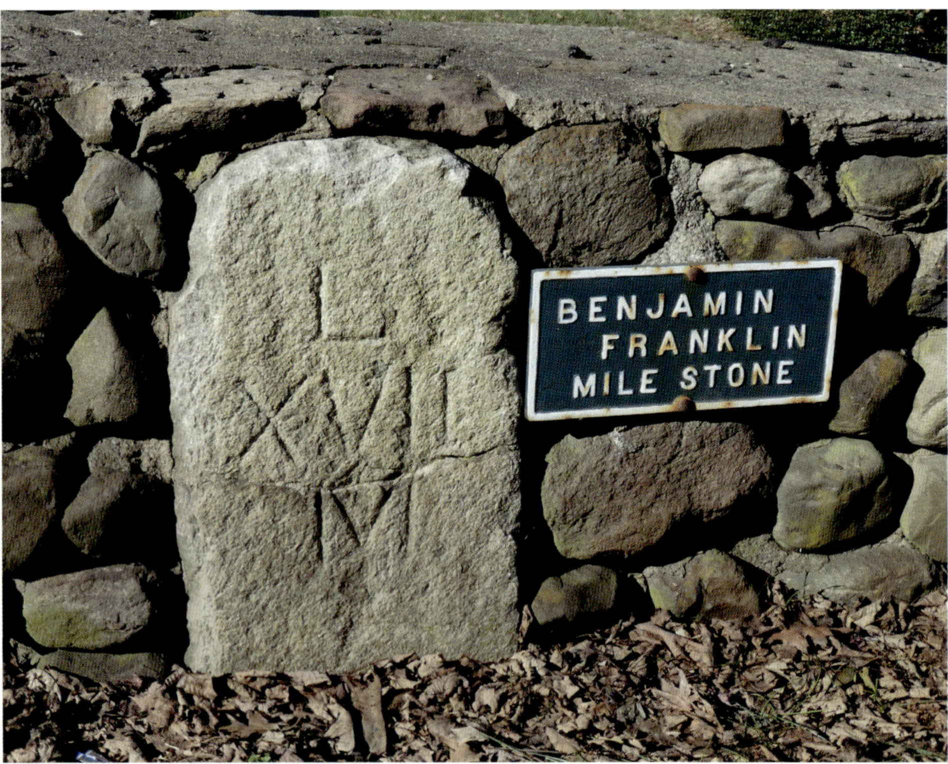

A few steps north of the Southbury border, the Benjamin Franklin milestone markers were placed every mile. Even though there were likely milestones through Southbury, too, none can be found at this time.

1

SOUTHBURY

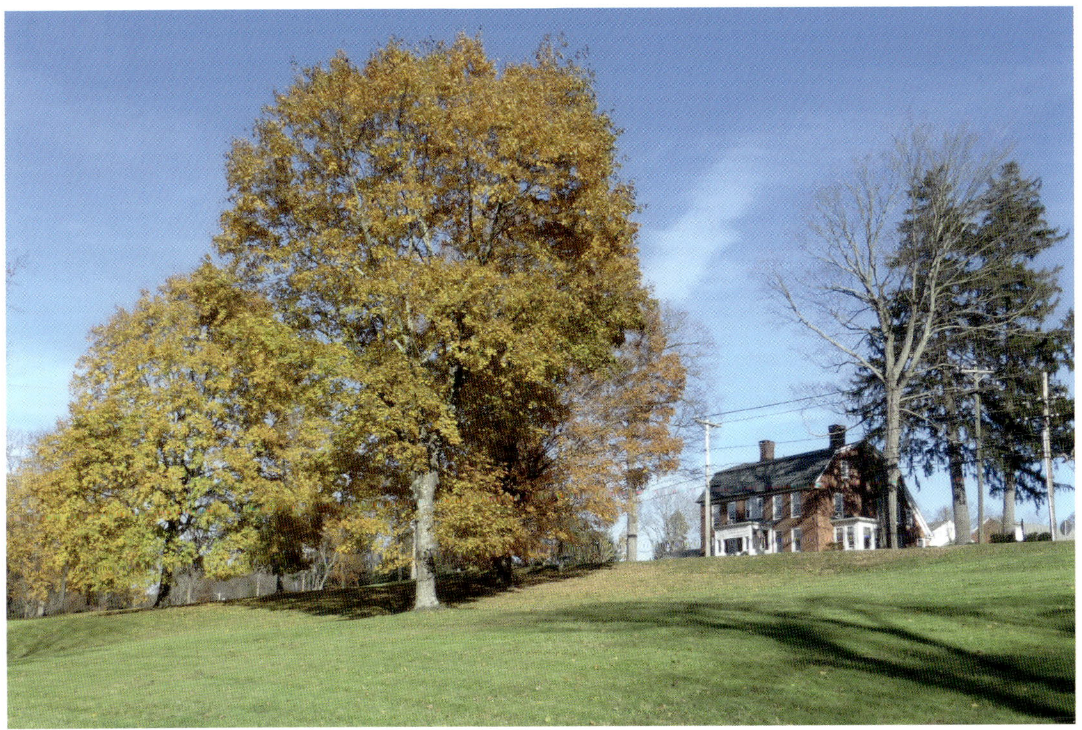

The first houses built in Southbury were located on the white oak plains where the settlers spent the first night in 1673. The land was a beautiful, fertile, level area with over 300 oaks scattered throughout. Even though it seemed a perfect place for homes, the spring freshet came through and washed away their efforts. Realizing that the location was not safe, new homes were built along the path to Woodbury, now Main Street North, where they still stand in the White Oak district.

The town continued to grow southward, towards what was then called the Bullet Hill district. The road split there, with one path going to Southford, and ultimately New Haven, while the other led to the ferry at Sandy Hook. This chapter follows the road and our history along Main Street North and Main Street South.

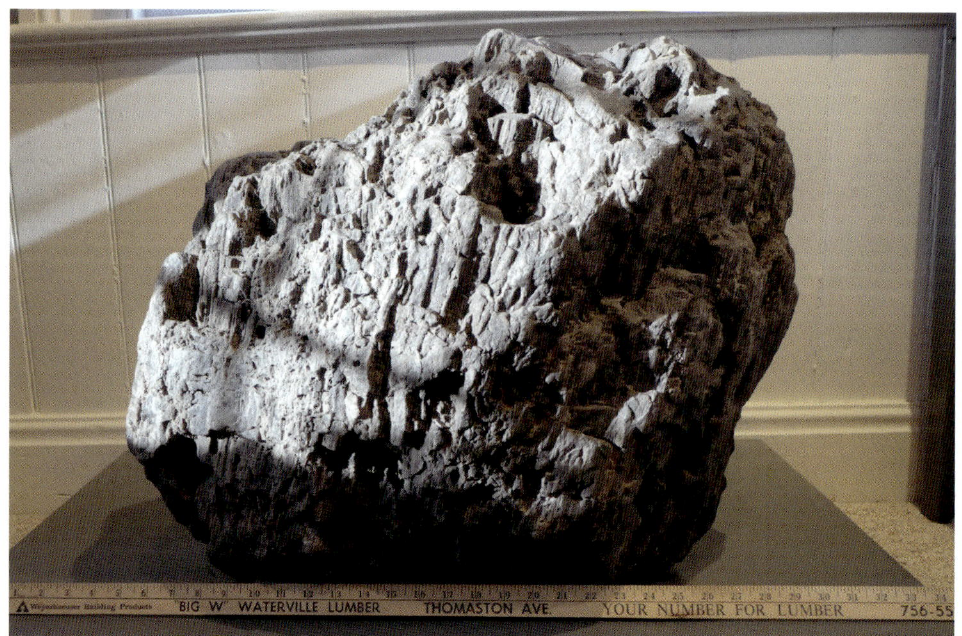

PETRIFIED WOOD: Two hundred to two hundred and fifty million years ago, a grove of conifers grew in a portion of South Britain. The species of trees was identified and named *Pomperaugoxylon connecticutense* during the 1980s when large pieces of petrified wood caught the attention of a geologist from Yale. Local residents had been aware of the stone tree stumps, branches, and pieces of petrified wood since the settlers arrived. An early farmer tried remove a stump with his axe, which broke in the process. Bill and Marta Hoyenski (below) found a large piece of the petrified wood in the 1970s and later donated it to the Southbury Historical Society.

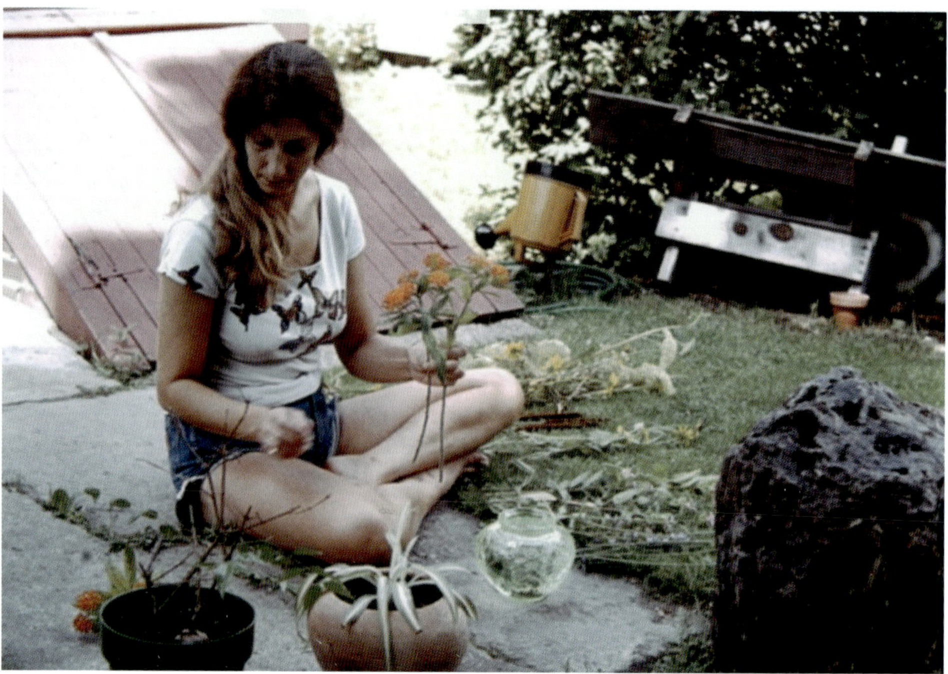

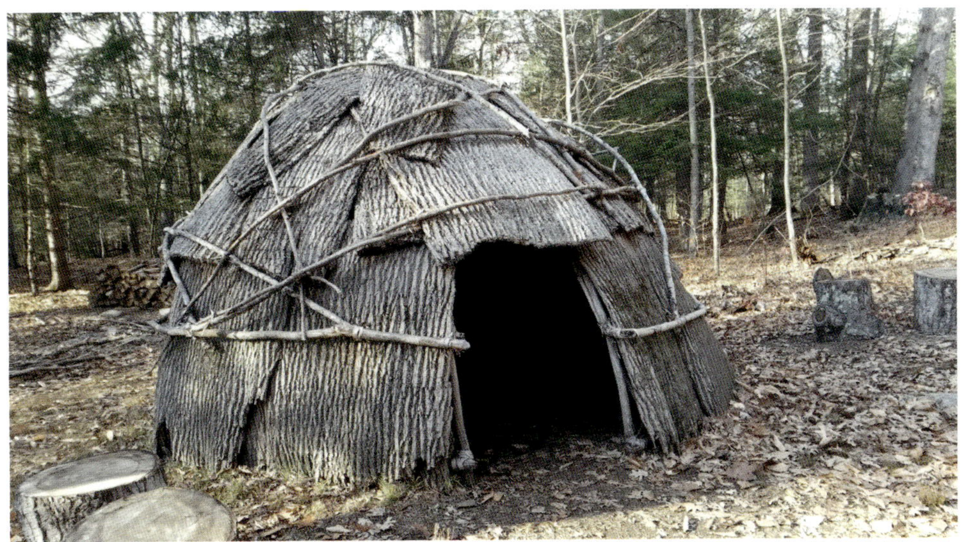

NATIVES: The Pootatuck tribe had a well-established encampment here in 1673 when the settlers from Stratford arrived. The natives lived in a village of wigwams near the river and grew crops of corn, squash, beans, and tobacco. The settlers meticulously bought the land from the Pootatuck representatives. Over 250 years ago, the Mitchell family promised the tribe that their burial grounds would be protected, and that agreement still holds. Arrow heads, spears, and other native artifacts can still be found in many places throughout Southbury. The arrowheads, scrapers, and drills seen in the below collection were found on the Perry Farm, now the Southbury Plaza, between 1800 and 1950.

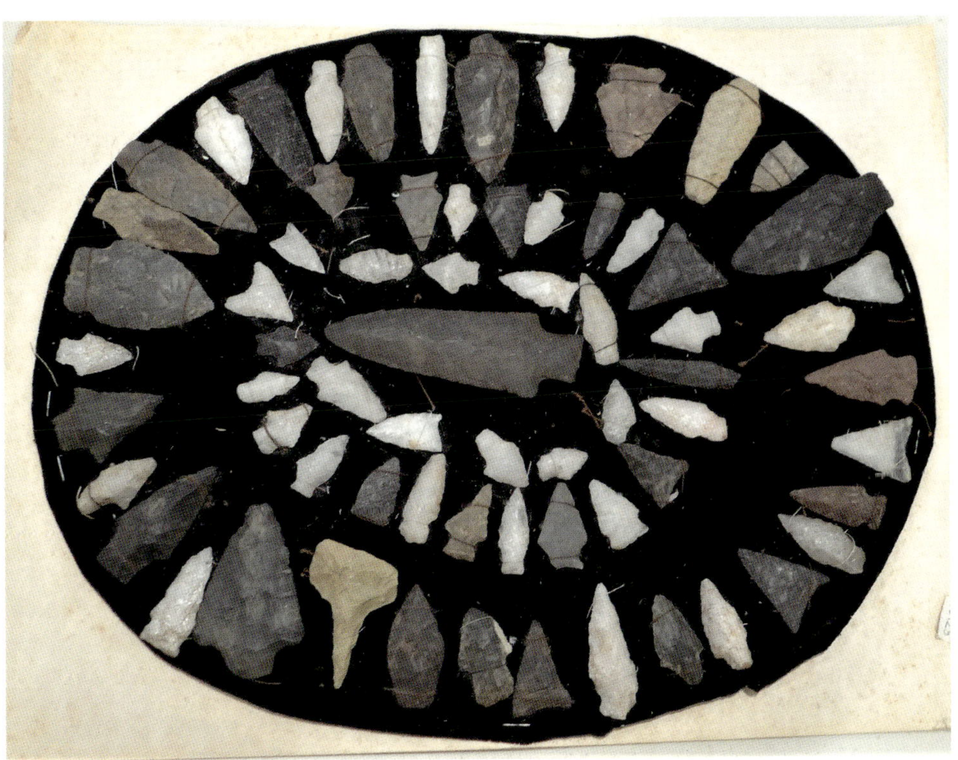

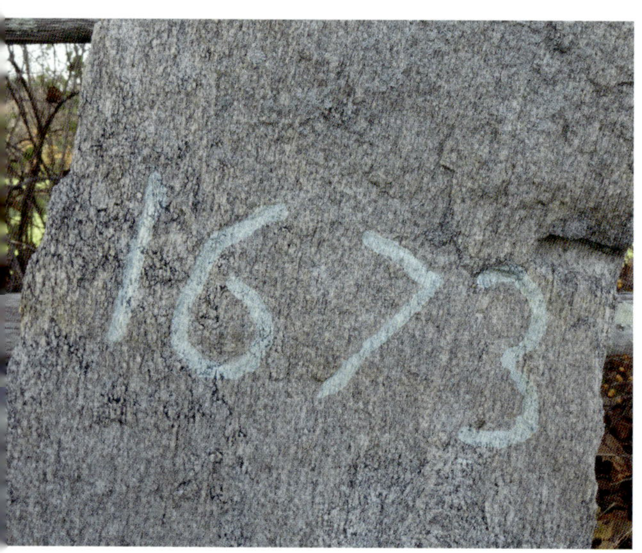

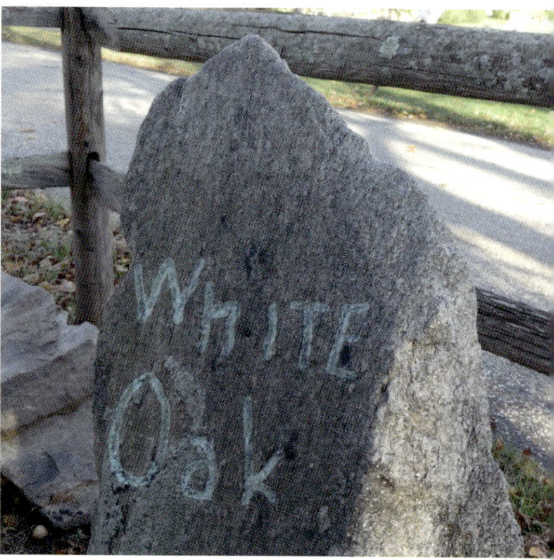

WHITE OAK MONUMENT: On the way to the Pomperaug Plantation, (Woodbury), the settlers stopped to spend the night by a large white oak tree. When the tree fell during a storm in 1808, Shadrach Osborn, first selectman, saved several pieces of the tree. At the site of the white oak, a granite pillar was placed in 1896, carved with the date of 1673, when the settlers arrived. The back of the monument is inscribed with, "White Oak." In 1996, a new monument was erected alongside the granite pillar, and surrounded by a new wooden fence. The monuments are in Settlers Park on Crook Horn Lane.

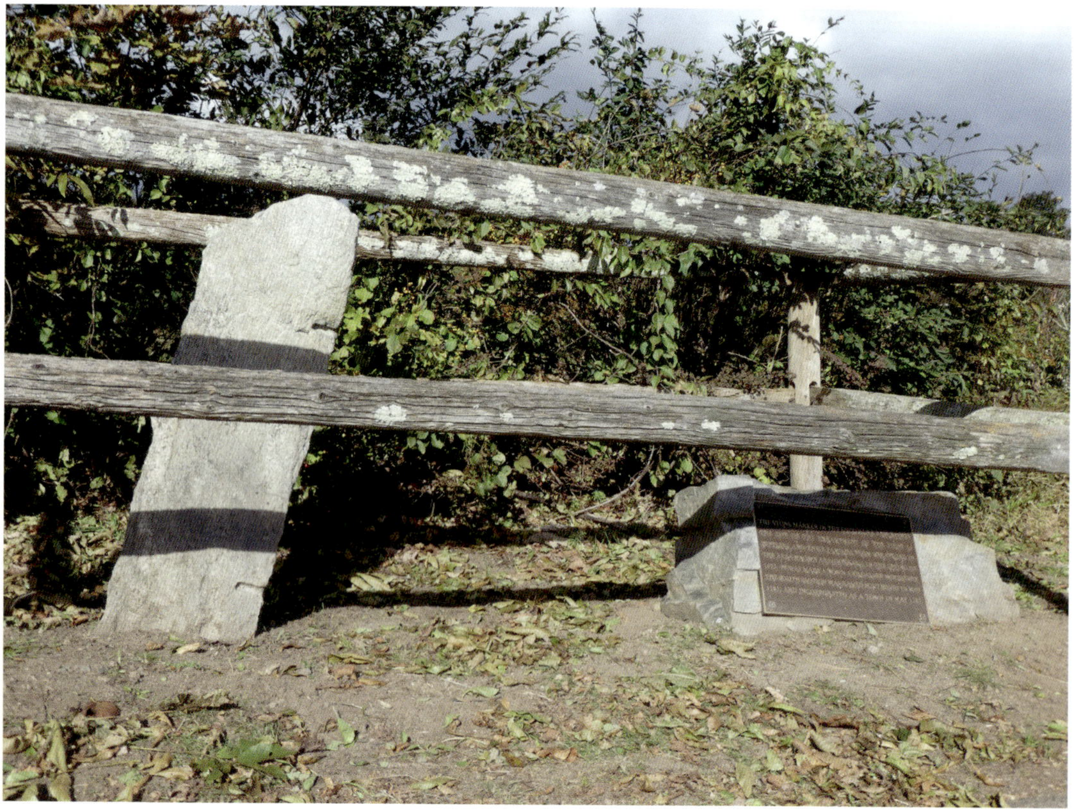

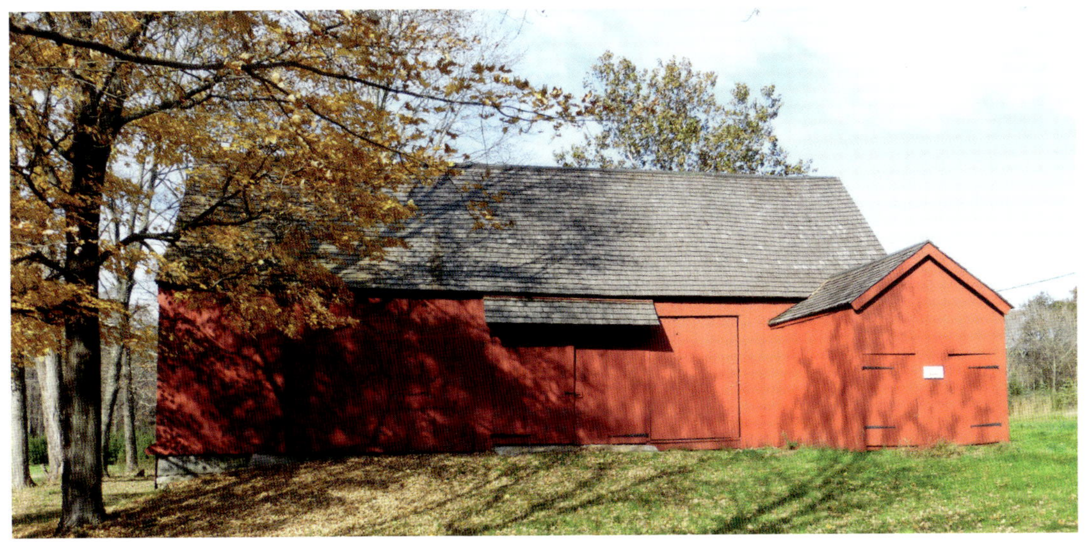

1690 BARN: The Stiles Barn was built by Benjamin Stiles in 1690 and is the oldest barn still standing in Southbury. This once-thatched barn was originally used to store the feed for the animals even before the house was started. Designated a "Bicentennial Barn" in 1976, the barn was renovated in 1985 using hand-hewn oak beams, carefully keeping to the original design. The structure is still proudly owned by the Stiles family. This area in White Oak was known for many years as Stilesville, due to the large number of Stiles family houses, farms, and mills. (RS)

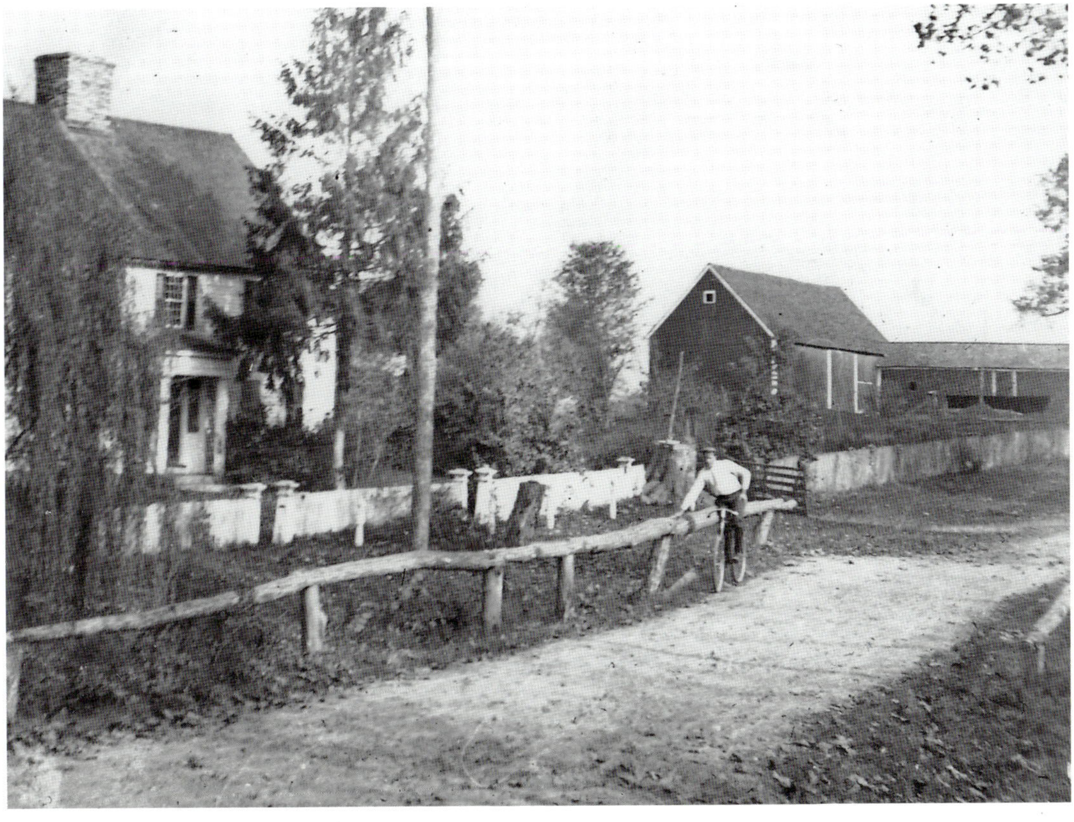

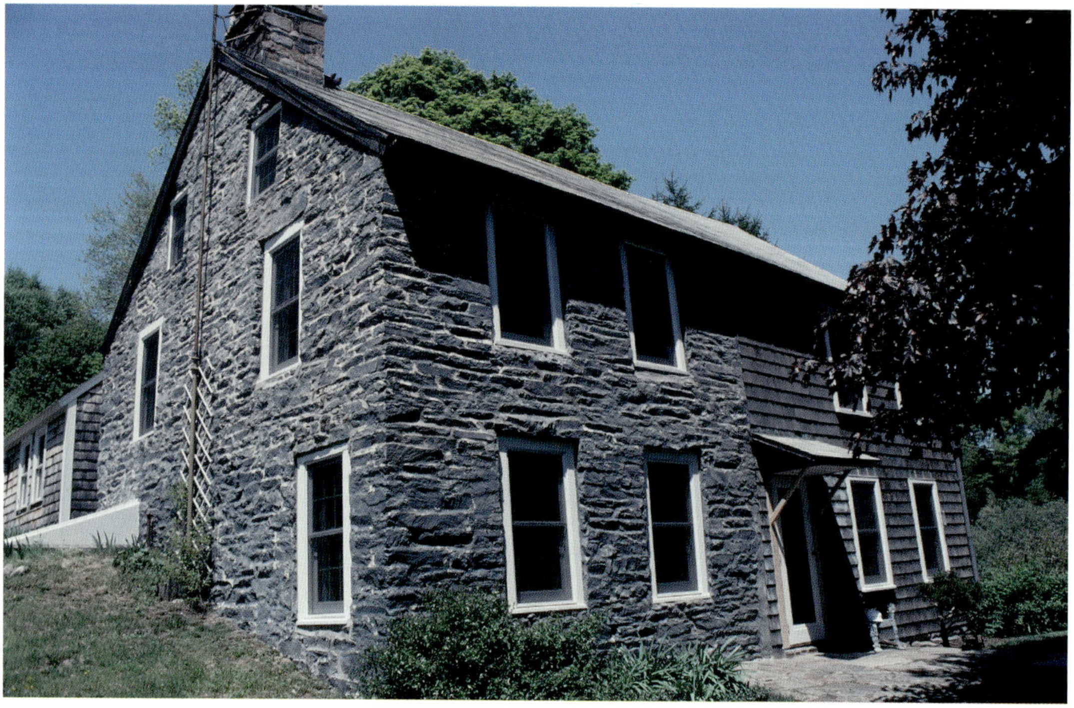

STONE HOUSE: Set well back from South Britain Road is one of the oldest buildings in South Britain. In 1704, the Bronson brothers moved granite from Mine Hill to construct a secure house. There was some concern in 1707 that the Pootatuck and Wyantenuck tribes were joining the French to fight against the colonists. A resolution was sent out "to provide a sufficient number of Well fortified Houses be built for the Saftie of their families." The stone house was fitted with a look-out tower on the roof, with a log palisade fence surrounding the building. After the danger passed, the building became a home.

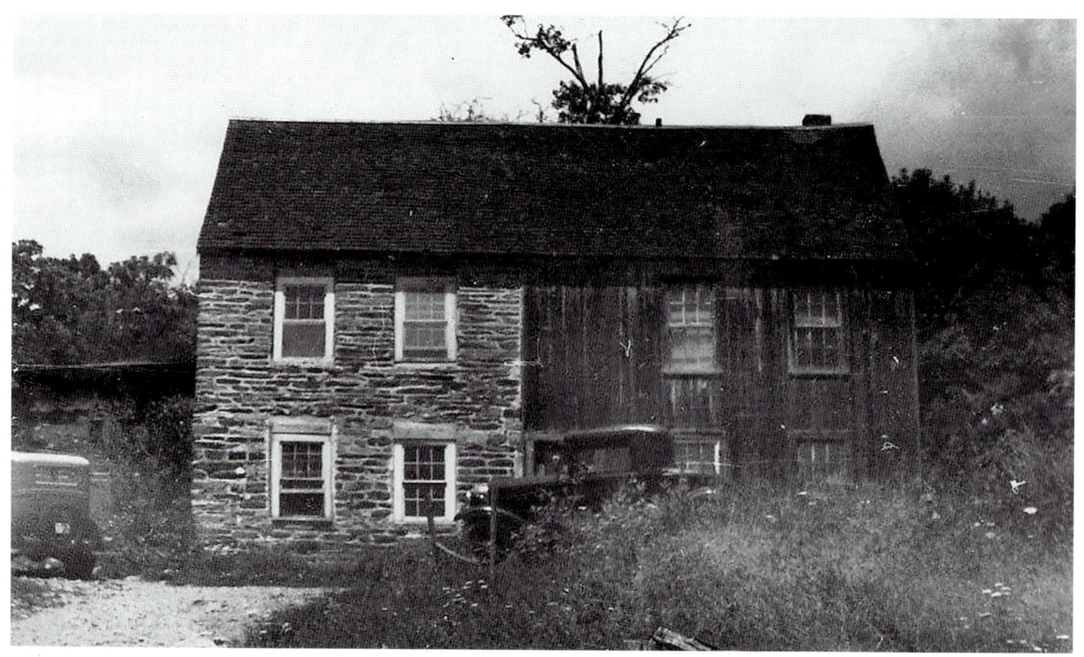

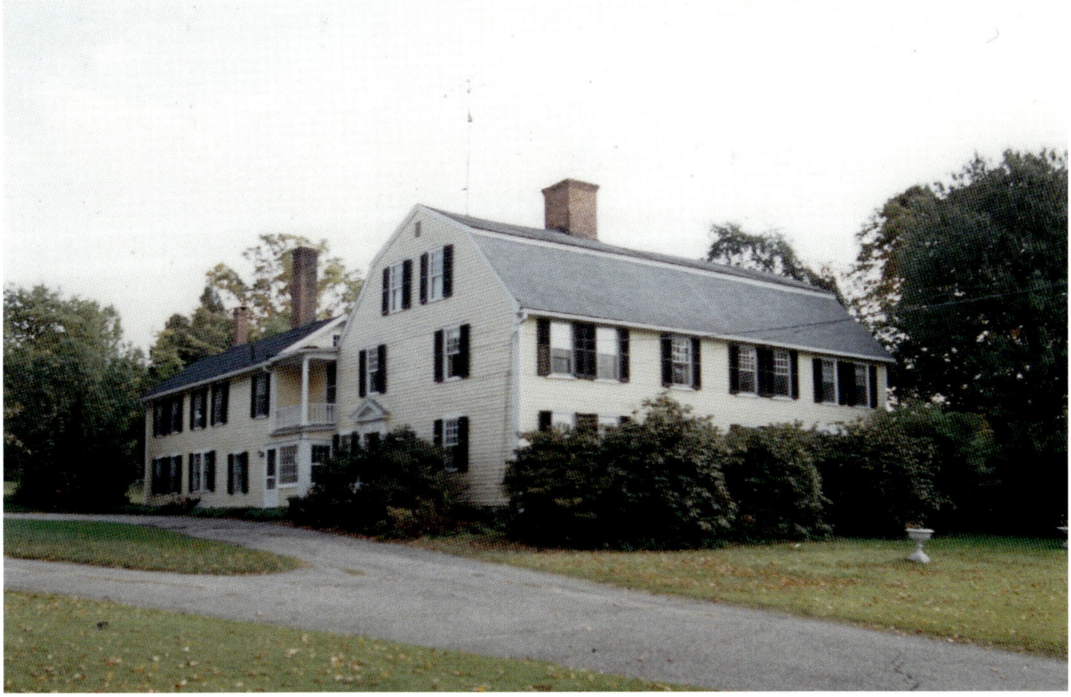

TAVERN: Now on the town line of Woodbury and Southbury, the Nathan Curtiss Tavern was built in the mid-1700s, and was a stopping place for many colonial travelers. Some of Rochambeau's officers stayed there during their march through town in a separate stone building which pre-dated the house. This structure was one of the required fortifications built for safety from a possible attack of the Natives. During renovations in 1900, the foundation of the fort was found near the flagpole and left undisturbed. The beautiful octagonal barn was built by A. A. Stone.

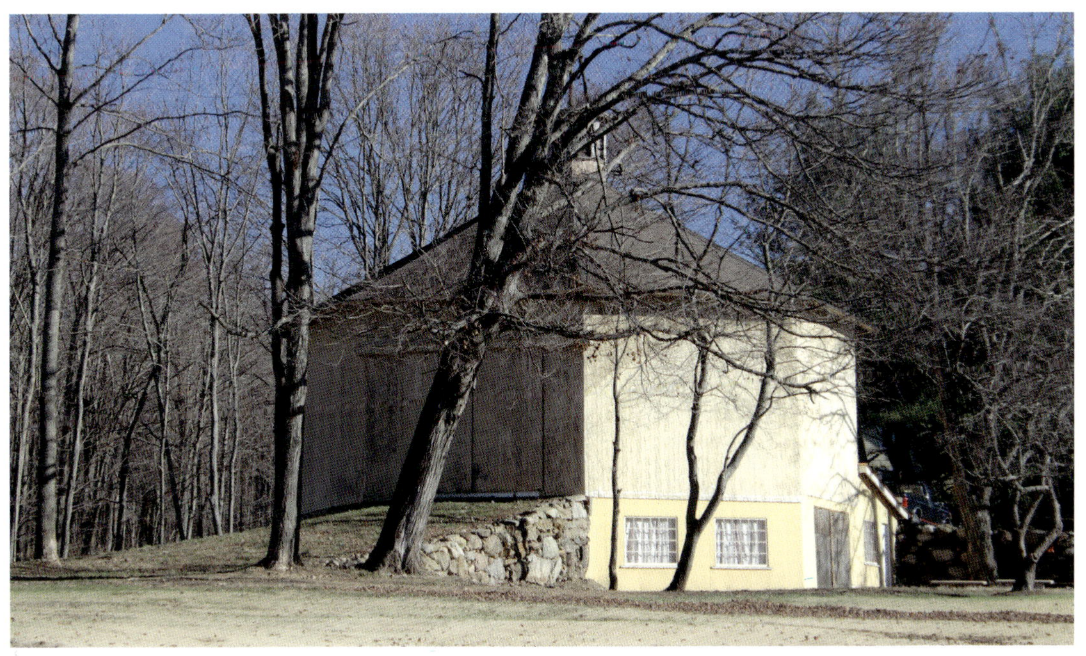

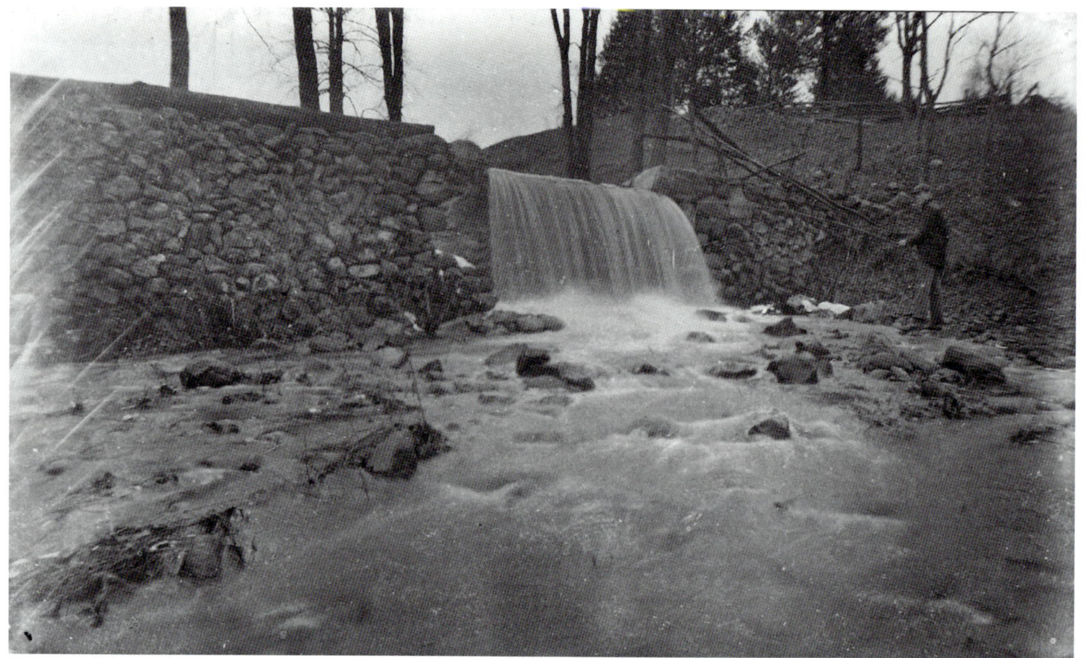

MILL DAM: Across from the Stiles Barn is a mill dam that stood for over 200 years, which was built for the Stiles lumber mill. The story is maintained that the dam was under construction before the Revolutionary War, but was left unfinished while the men served in the Continental Army. The dam was completed when the man-power was once again available and it was a splendid sight to see for many generations. The dam broke down within the last twenty years and was rebuilt twice at great cost. Unfortunately, this iconic mill dam has fallen down again. (RS)

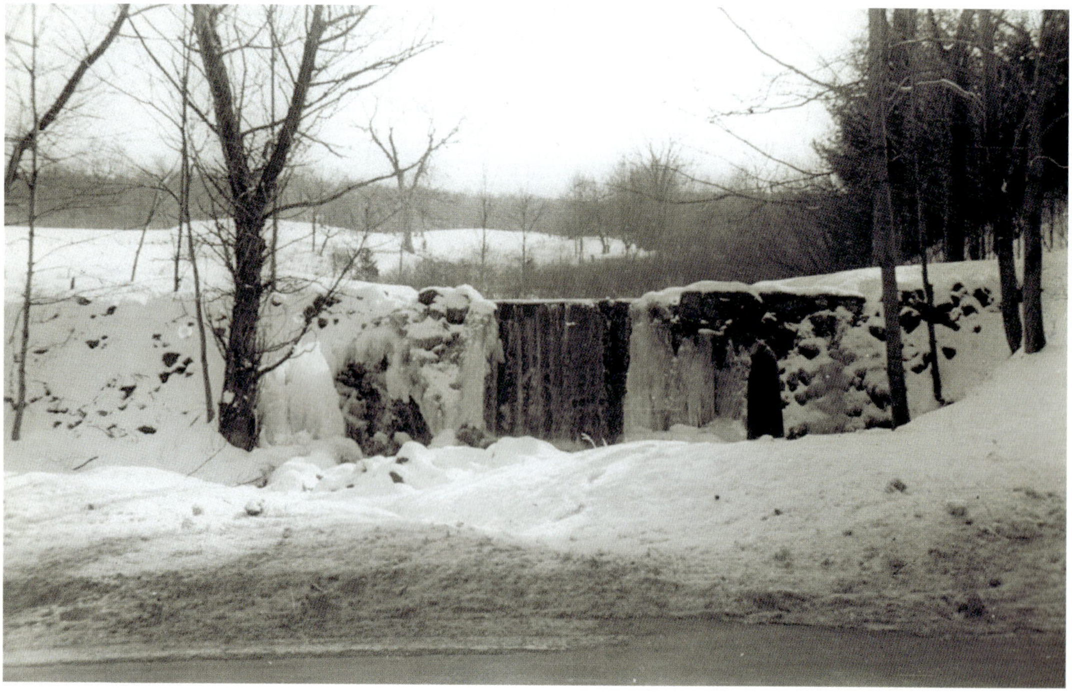

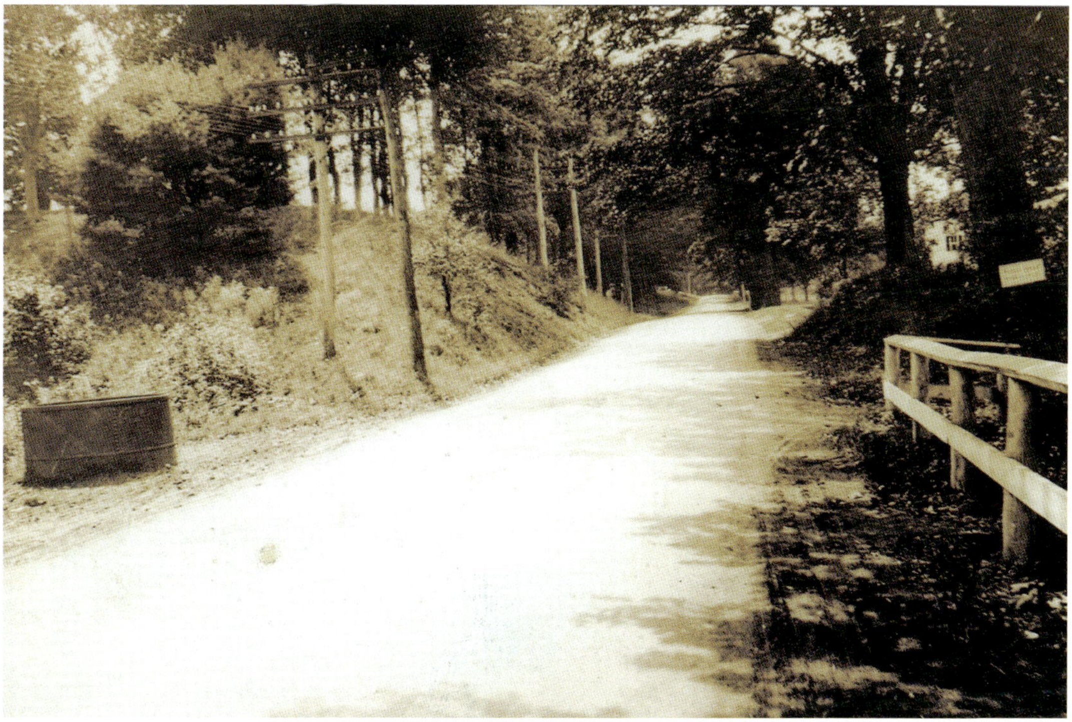

TROUGH REMOVED: Along Main Street North, located near the Stiles residences, was a watering trough along the road to give a place for horses to have a quick drink of water. Eventually, the narrow dirt road was shared by horses and early automobiles and was paved in 1919. In the 1970s, the watering trough was converted to a lovely planter. It was removed when the road was widened. (KSL)

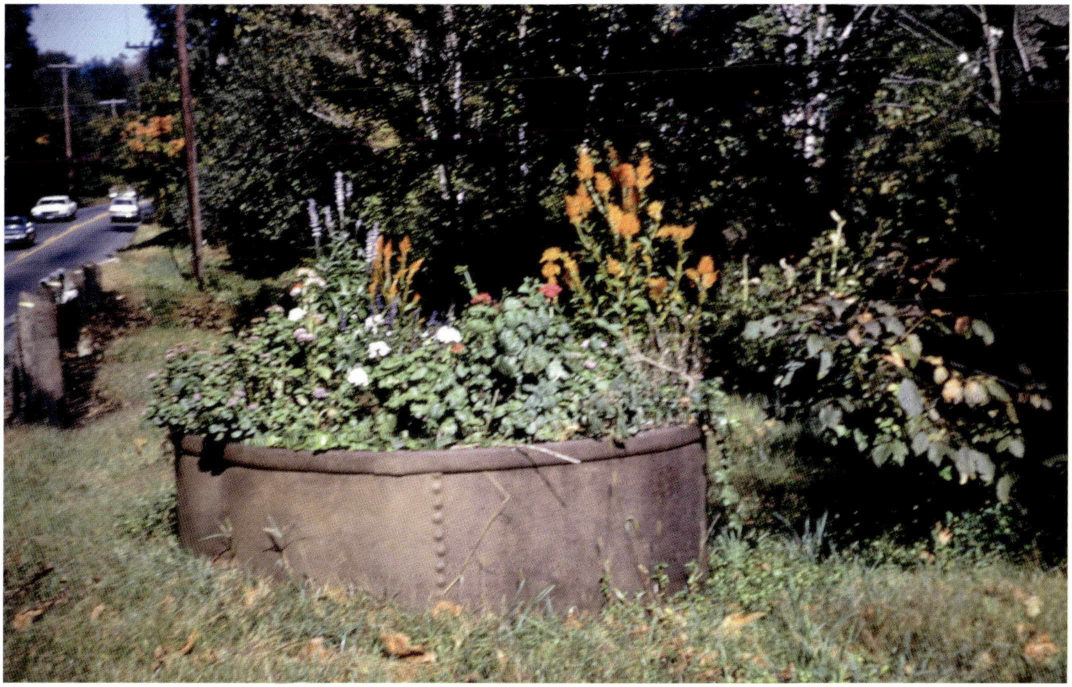

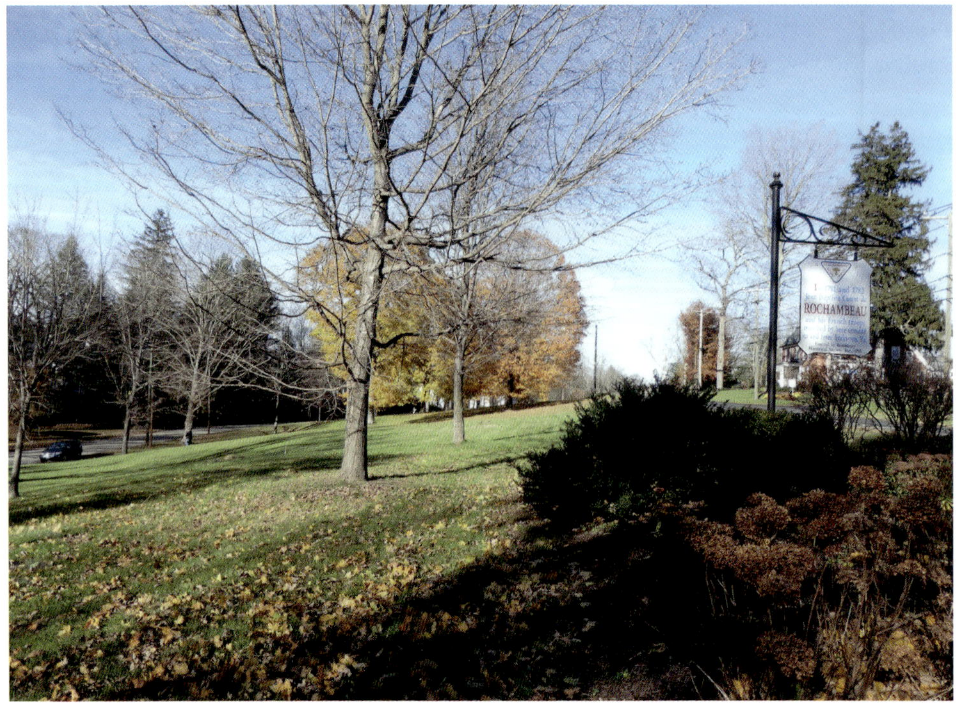

KINGSLAND: The "Indian Trail" or "Pomperaug Trail" had already been in use by the local tribes when the settlers arrived from Stratford. The early proprietors built their houses surrounding the green area now known as Kingsland, and the first Meeting House in Southbury was built here in 1735. At times, the land was common land used for grazing animals. French General Rochambeau, who brought an army to help General George Washington during America's Revolution, marched his troops along this area.

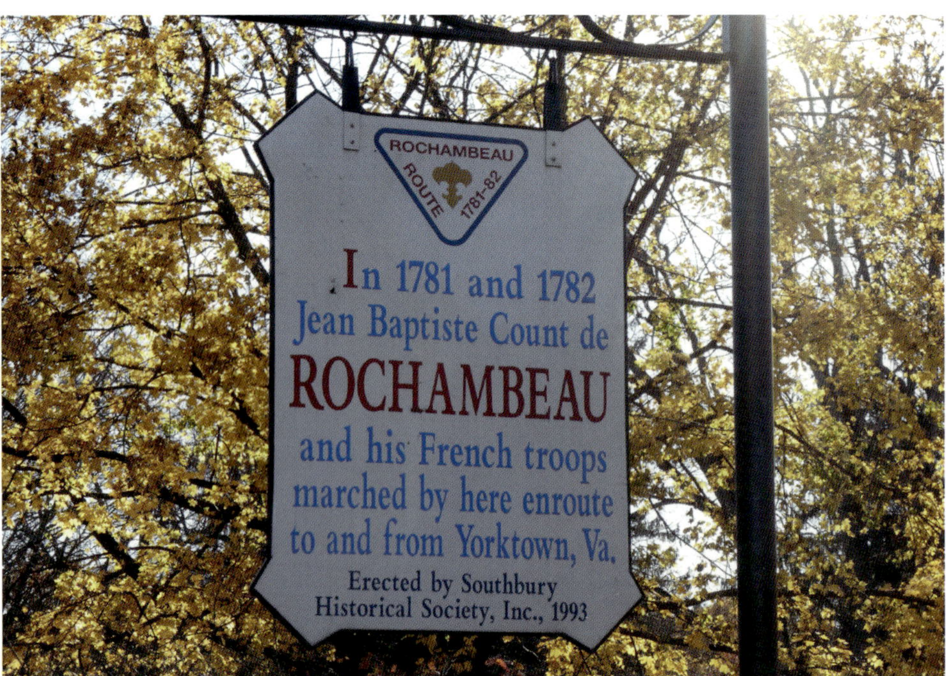

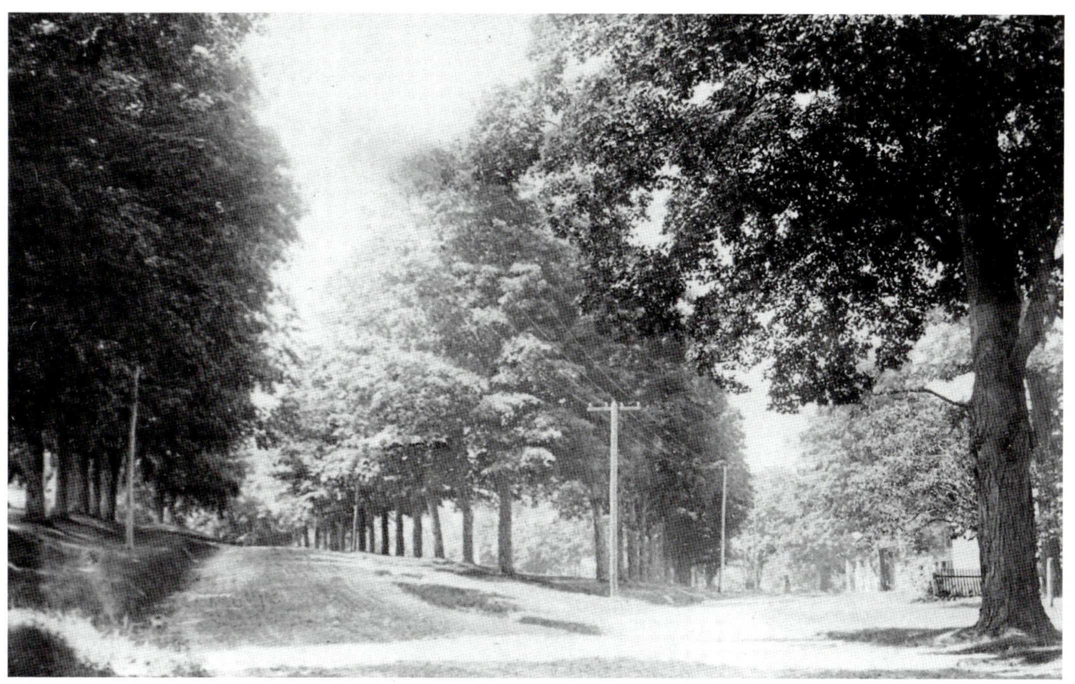

MANSION HOUSE ROAD: The road from Woodbury divided shortly after entering Southbury, with Kingsland the land in between these roads. One of the houses along the road was called the Mansion House, built in 1828 for the Mitchell family. Other homes belonged to the Stiles and Hinman families. The road, with its old houses, is still a beautiful side route to travel especially in the fall. The above photograph shows the intersection as it looked in the early 1900s. The road to the right is Mansion House Road. The bottom photograph is taken halfway down the road with Kingsland to the left, with the Beecher House to the right.

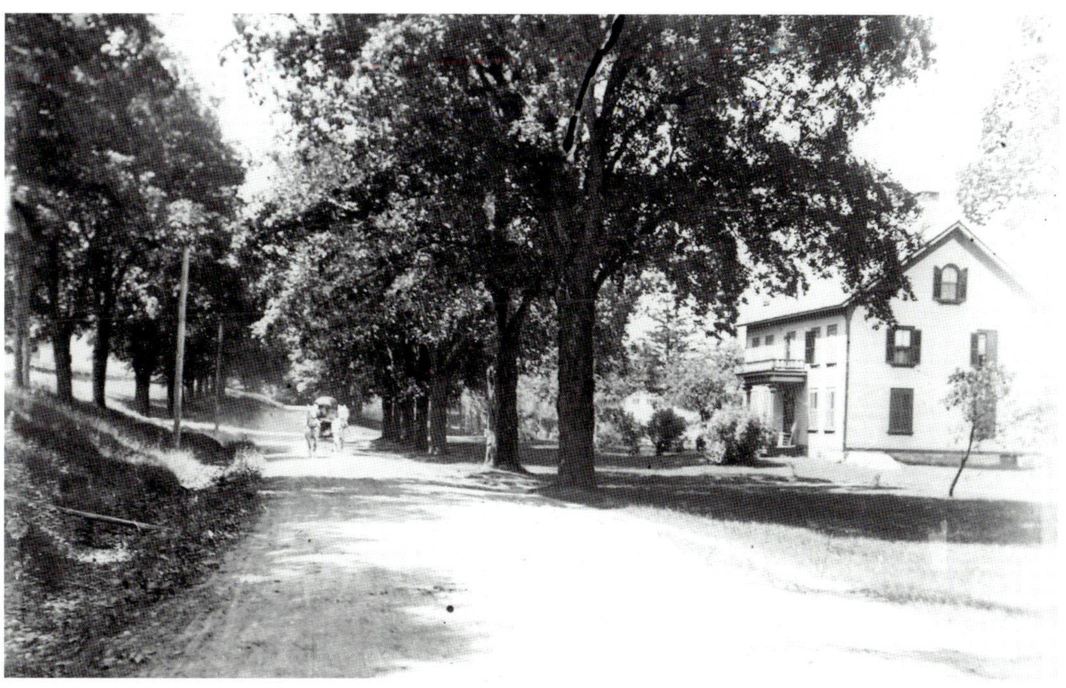

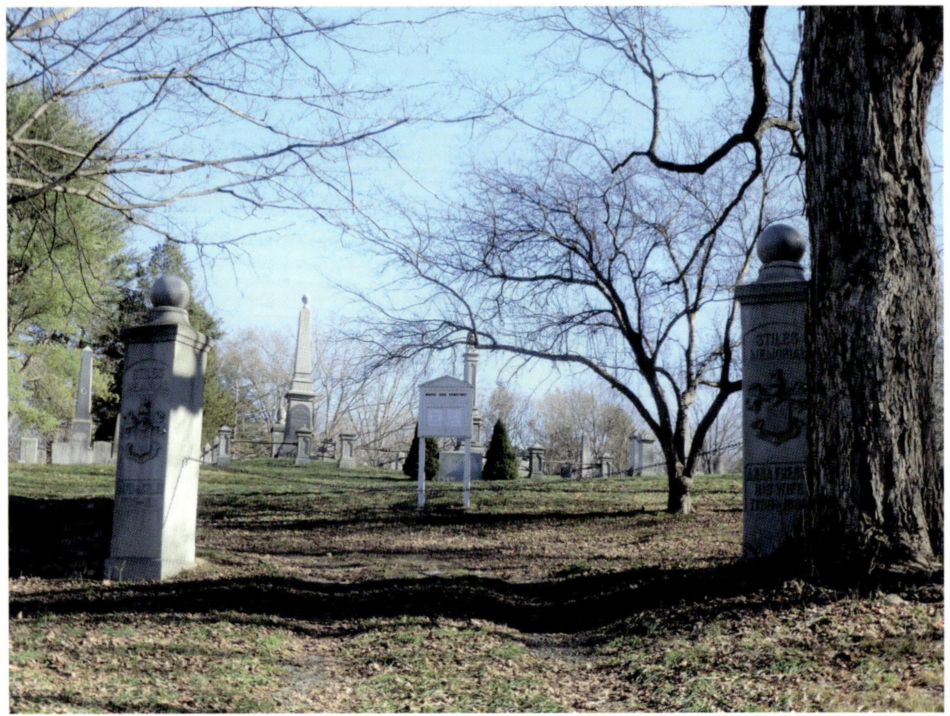

FIRST BURYING PLACE: The White Oak Cemetery, also known as the Stiles Memorial Cemetery, was started in the early 1700s. The oldest headstone still visible is made of red sandstone for Moses Johnson, who died in 1713. Monuments can be found for many of the town's first residents, including the Stiles, Curtis, Hicocks, and Hinmans, along with Revolutionary War soldiers. A sign at the cemetery says, "The story is told that slaves are reported to have been buried in the driveway." This is a startling reminder that even Southbury had slaves. Several local slaves served in the Revolutionary War and gained their freedom.

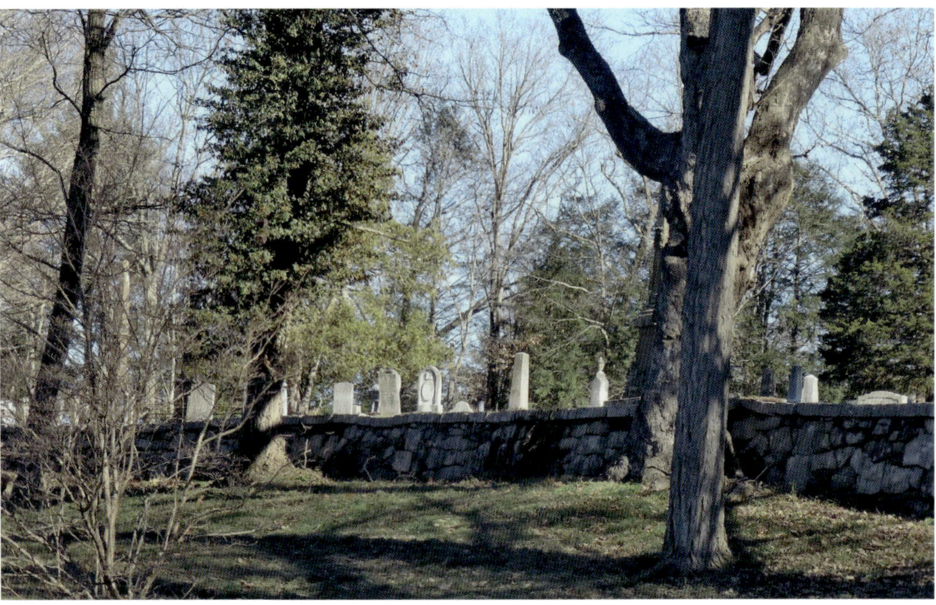

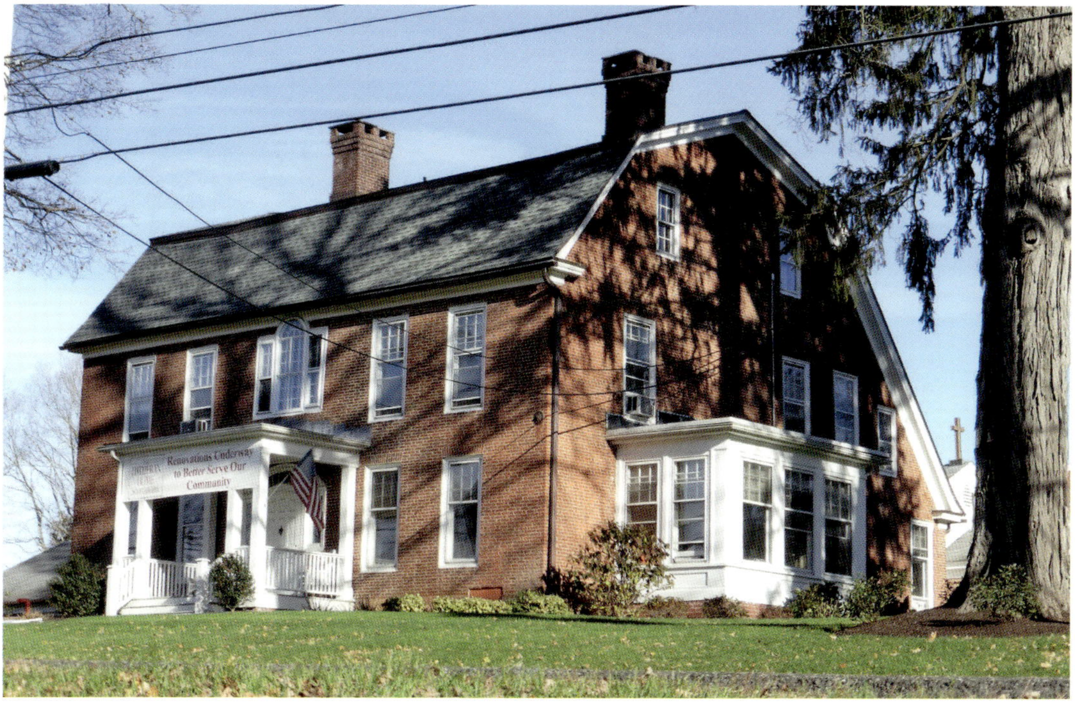

LUTHERAN HOME: The large, brick house was built *circa* 1760 for Sherman Hinman, a gift from his father, Benjamin Hinman. After many owners, the house was purchased by Samuel G. Goodrich, where he lived from 1857 to 1866. Goodrich wrote the first history text books for children, telling stories as Peter Parley. His time in Southbury was filled with community activities, as he was writing a book on nature and invited all the children to bring him leaves, seeds, and bugs. In 1918, the home was converted to the German Lutheran Home for the Aged. The Lutheran Home is still in operation and home to 200 residents.

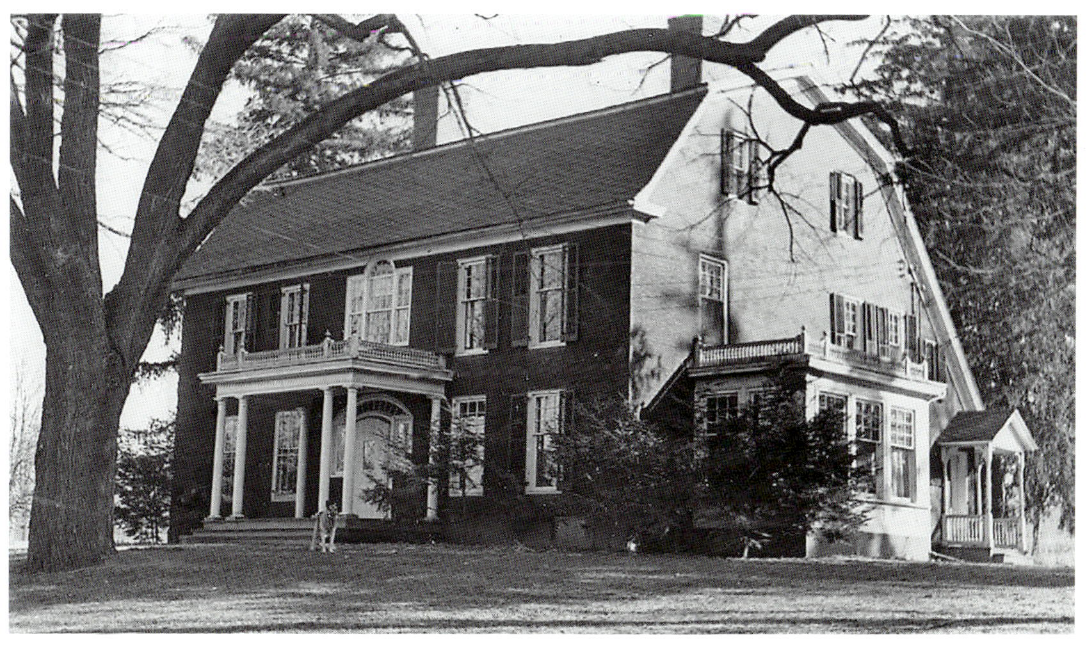

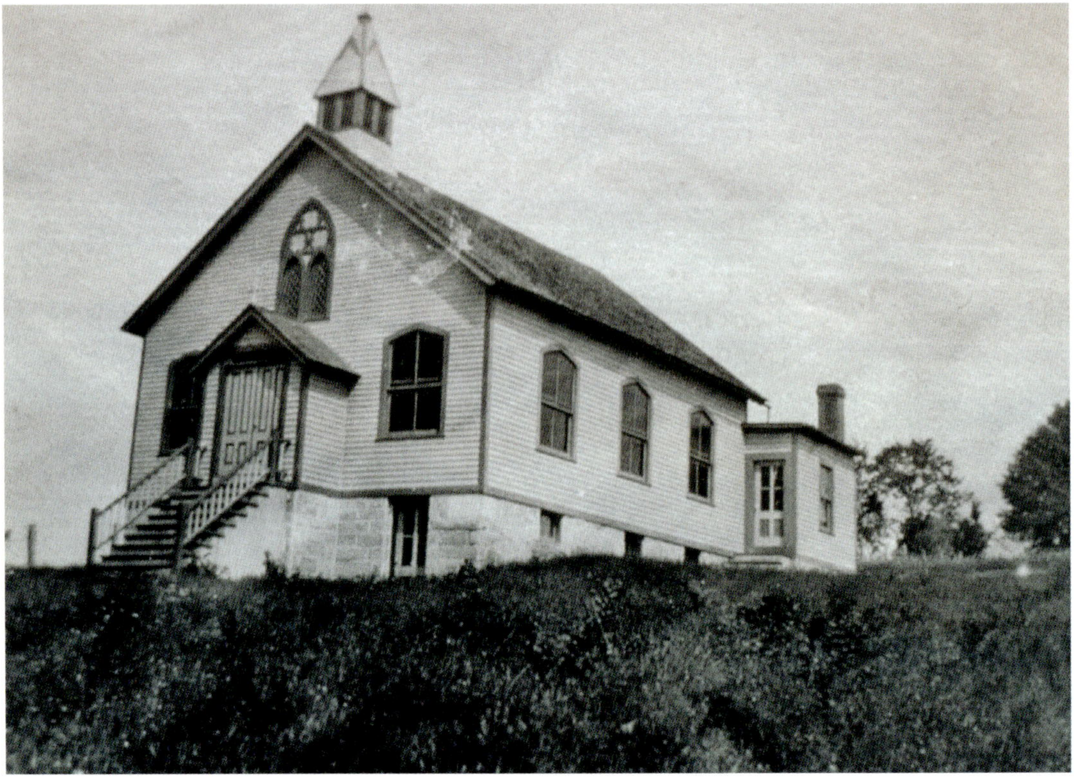

SACRED HEART CATHOLIC CHURCH: In 1844, there were forty Catholic families in Southbury, many of them with Irish origins. The mission church was built on land donated by Dennis Hunihan. The first mass was held on Christmas 1884, and in 1890, the land next door was purchased for a cemetery. As the congregation increased, space for a larger church was found in 1958. The small church was no longer needed and was demolished. The cemetery, next to White Oak Schoolhouse, is still in use.

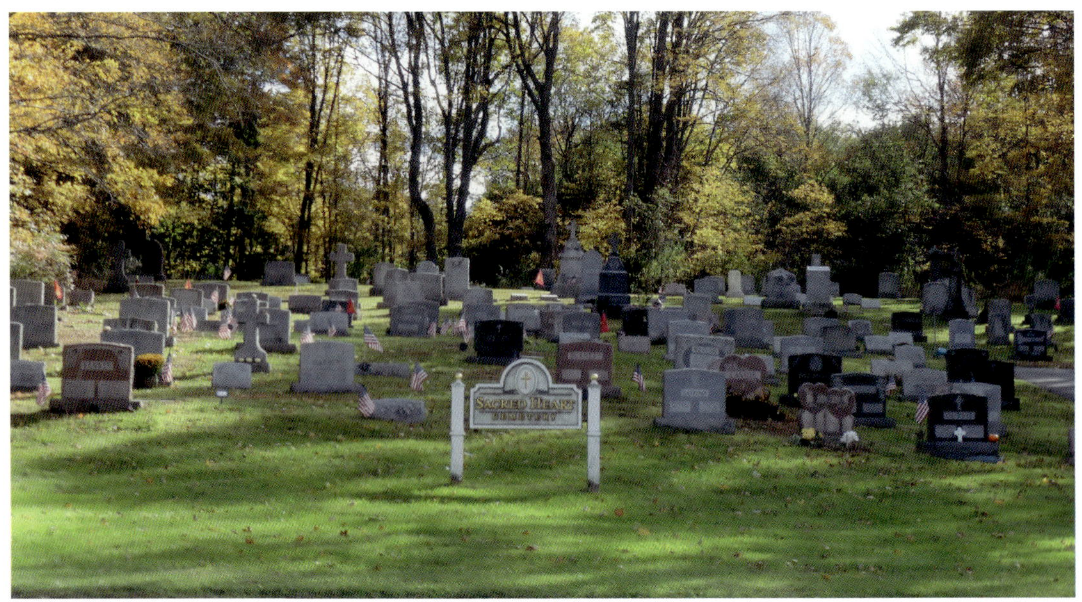

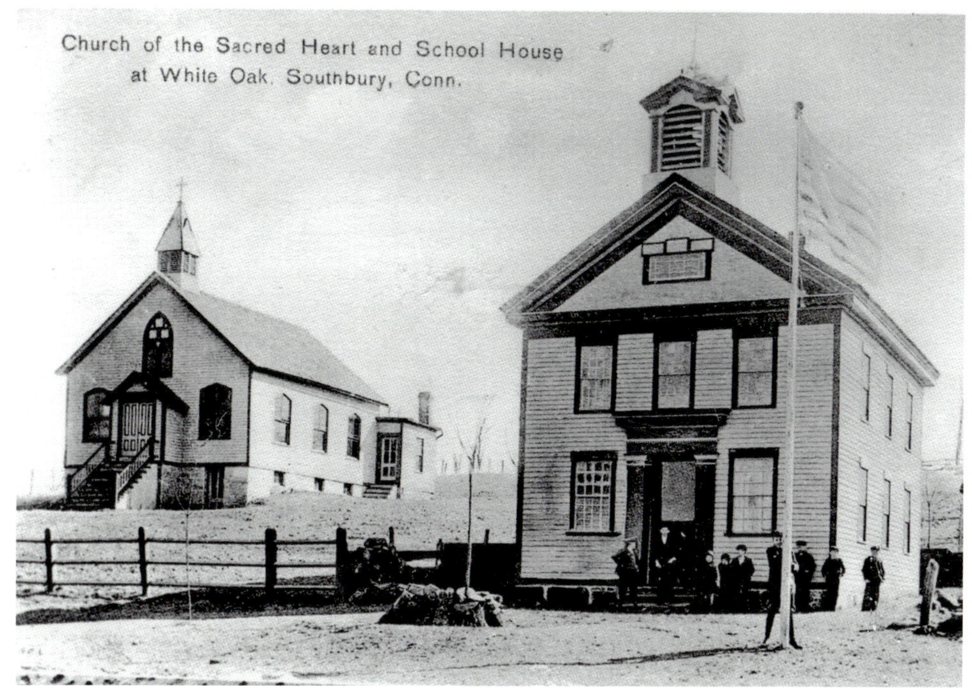

SCHOOLHOUSE: The two-story White Oak District schoolhouse was built in 1840, across from Kingsland. While the main floor was used as a school, the upper floor was used for community events until the 1920s when it was needed as a school room. The school was closed in 1941 while the children were on their Christmas break. On January 5, 1942, all the town's elementary school students attended the Consolidated School for the very first time. The building was sold and used as an antique shop for many years.

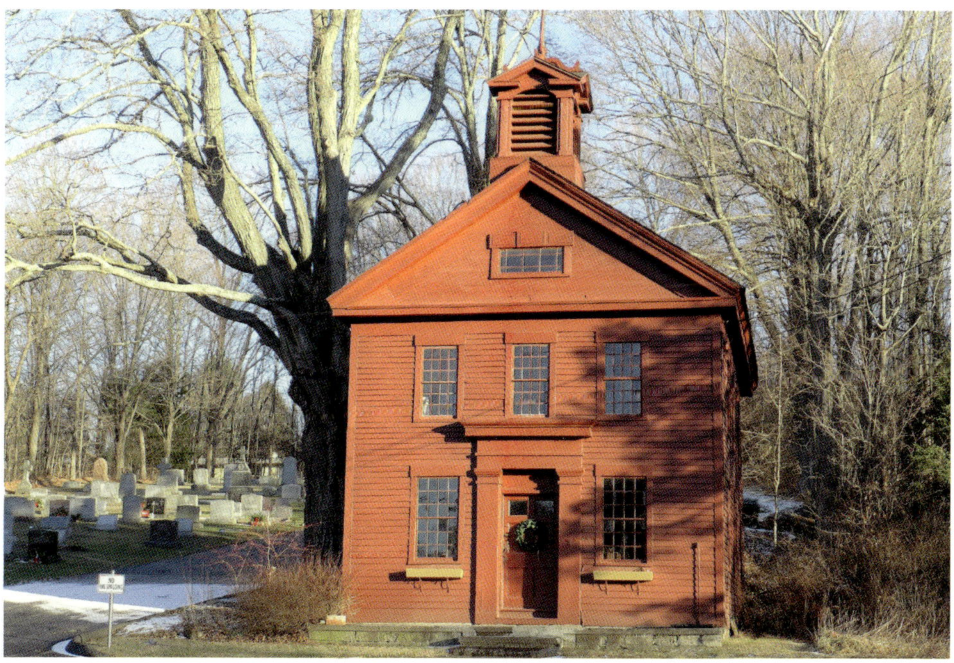

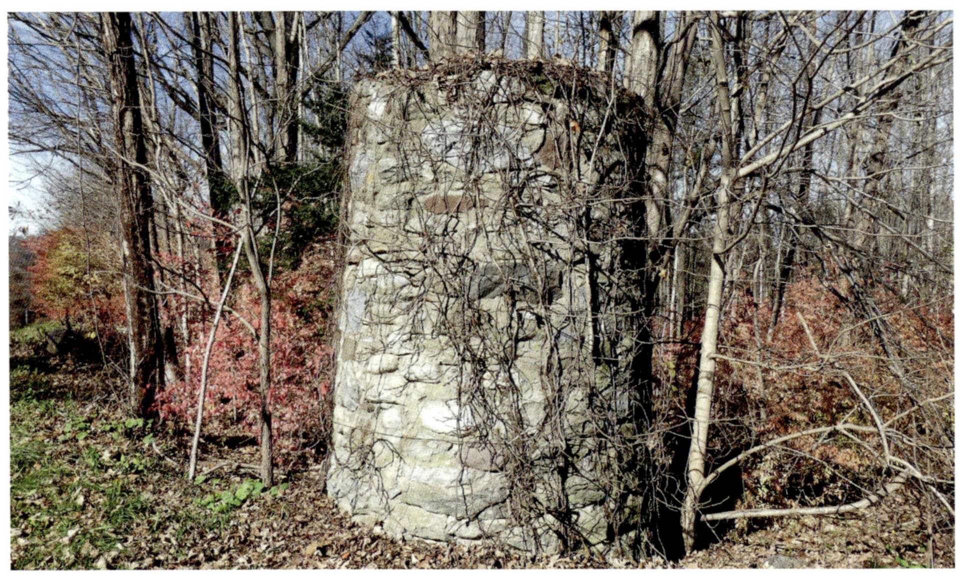

MYSTERY: At the corner of Route 67 and Old Field Hill Road, this stone pillar stands tall and imposing in the winter, but is hidden behind ivy during the summer. One guidebook claims that the pillar marked the location of the Southbury's second Meeting House, from 1767 to 1844. Another historian claimed that the pillar was placed by the Hinman family, marking the boundary between White Oak and Bullet Hill school districts. The Hinman and Brown families agreed that the school district border would go between their houses because each family had a large number of children. Below is a drawing of the Second Meeting House that was signed as C. G. S. and is attributed to Clarence Stiles.

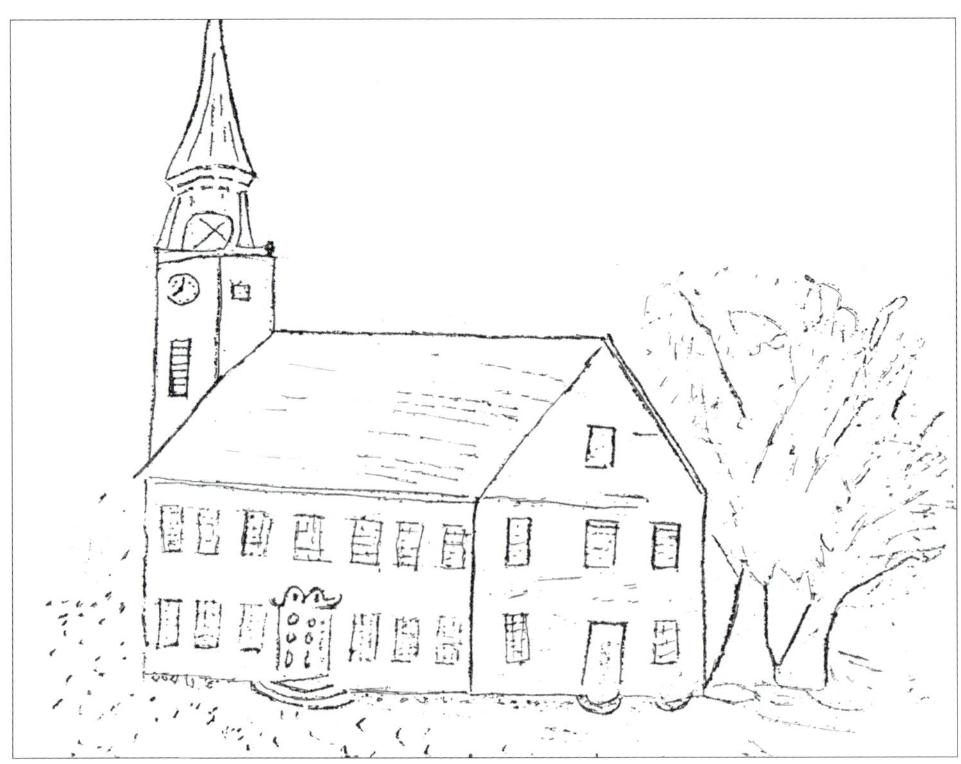

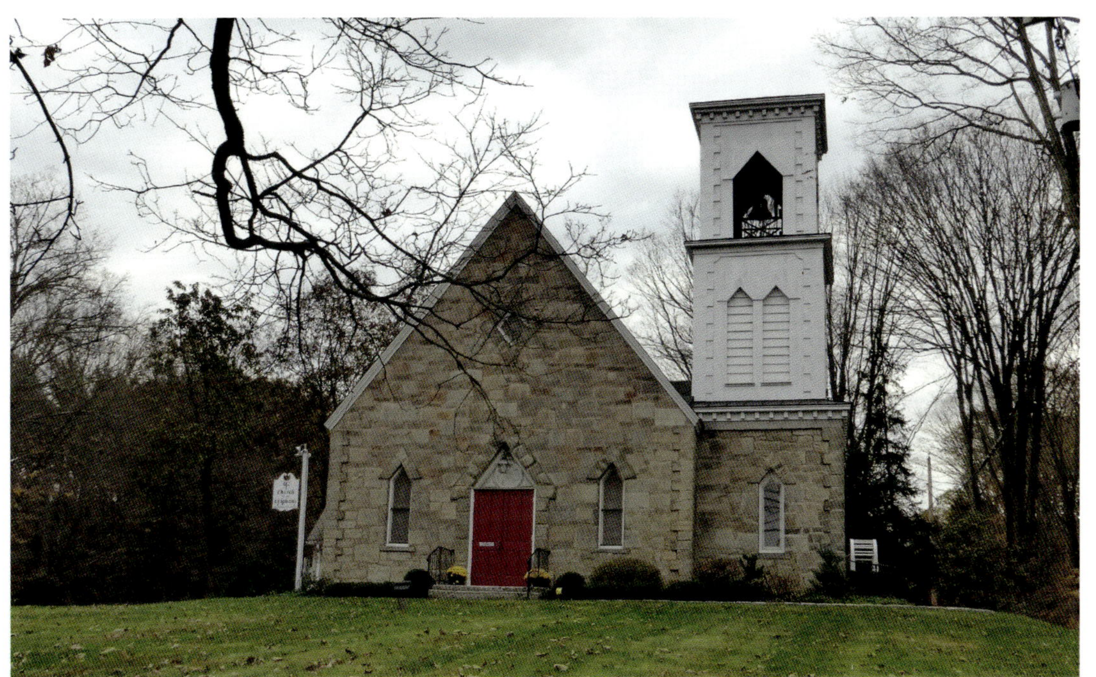

EPISCOPAL CHURCH: The Episcopal Society was organized in the upper room of Bullet Hill School on April 18, 1843, and they called themselves the Church of the Resurrection. In 1857, land was deeded to the congregation for a church building from Frederick Harriman, on land once owned by Shadrach Osborn. The group later changed their name to Church of the Epiphany. Obtaining quarried granite from Roxbury, the construction commenced with the cornerstone being set in place in 1863. The building was consecrated in 1867 and the wooden bell tower was added twenty years later.

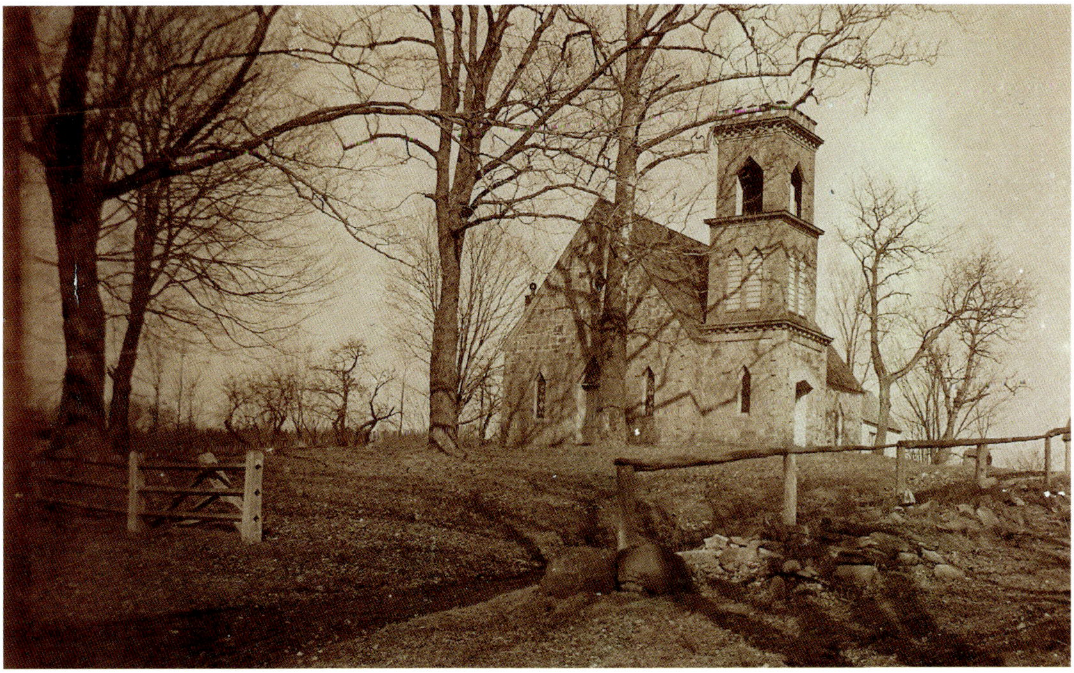

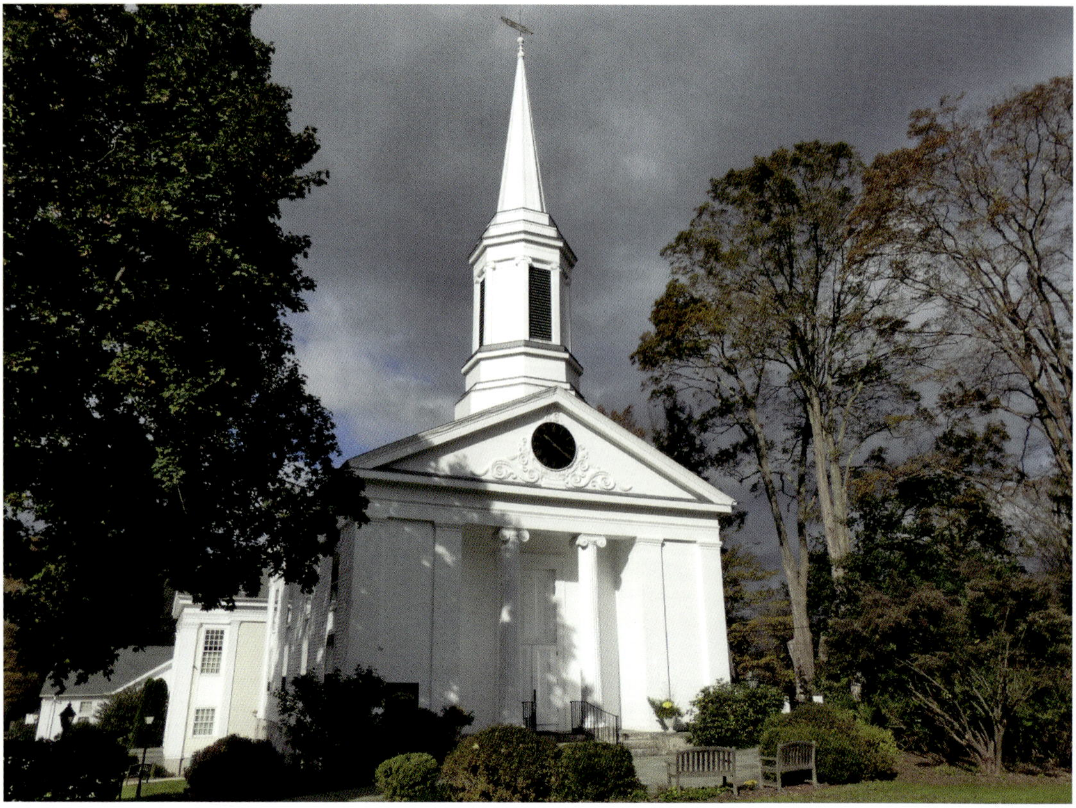

MEETING HOUSE: The United Church of Christ began as the third Meeting House of the first Ecclesiastical of Southbury, built in 1844. Meeting Houses were used for religious instruction and town meetings. In 1922, the congregation decided to join with the Methodist for one year to save money. The congregations alternated their meeting places: six months at the Methodist Church and six months at the Meeting House. The churches decided to join and changed their name to the Federated Church of Southbury.

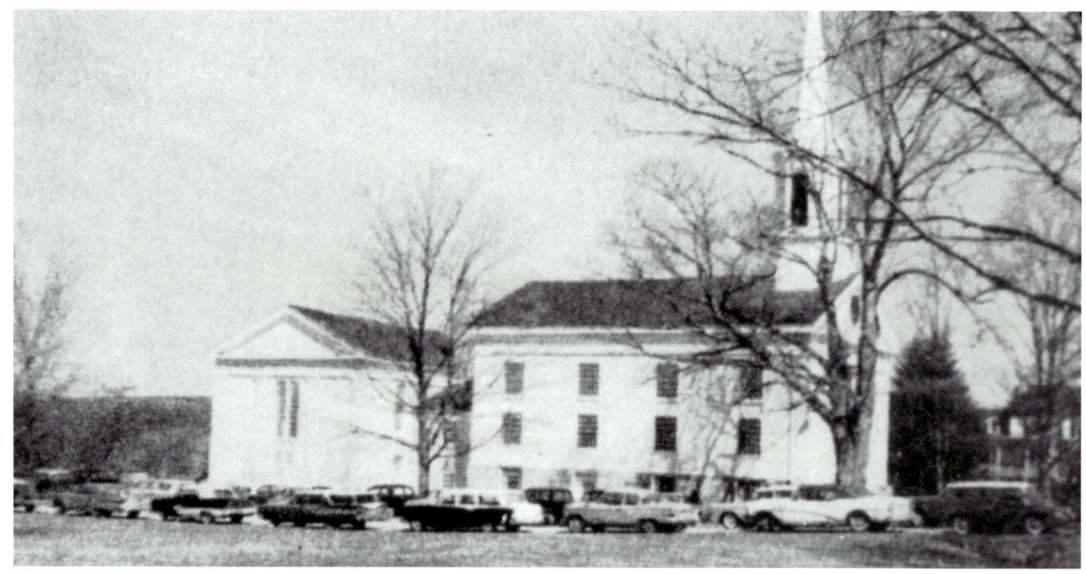

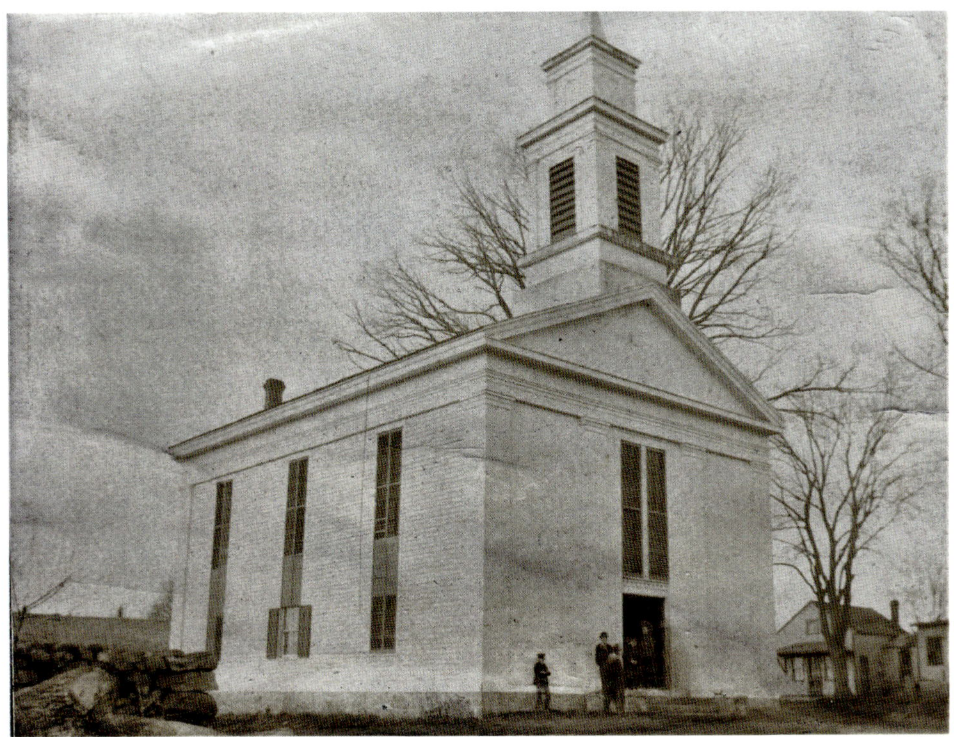

METHODIST: The Methodist circuit preacher started coming to Southbury as early as 1790. A congregation was started in Southbury in the Bullet Hill School. They built their church in 1847 between the schoolhouse and the Meeting House. The contractor who built the Meeting House, now the United Church of Christ, was also responsible for the building of the Methodist Church. In 1957, the Methodist Church was closed, and skillfully moved and attached to the United Church of Christ. It is painted a pale yellow and can easily be identified.

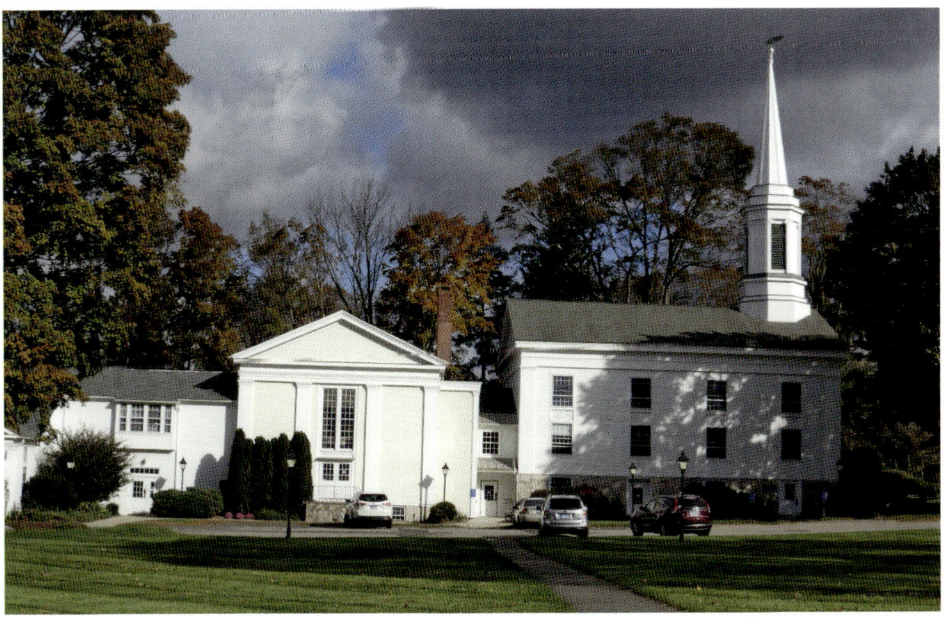

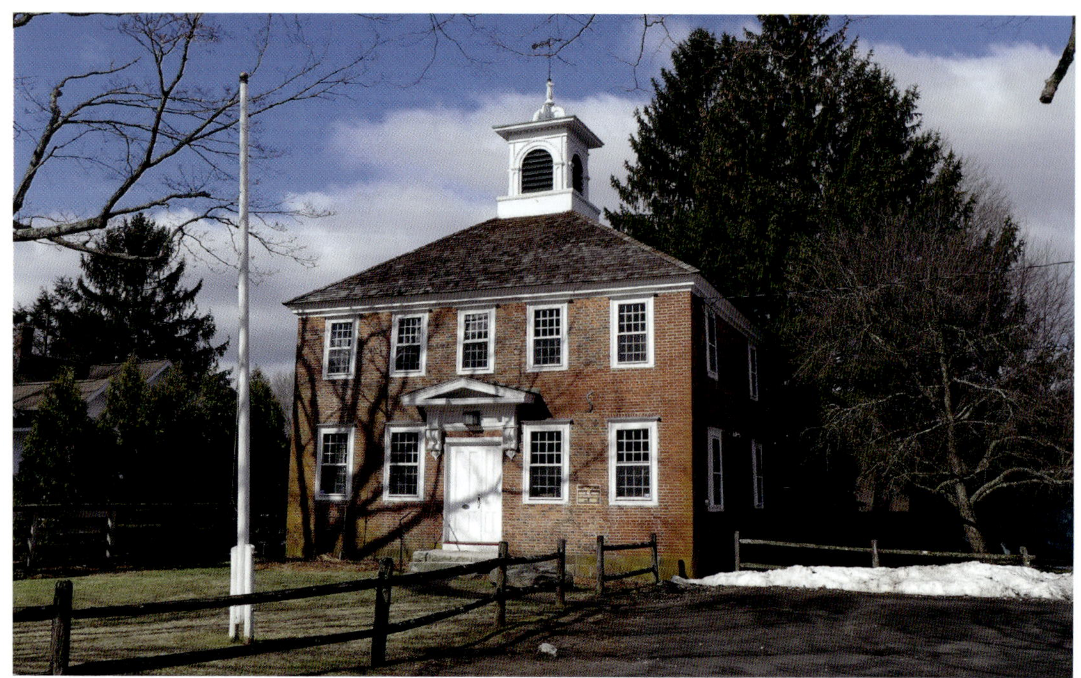

OLDEST TOWN BUILDING: The Brick Schoolhouse was built in the Bullet Hill district of the town sometime in the late 1700s, the accepted date being 1789. The main floor was used for school, while the upper room served many community purposes, including town and church meetings, dances, and lectures. The second floor was used for schooling beginning in 1928 until the school closed in December 1941. Bullet Hill School is the oldest town-owned building in Southbury. Every year, each second-grade class in the region spends a day at the Bullet Hill School.

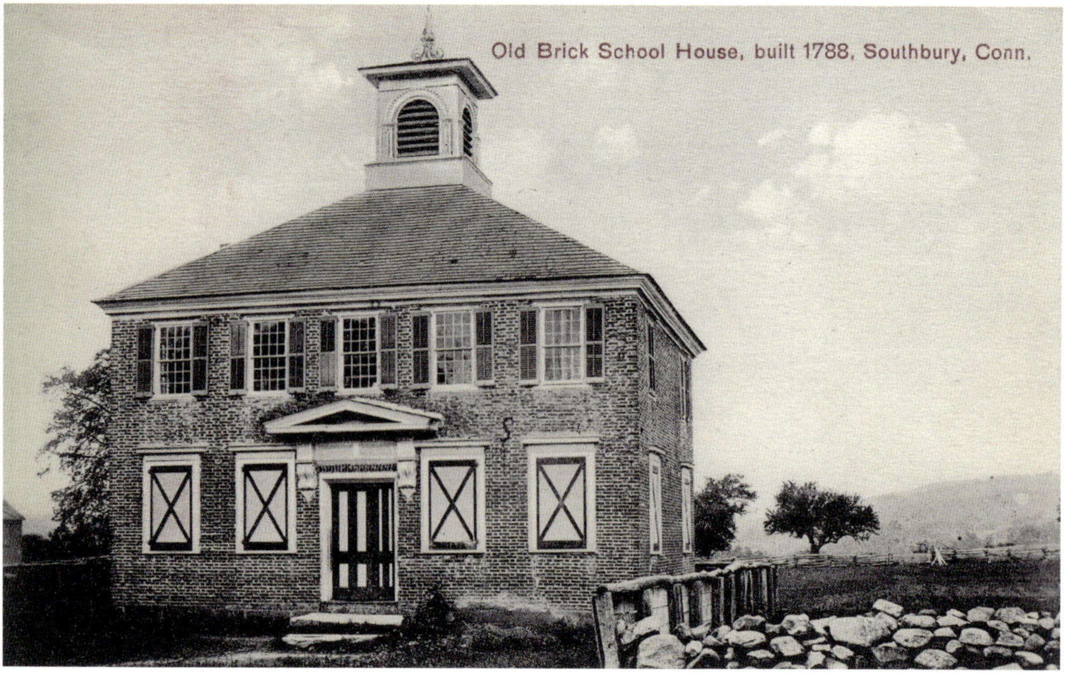

Old Brick School House, built 1788, Southbury, Conn.

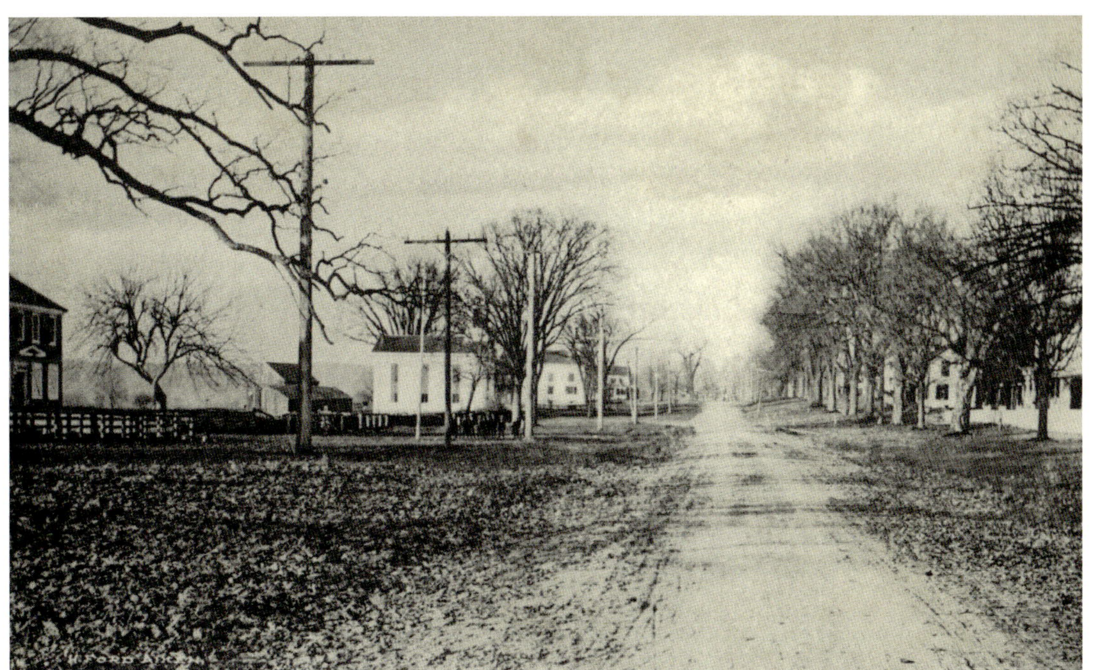

ROAD VIEW: In this wonderful old scene along Main Street North, you can see a portion of Bullet Hill School on the left side of the dirt road. The white building with the tall, narrow windows is the Southbury Methodist Church in its original location, with the United Church of Christ a little beyond. In the postcard below, the old intersection between Route 6 and Route 67 is clearly visible. Before Heritage Road was built in the 1970s, Route 6 ran diagonally through what is now Garage Road, where Main Street North made an easy transition into Main Street South.

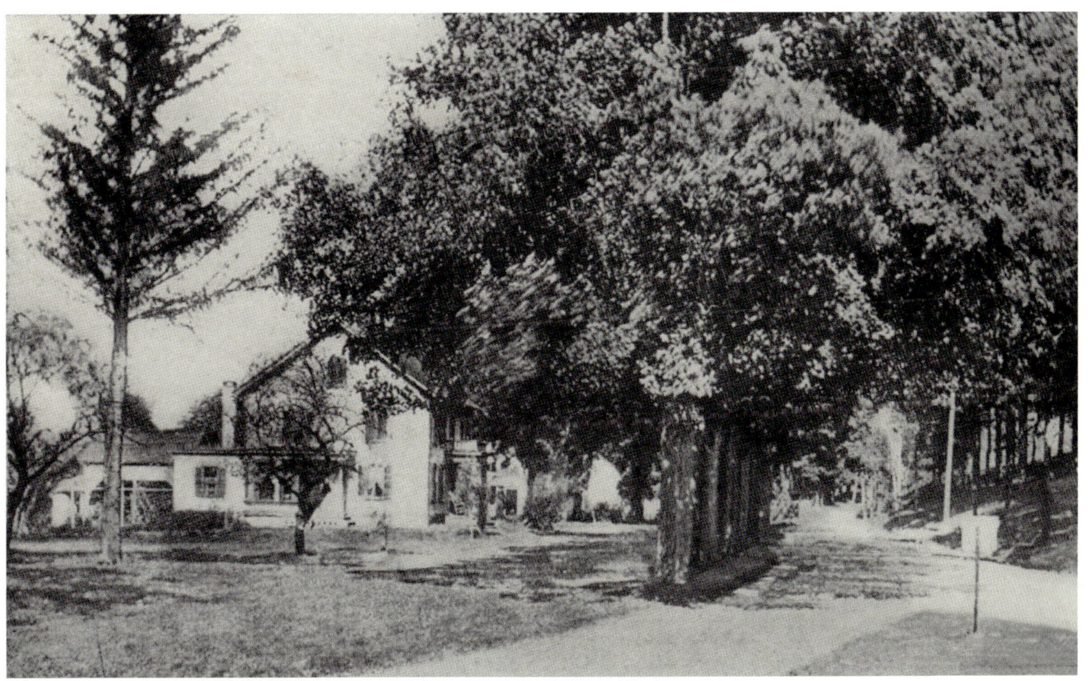

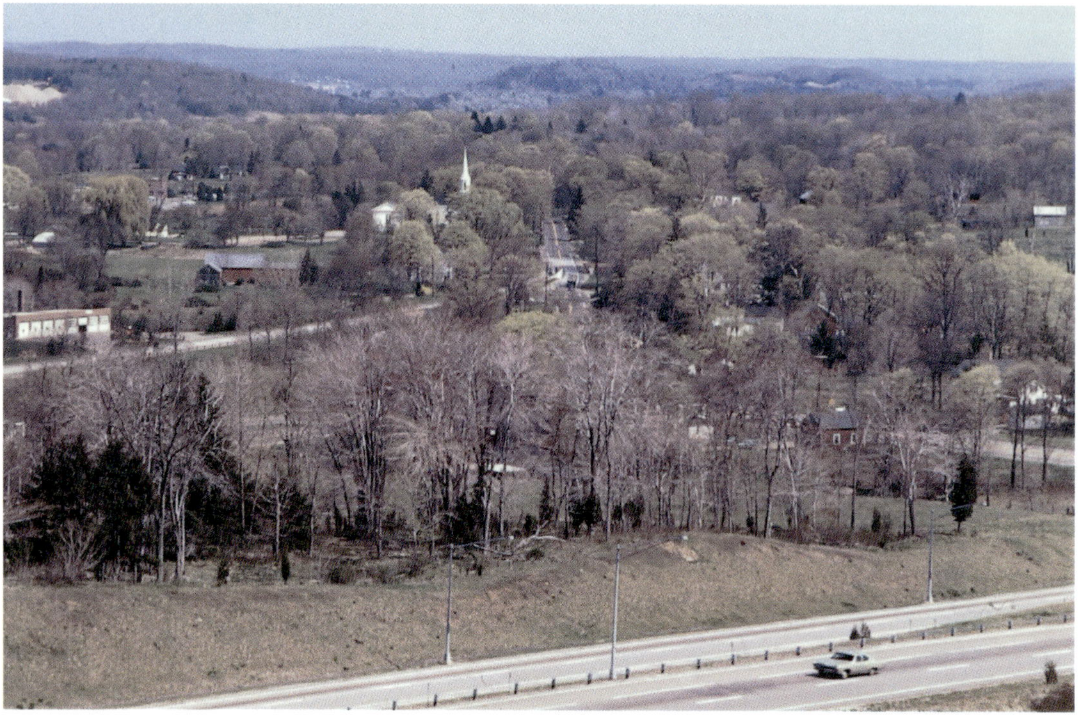

VIEW FROM I-84: This view of the town was taken in the 1966, shortly after Interstate 84 opened here in 1963. Off to the left, the land is being cleared for Heritage Village. To the far middle right is where the Southbury Plaza now stands. Along the middle, the steeple of the United Church of Christ is clearly visible and the main roads of Route 67 and 6 meet at a pleasant triangle. The original portion of the red barn now known as the Romanauskas barn was constructed around 1780 by Timothy Hinman. The earliest portion was built close to the house and expanded through the years. In the 1920, the barn was enlarged for a cow barn and a silo was added. In 1974, the Romanauskas family purchased the land and carefully restored the barn. (WB)

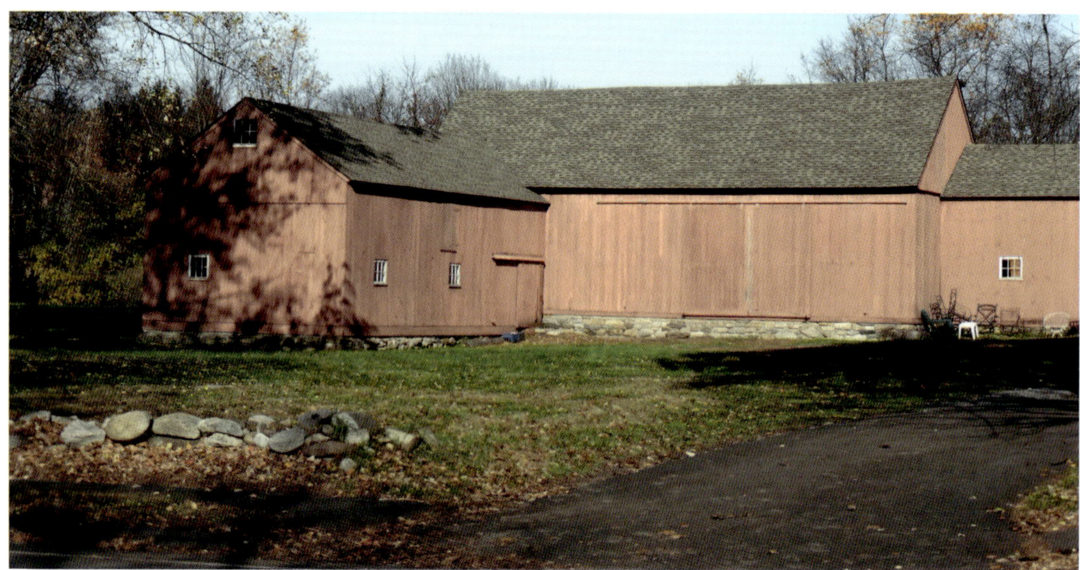

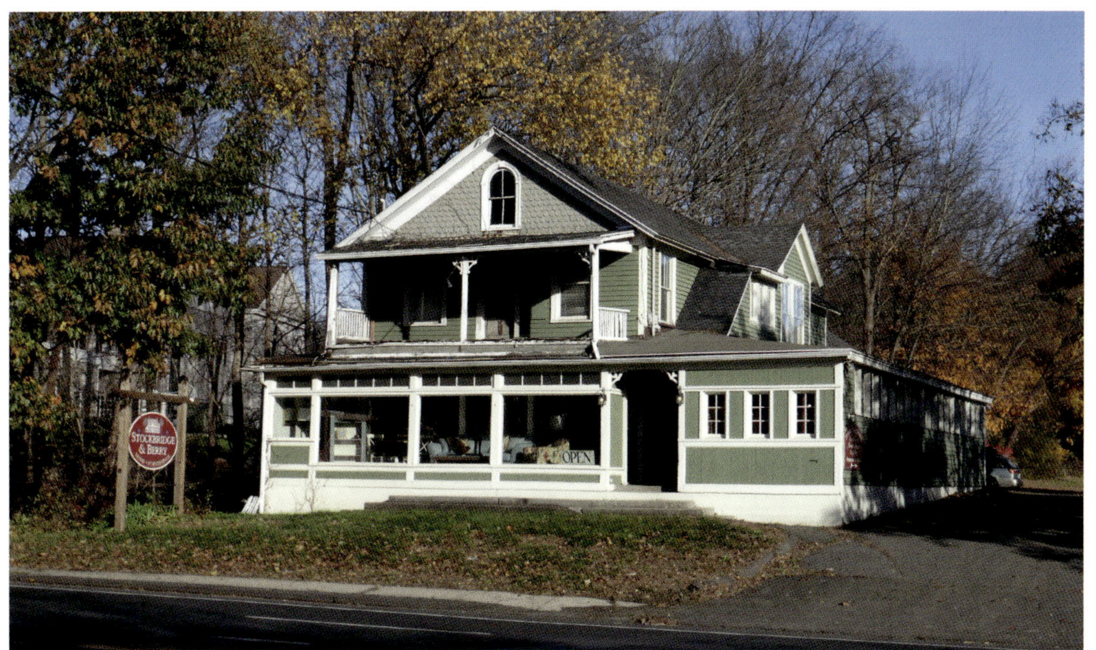

GENERAL STORE: Located a short distance north from the Southbury Plaza entrance is a building that has been a store since 1886. The first general store was run by C. K. and Burritt Osborn. In the early 1900s, the store was operated by C. L. Graef. Even when owners changed throughout the years, the general store was a favorite destination. Many people still have memories of visiting the Tyler Store or later the Green Store for the best penny candy selection in town. Postal services were part of the store from the early days until a town post office was built. Despite housing several businesses since the general store closed in 1977, the building has retained a similar façade throughout the years.

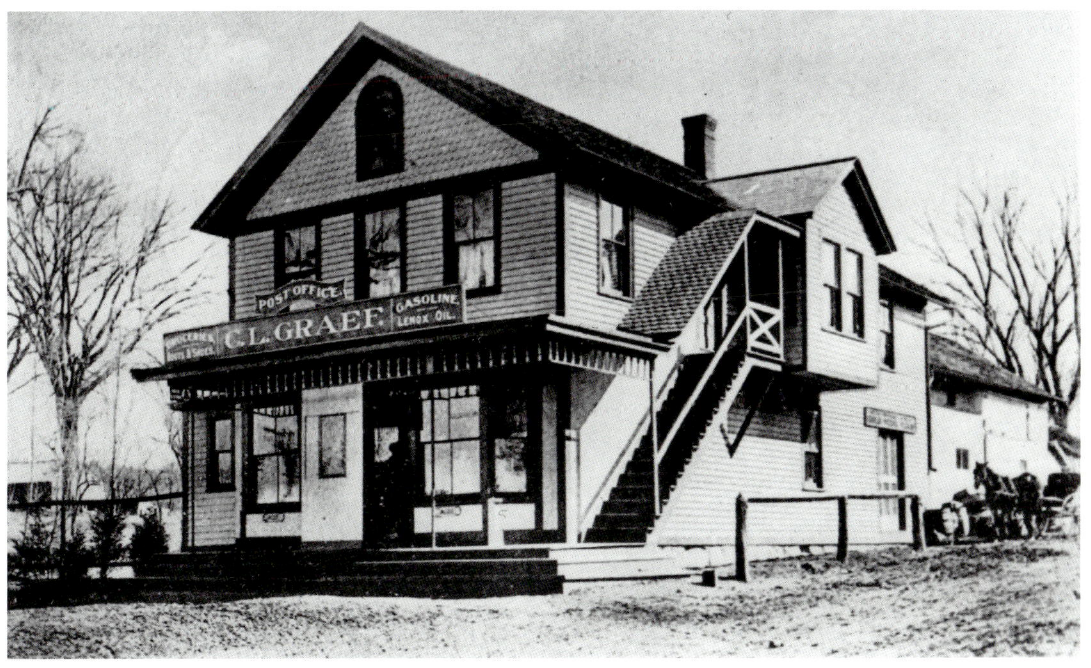

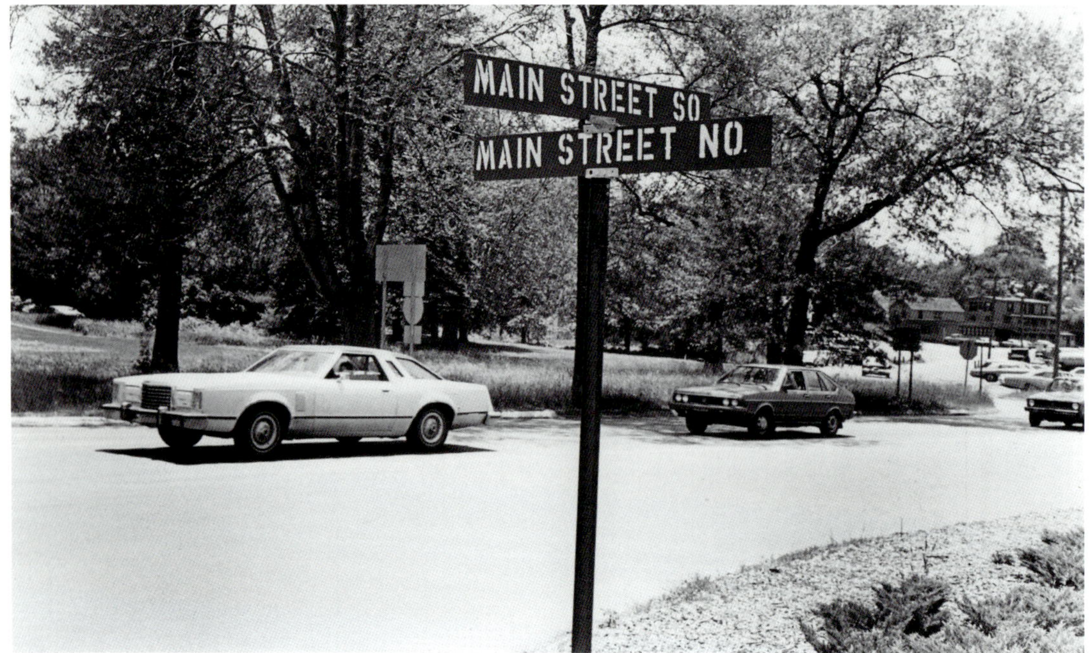

Big Change: The intersection of Main Street North and Main Street South as we know it now was made when exit 15 at Interstate 84 opened. For many years, there were not any traffic lights, only a stop sign. In the photograph above, the white car is next to Playhouse Corners, with the Oak Tree Inn clearly visible in the background. The bottom photograph was taken early on a Sunday morning from the Southbury Plaza looking toward Main Street North, with Playhouse Corner to the left.

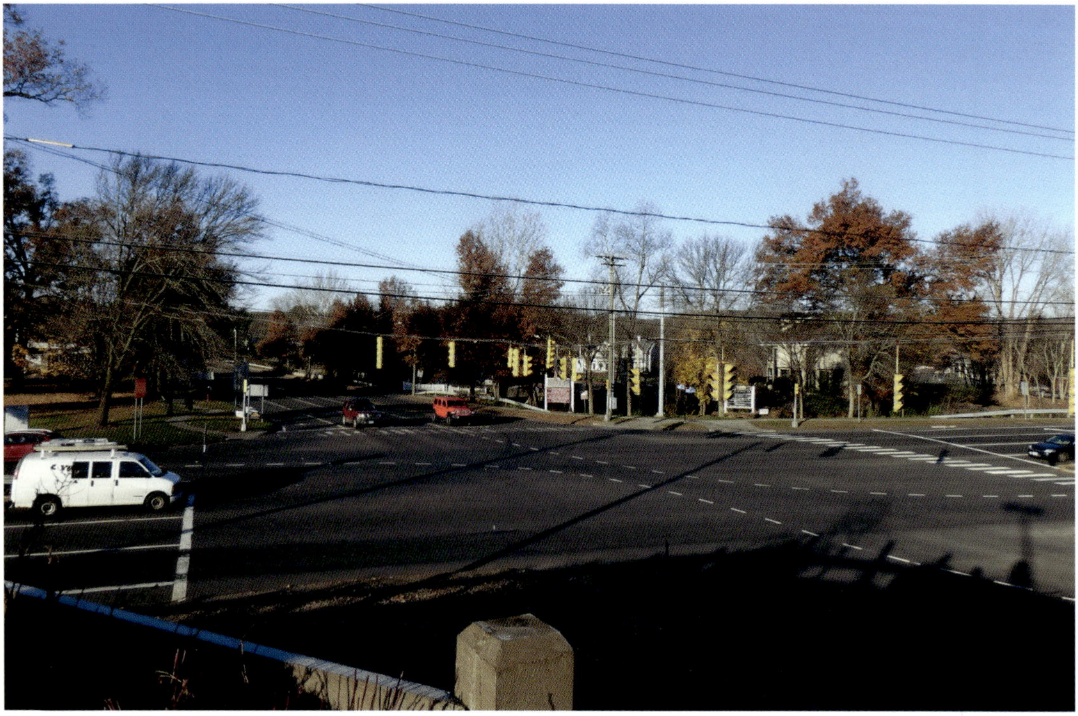

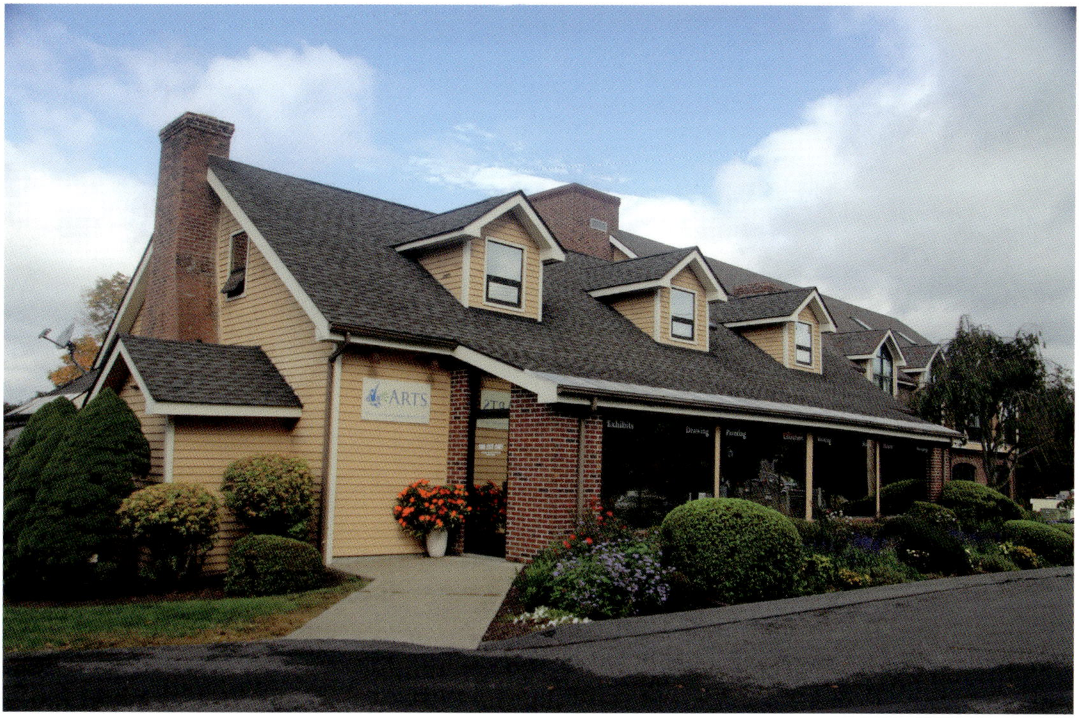

ICE CREAM: Briarwood Farms was a popular ice cream parlor and restaurant in the 1940s. The photo shows a large neon coffee cup with drips of coffee sliding down. Briarwood was a hangout for children leaving the nearby elementary school, and a stopping place for dinner after a show at the Southbury Playhouse. The restaurant changed owners and was at one time called, "The Three Gables Bar and Restaurant" and later, "Sabills." The Rathkeller was built on the lower level.

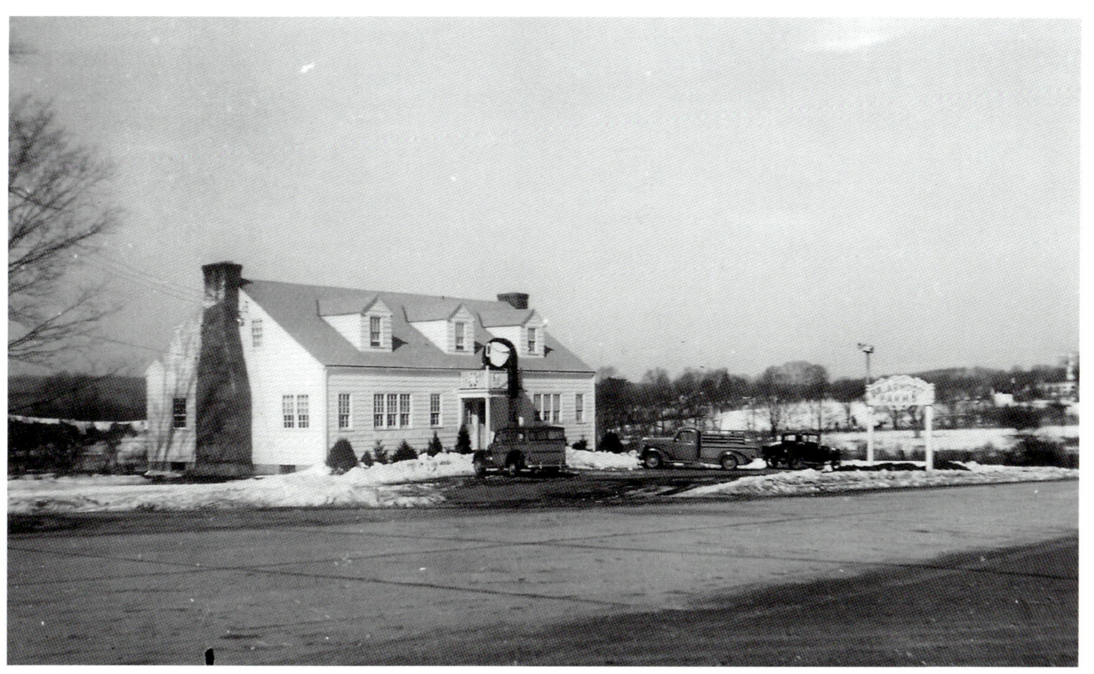

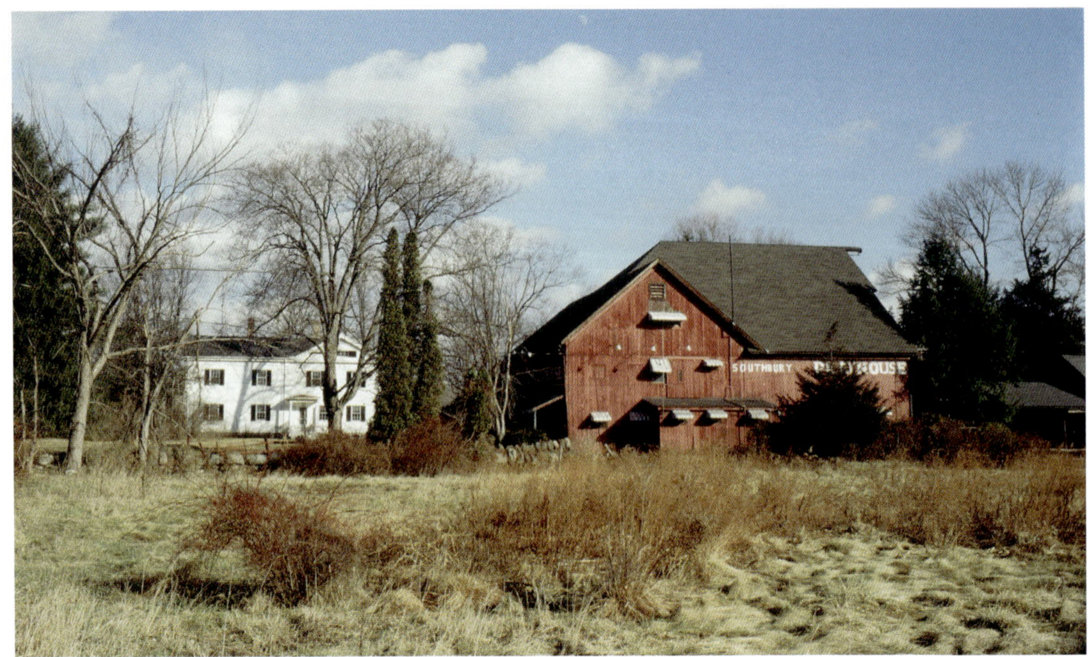

PLAYHOUSE: The Southbury Playhouse started as sturdy barn built around 1887 on the Hicock property. Built of chestnut beams and wooden pegs, it was once a tobacco barn and much later was used as a livestock auction barn. The animals would be unloaded from the local train station and brought down to the fields around the barn. Jack Quinn's Southbury Playhouse began in 1945, and continued under two other owners and hosted over fifty productions until 1985. The Southbury Playhouse was demolished in 1989. (KSL)

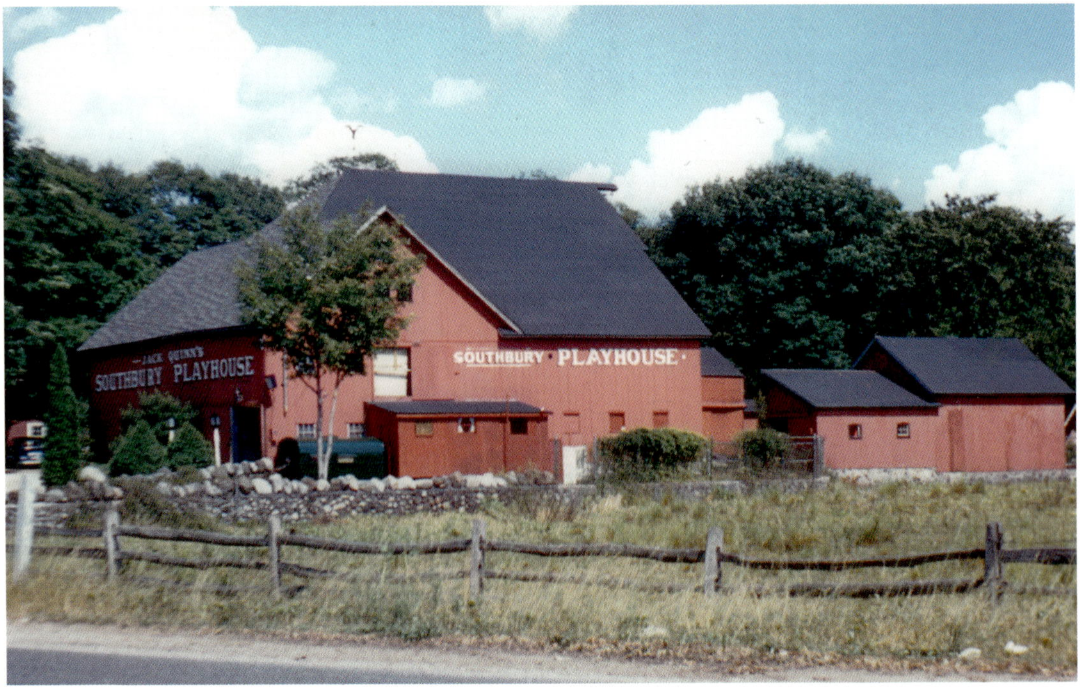

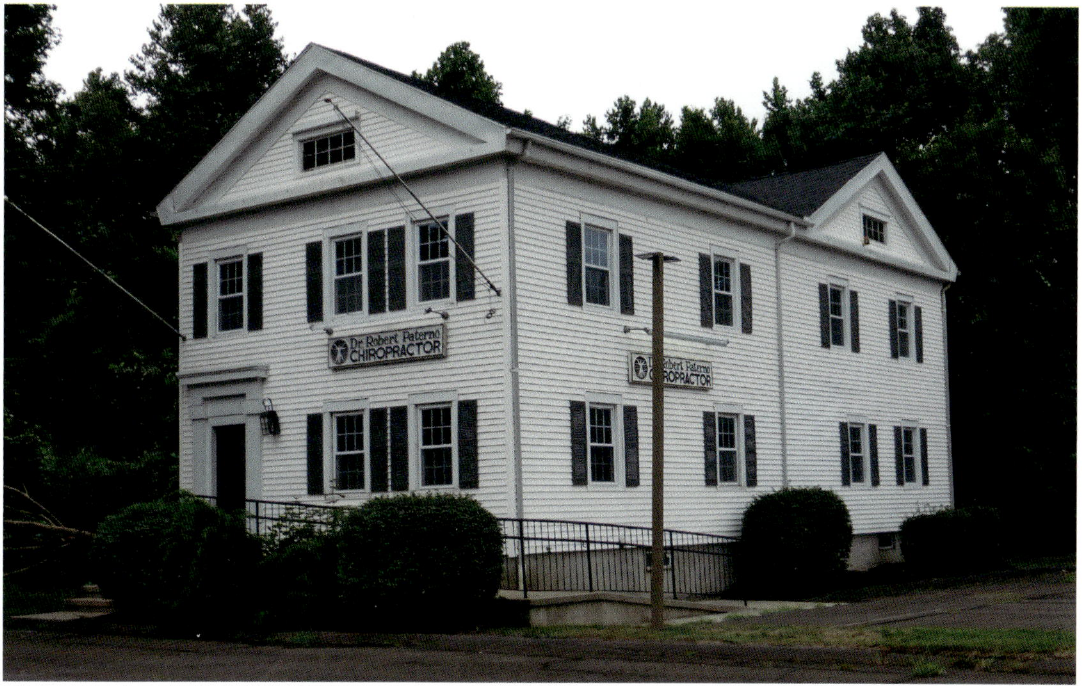

HOUSE MOVED: The building known as the Shelton House was once owned by the Hicock family on what is now the Playhouse Corners. At one time, the family had several buildings on the property, including barns and a mill. The Southbury Playhouse was the barn on the property. After the barn was razed, the house was moved off to the side corner of the new development. The bottom photograph shows two houses. The house on the right was dismantled in 1928 and taken to Darien, where it was reassembled.

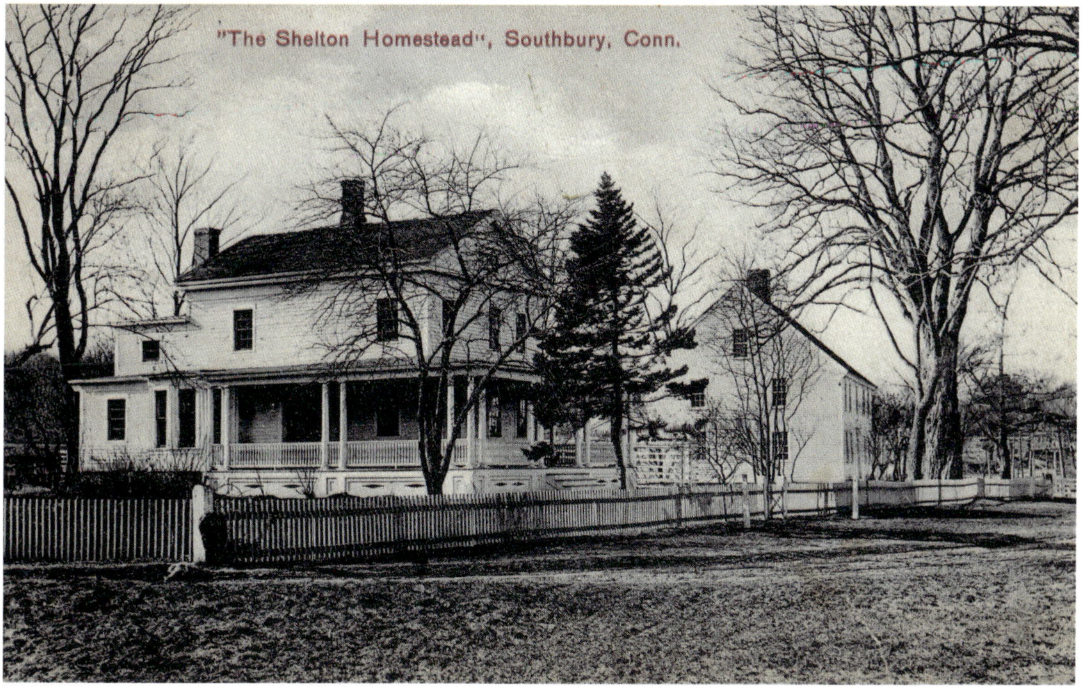

"The Shelton Homestead", Southbury, Conn.

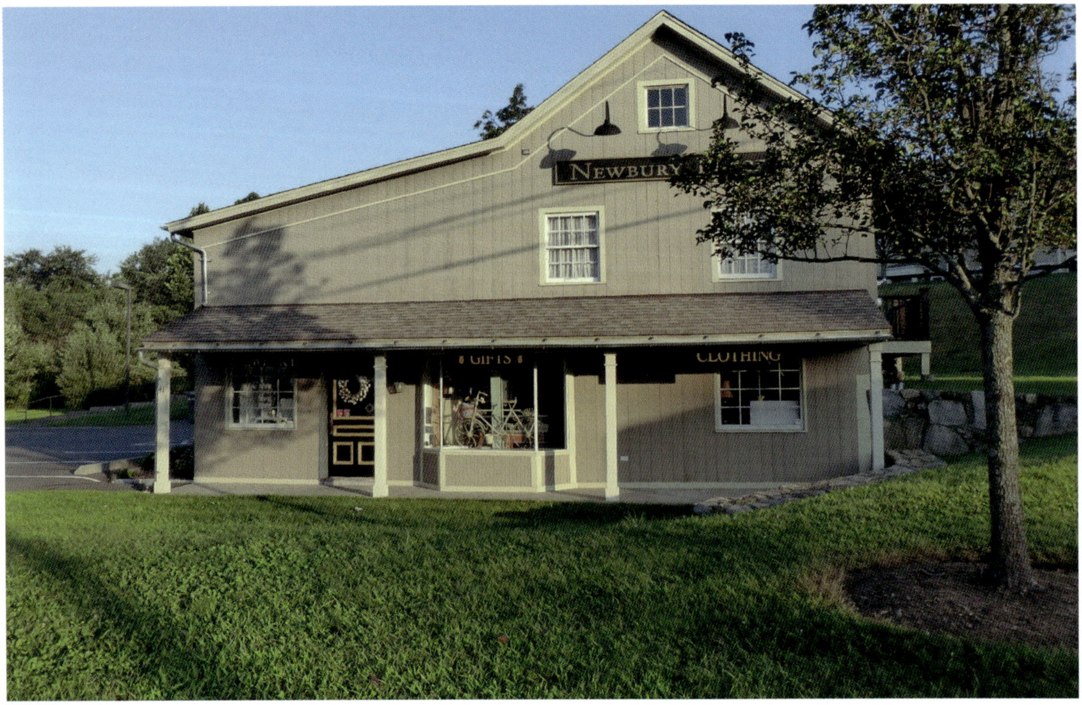

A. A. Stone & Sons Groceries: Andrew Alonzo Stone moved to Southbury before 1850 and purchased land from the Shelton family to open a general store, selling just about everything needed for a household or farm. In the rear of the building, he had supplies of lumber, coal, and grain. The cellar housed a grist mill where the grains were processed. The store later became C. L. Adams and Company and the mill was discontinued. Next it became Bullet Hill Supply which sold hardware along with feed and coal. Now, the Newberry Place graces the building. The old grist mill workings are still located in the cellar; however, they are sealed beneath a layer of concrete. The photo was taken in 1888.

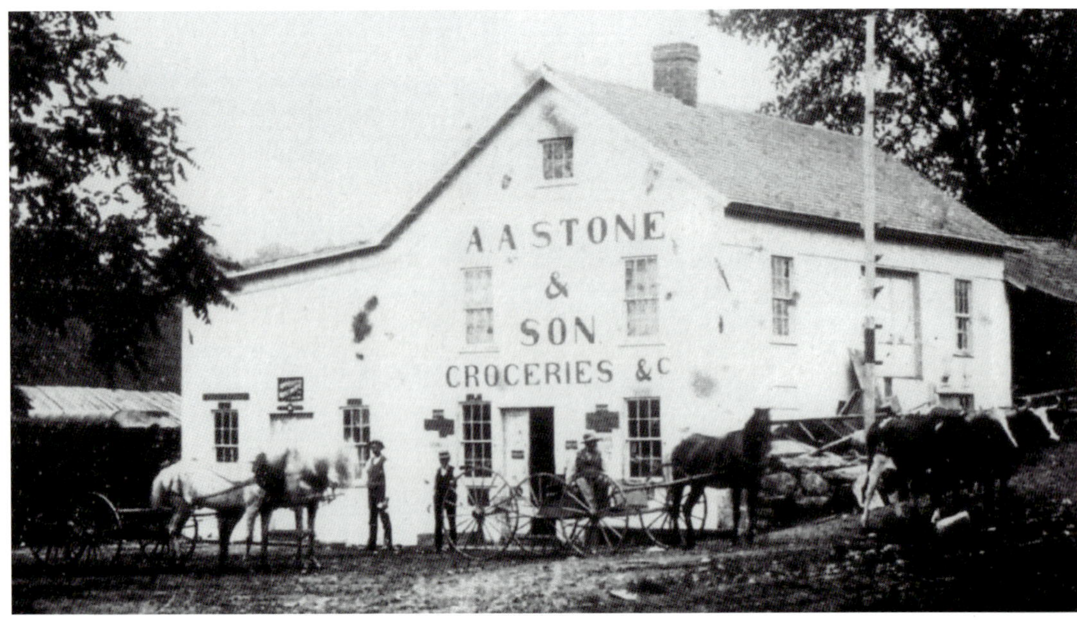

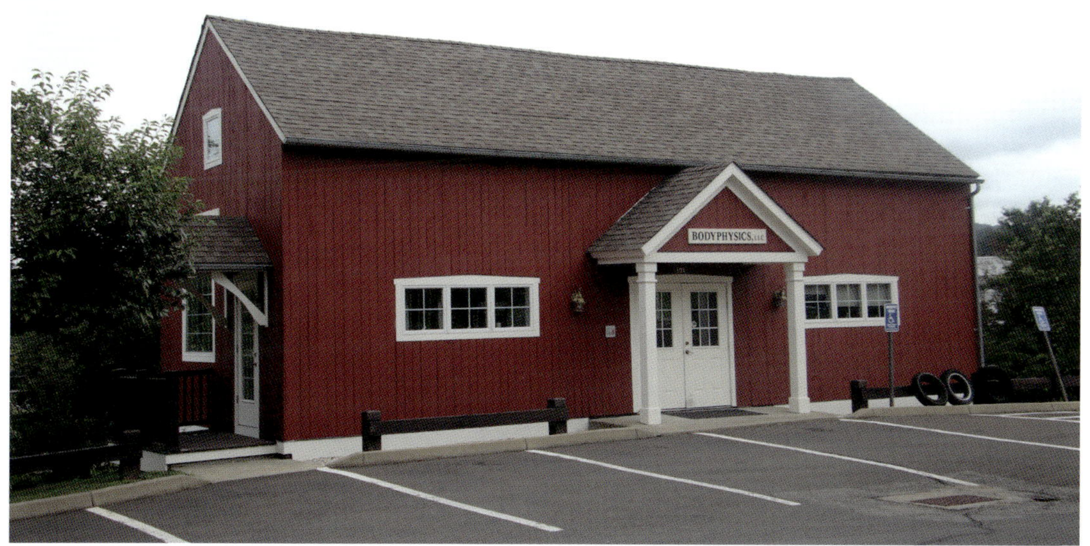

OXEN BARN: Located near Oak Tree Inn and A. A. Stone's Supply, the barn was once used to house oxen. The animals were kept there until they were needed to deliver supplies from Stone's or to be rented by a local farmer. A large scale, used to weigh loads, was located in front of the store. Later the property was owned by the St. Pierre family. When Mr. Metcalf purchased the property, he moved the barn well away from the road and renovated it into a two-story building.

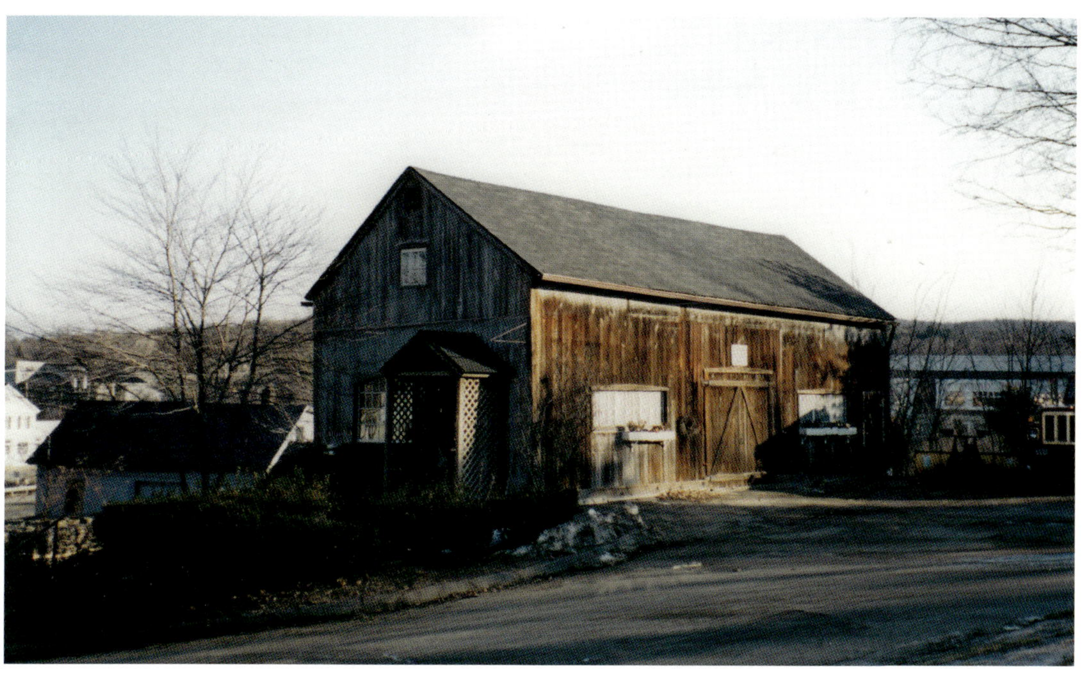

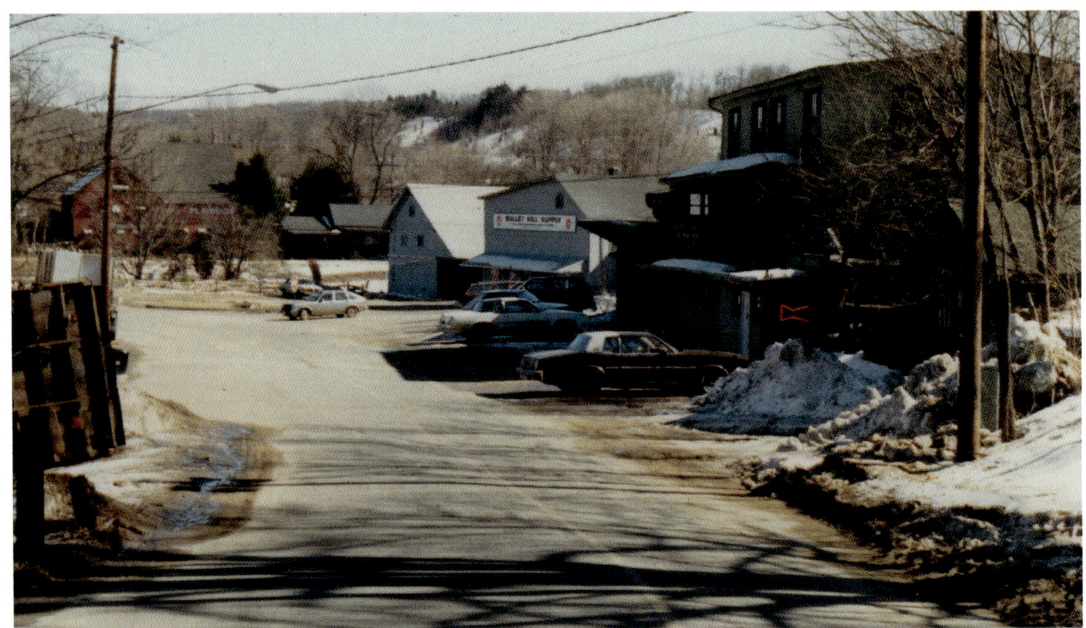

Bullet Hill Road: The above photograph shows a street view that looks past the Oak Tree Inn to the Bullet Hill Supply, with the Southbury Playhouse in the distance. Hine Brothers gas station is to the left. The old Southbury train depot used to be just up the hill to the right. The bottom photo is an early view in the reverse direction of the intersection, looking directly at the Oak Tree Inn. Off to the left would have been the busy feed store, and the road up to the depot. Fenced in on the right is where the Hine Brothers now have a gas station. As you can see, the road was very wide and muddy.

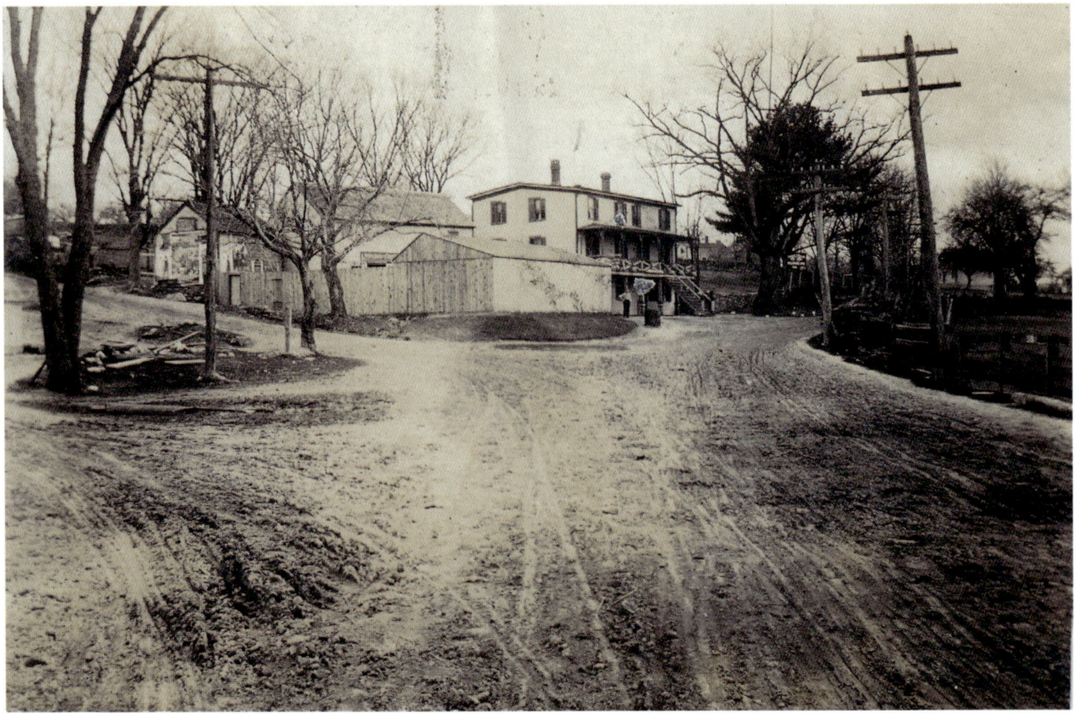

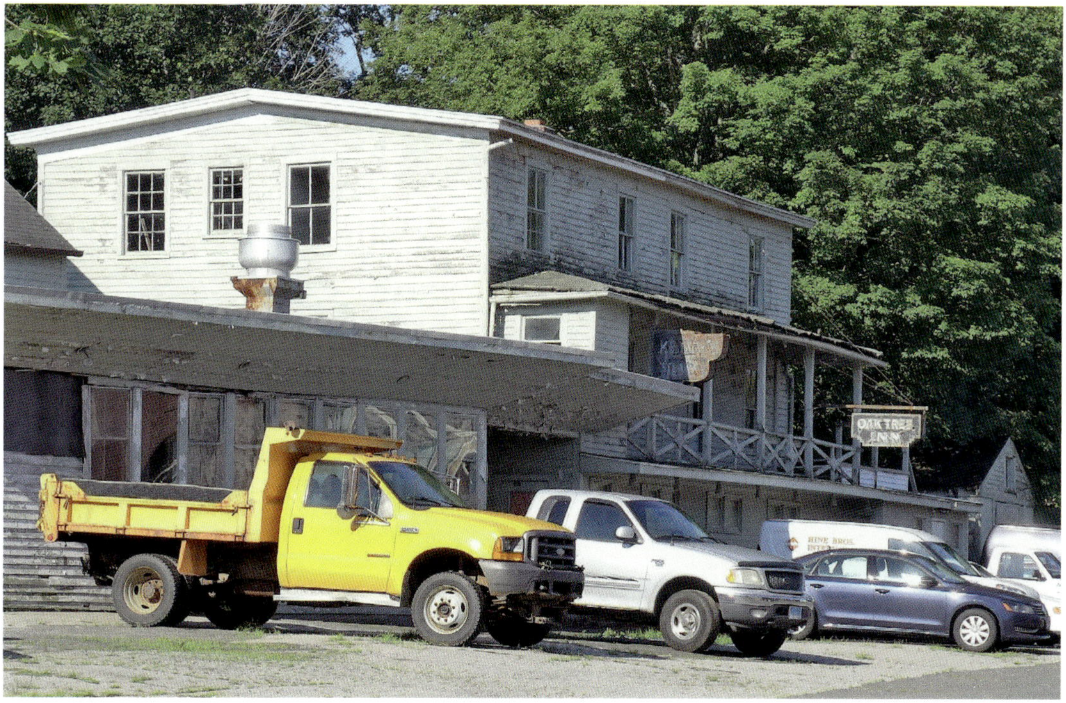

OAK TREE INN: Located in the heart of the activity near the Southbury train depot, the Oak Tree House was the place to stay in nineteenth century. The name came from the large old oak in front of the building. There were many owners through the years, including Wallace Nutting who was known for his hand-colored photographs. The name was changed to the Oak Tree Inn and the Kelly family owned the building from 1936 for almost sixty years. A search through old newspapers shows the Oak Tree Inn was a popular place for celebrities to meet after a show at the Southbury Playhouse, and a venue for wedding receptions or celebration events for groups as large as 200 people.

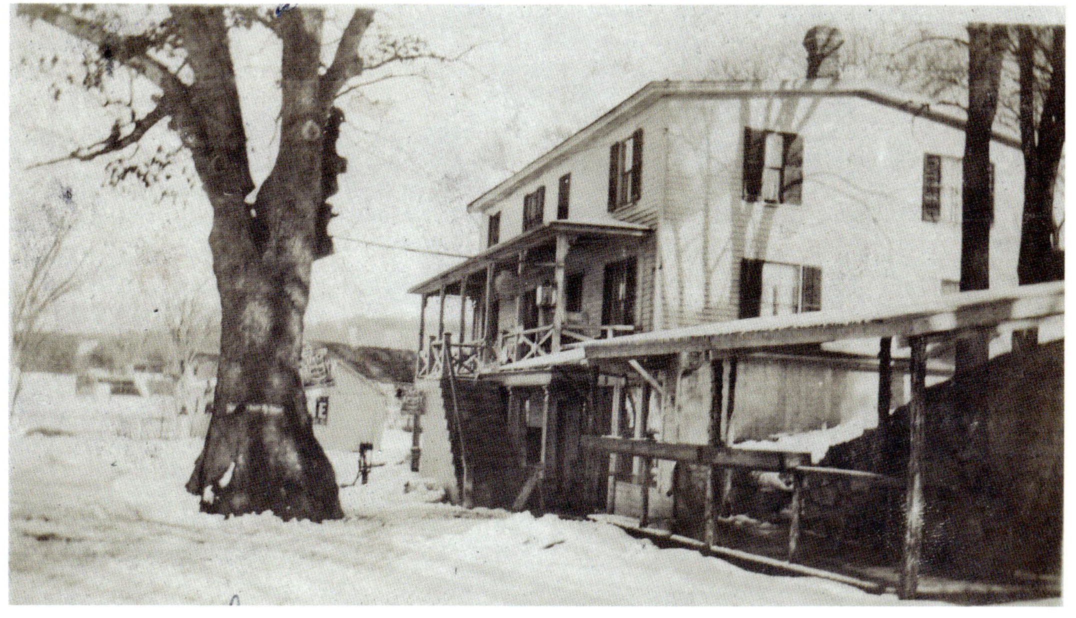

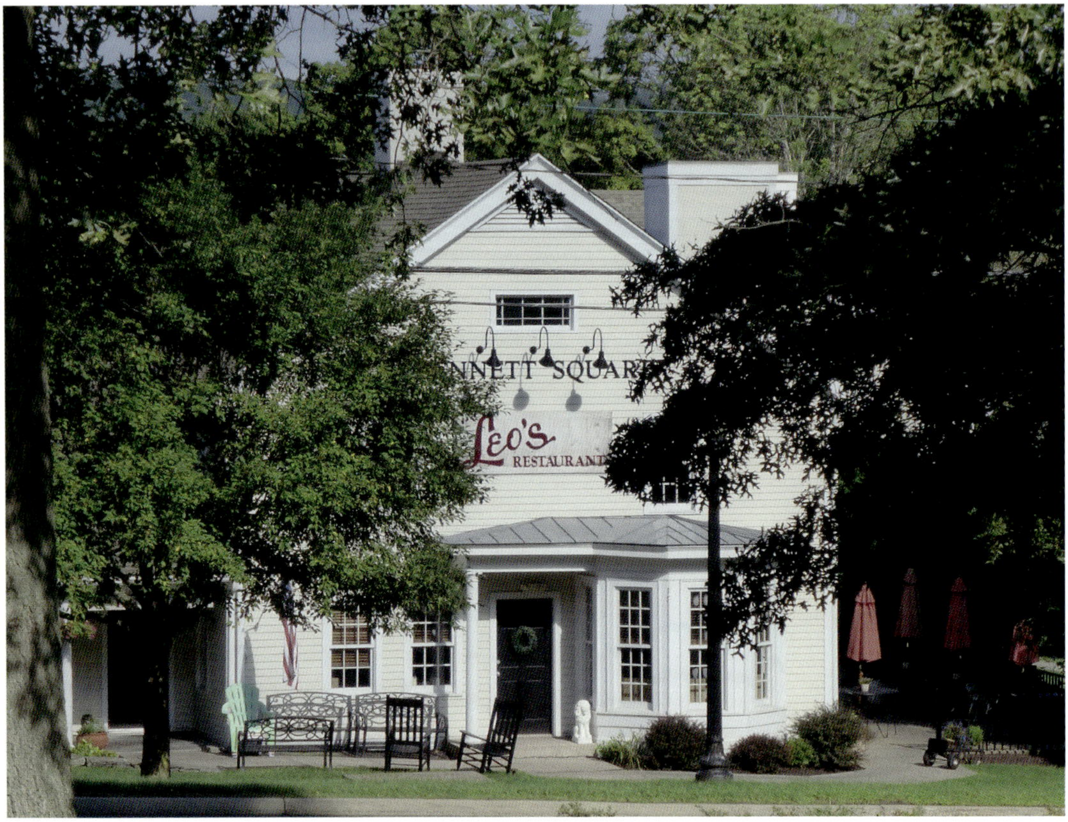

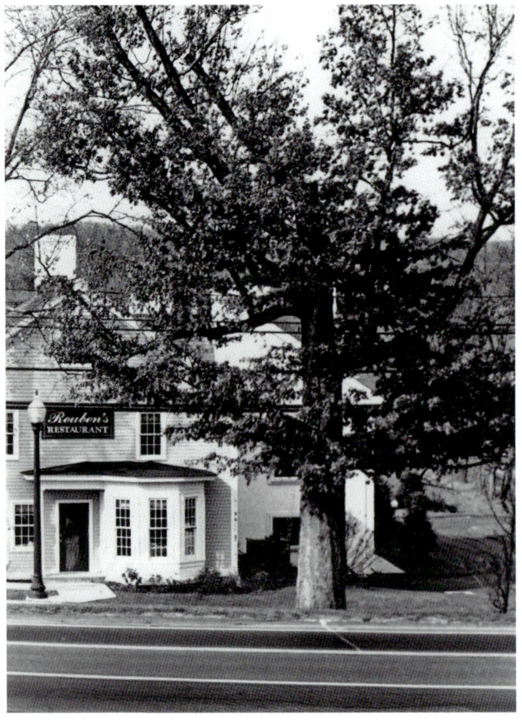

LEO'S: Originally a home owned by the Hicock family, the building later became the residence of Henry B. Russell, who served Southbury as the town treasurer, first selectman, and a lawmaker for forty years. In 1902, Russell attended the Constitutional Convention in Hartford as Southbury's representative to discuss making changes to the state's constitution. The building was renovated and expanded to include office space. The old house is now used as Leo's Restaurant, which has old exposed beams and two old fireplaces.

CONSTITUTION OAK: Once located in front of the current Leo's Restaurant, the large pin oak was a fixture on Main Street South. At the Constitutional Conference, each town was given a seedling in remembrance of the Charter Oak in Hartford, where the Connecticut charter was placed in hiding to prevent the British army from finding it. A monument was placed by the Constitution Oak tree in 1991 by the granddaughter of Henry B. Russell. The oak tree was removed in 2002, because it had become a safety hazard due to a rotting trunk. The monument is now at the Old Town Hall Museum, along with a polished slice of the tree.

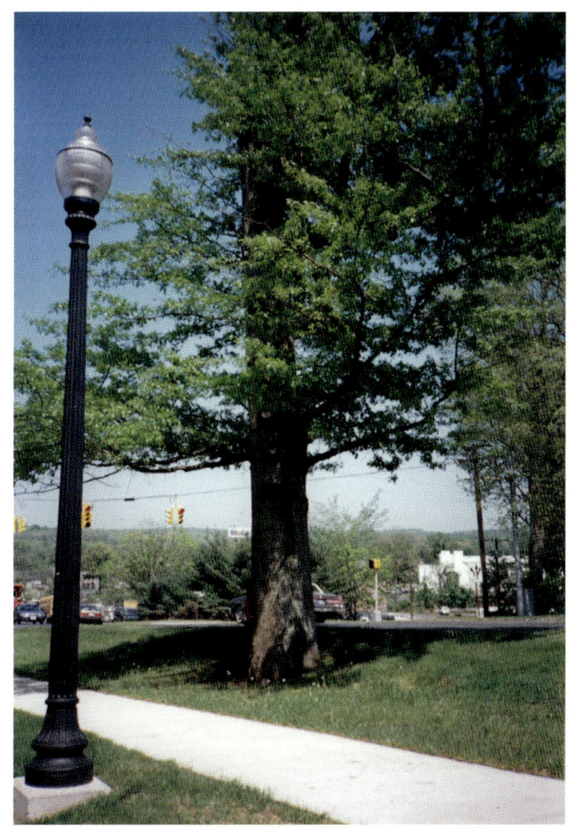

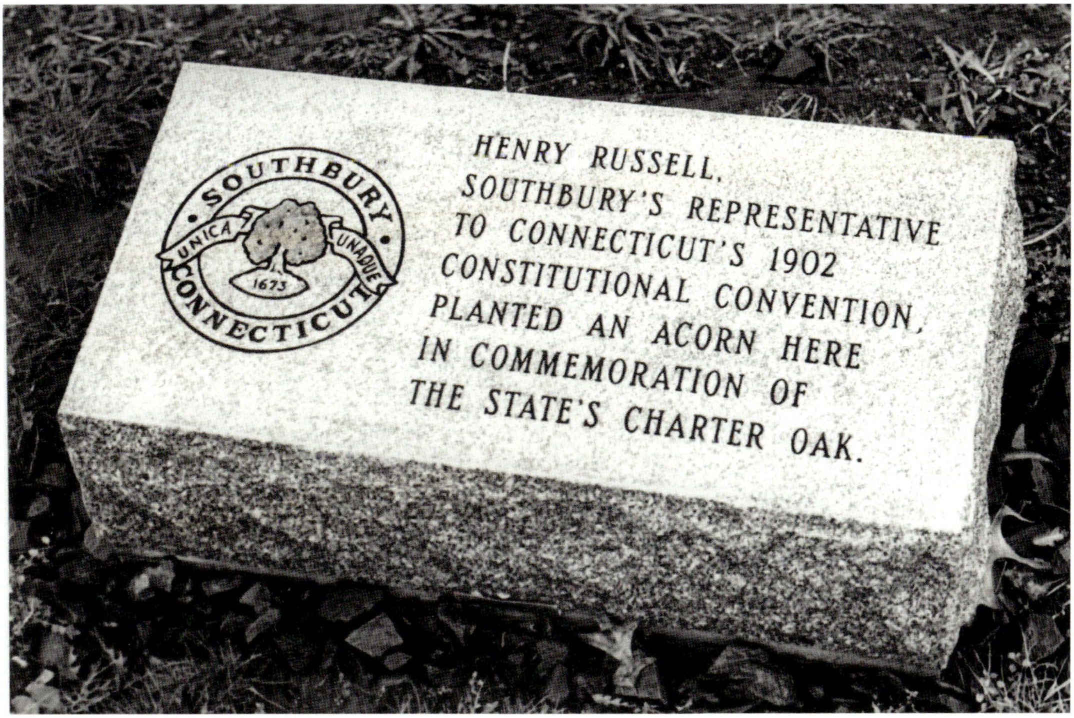

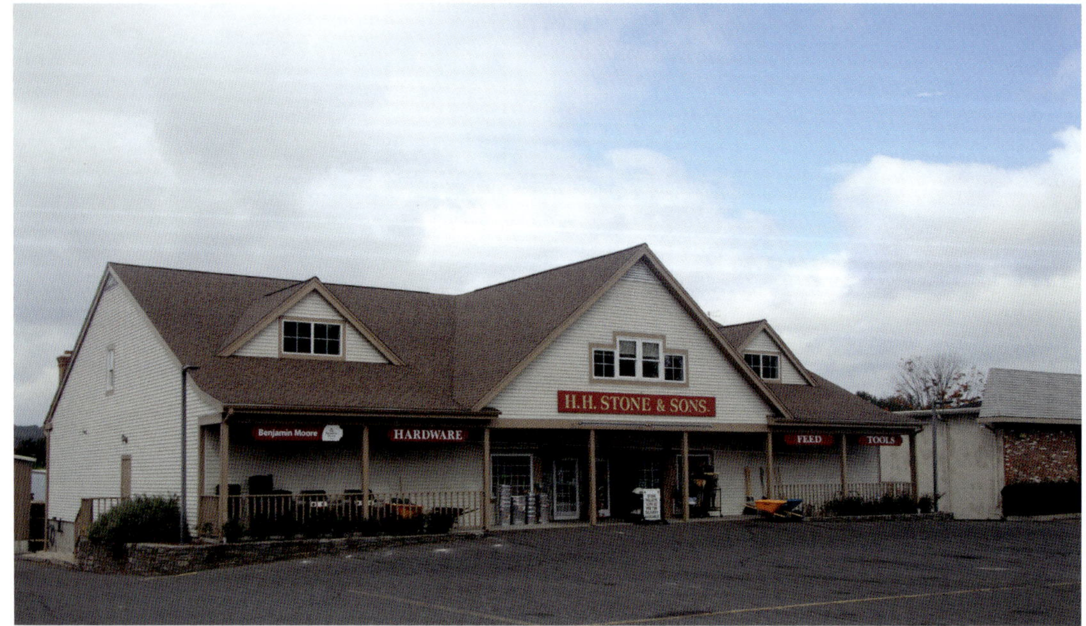

HARDWARE AND MORE: Harvey Harry Stone, grandson of A. A. Stone, purchased land next to the train depot in 1893 for a feed, grain, and coal business. When the railroad was in its final days in Southbury, Stone moved his business to Main Street South, next to the Southbury Food Center. That building is no longer there, being replaced by the present H. H. Stone and Sons. The bottom photograph was taken in the mid-1960s, and the top photograph was taken around 1985. (WB)

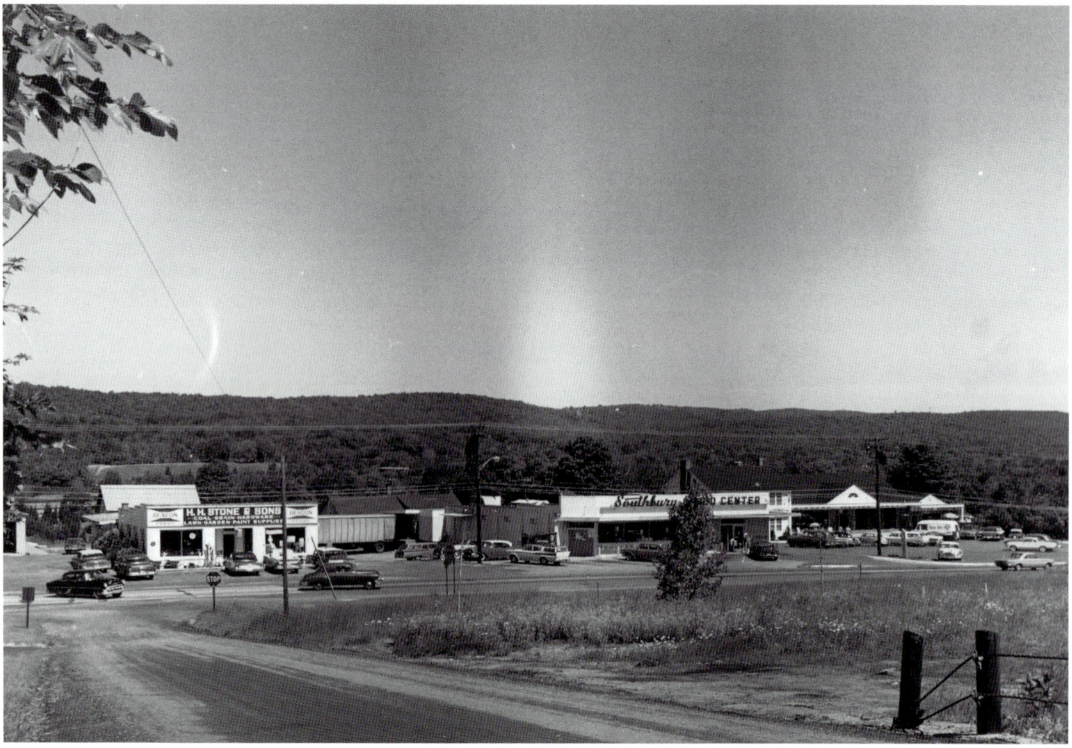

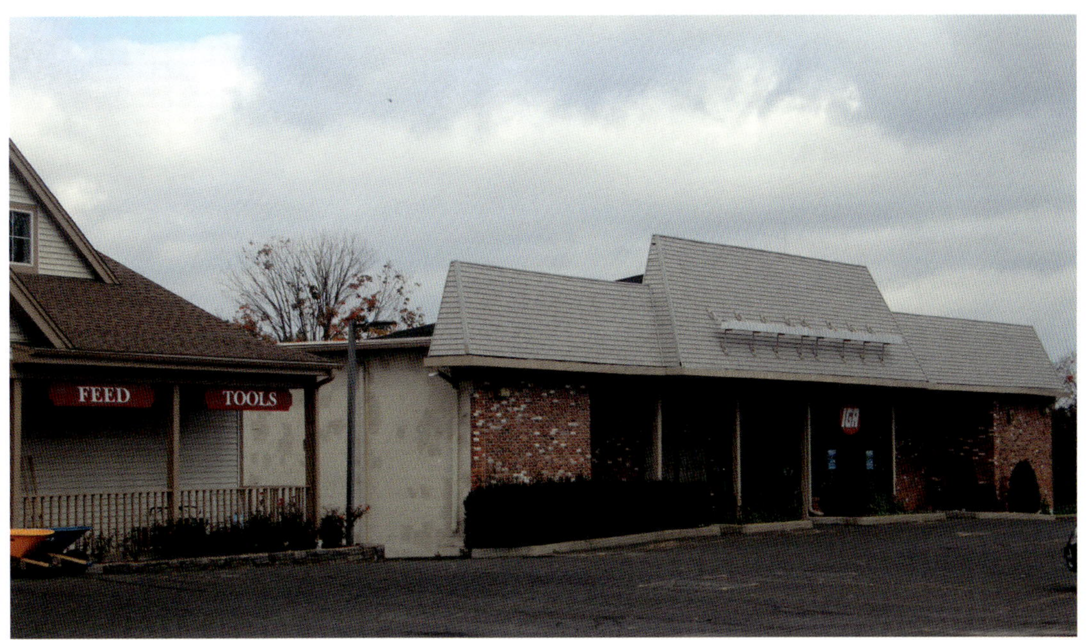

SUPERMARKET: The Southbury Food Center was built about 1941 and was the first "modern" grocery store in town. George Tomey started the business with the goal of good customer service in a clean store. The store was kept in the family for over sixty-six years, before it went through a couple of owner changes, and eventually closed in 2015. At the store entrance near the carriage collection plaza was an endearing brass sign which said, "Be an angel, bring back your cart."

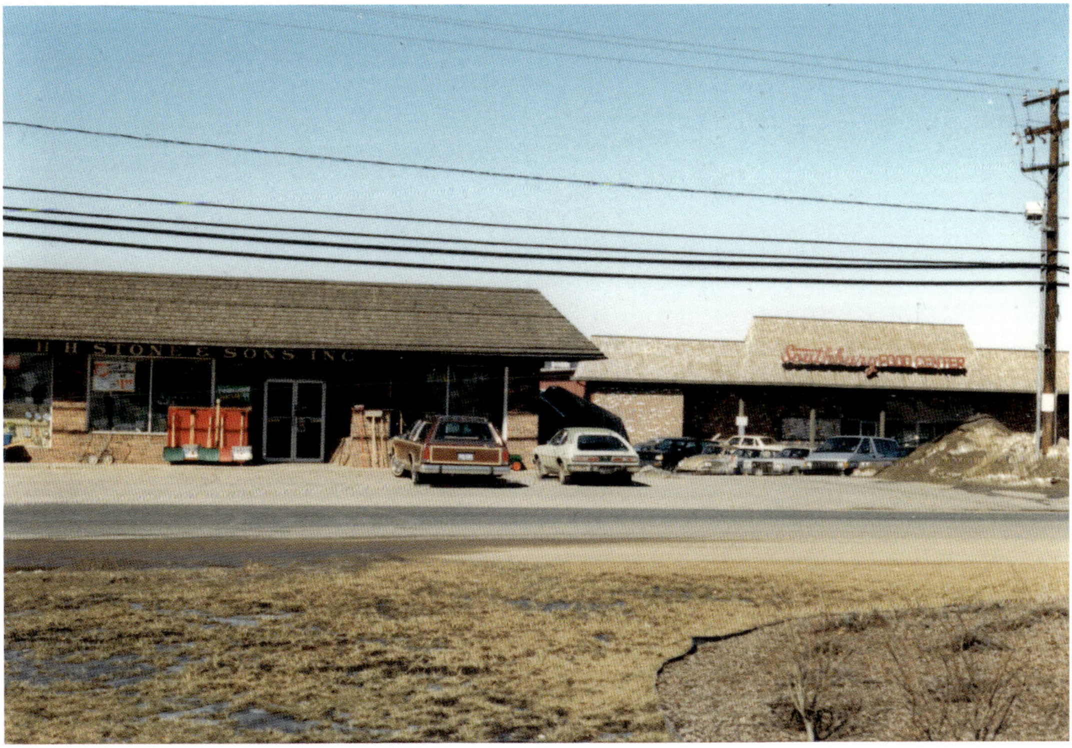

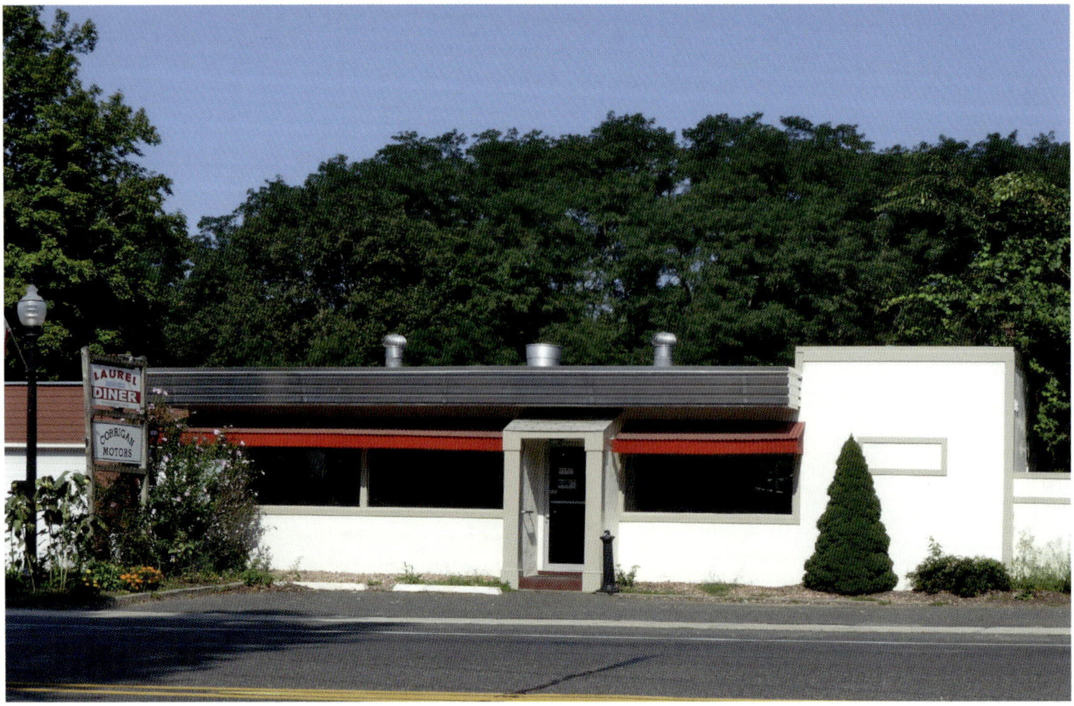

DINER: Since 1949, the Laurel Diner has been a fixture in town. Named after the state flower, it was built in the pattern of many diners of the time, including counter seating with high stools, and a few tables along the windows. The garage next door was once the Laurel Shell, selling Shell gasoline, making this a handy quick stop for both cars and passengers. The Laurel Diner, the oldest eat-in restaurant on Main Street, is still a favorite local stop for breakfast and lunch.

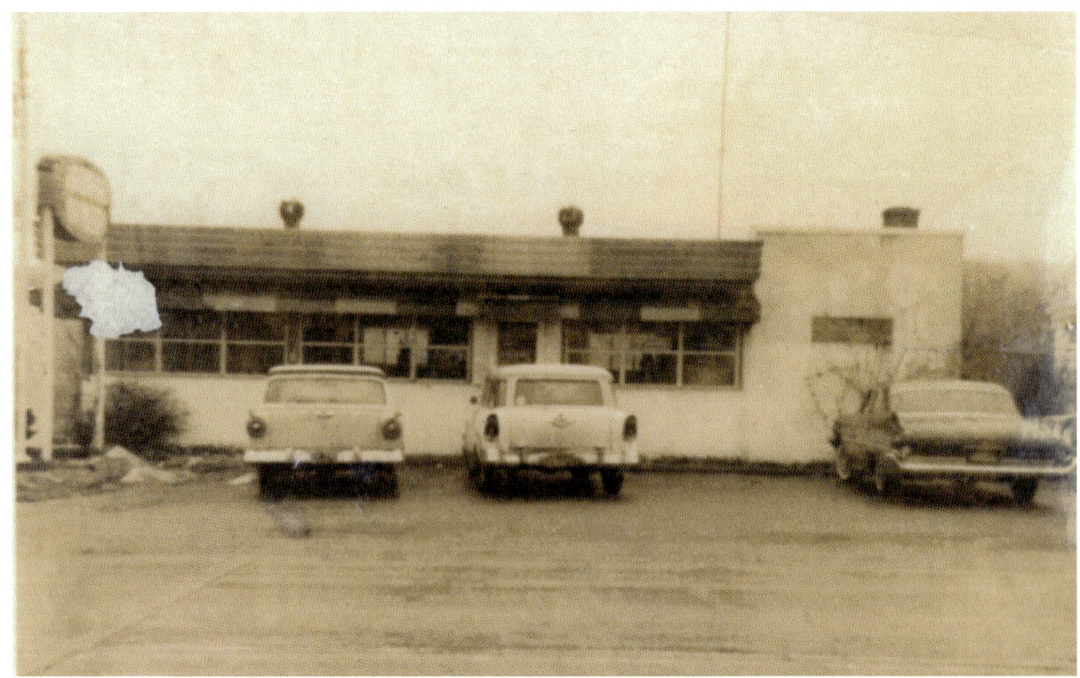

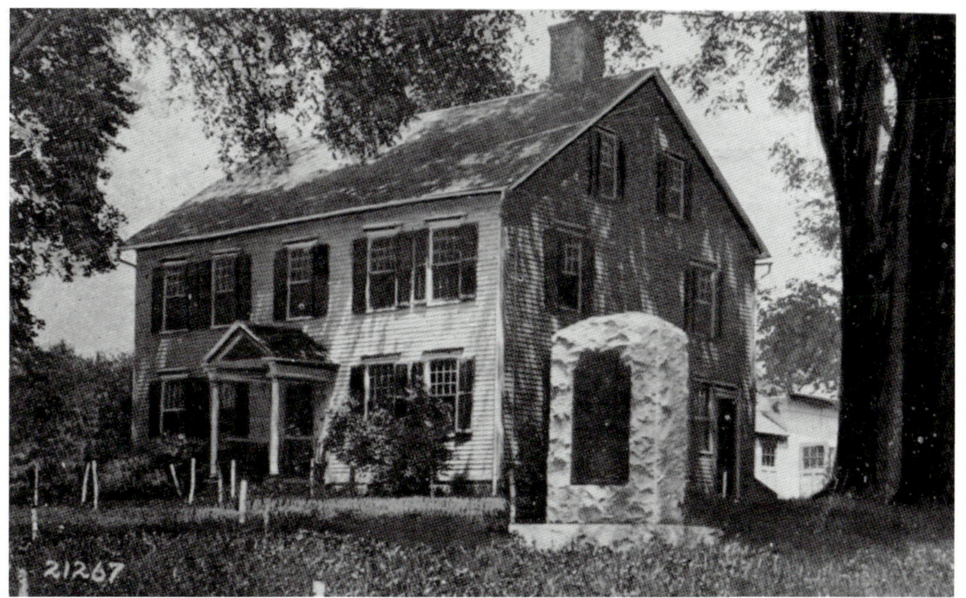

MONUMENT: The Southbury World War I monument looks similar to many other such monuments around the state, listing the names of the brave soldiers who fought from 1917 to 1919. This one, of course, tells the story our local heroes. The monument was originally placed at the old UCC parsonage at the corner of Route 67 and Old Waterbury Road, where it stayed until the road was widened and the intersection changed. It was moved to what is now the Veteran's Green, even before the Town Hall was constructed in the 1970s. Additional monuments and park benches have been installed in Veteran's Green to honor the sacrifice of our soldiers.

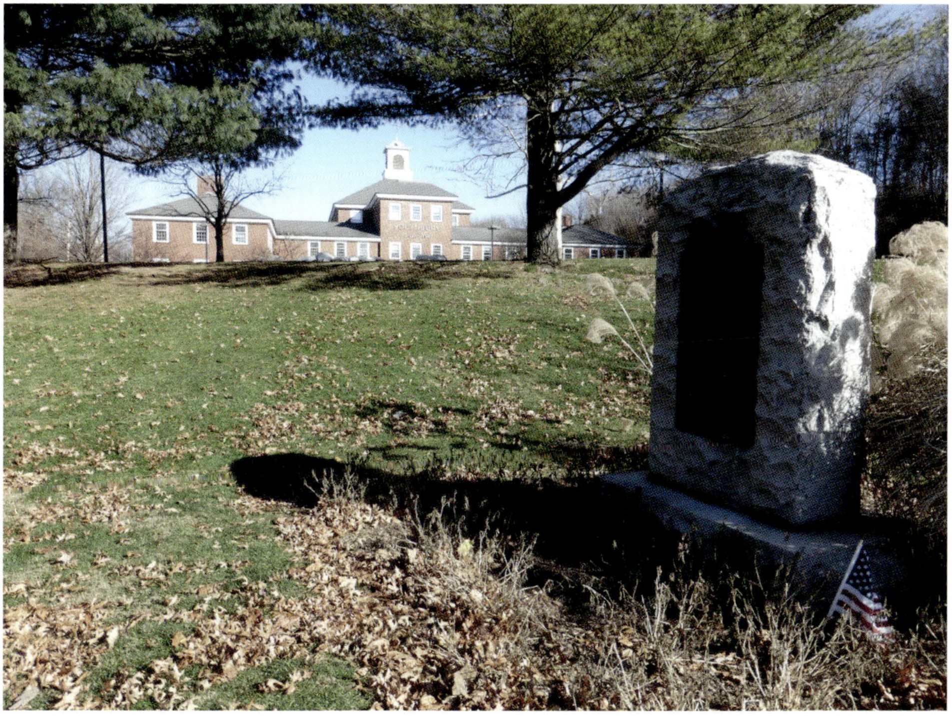

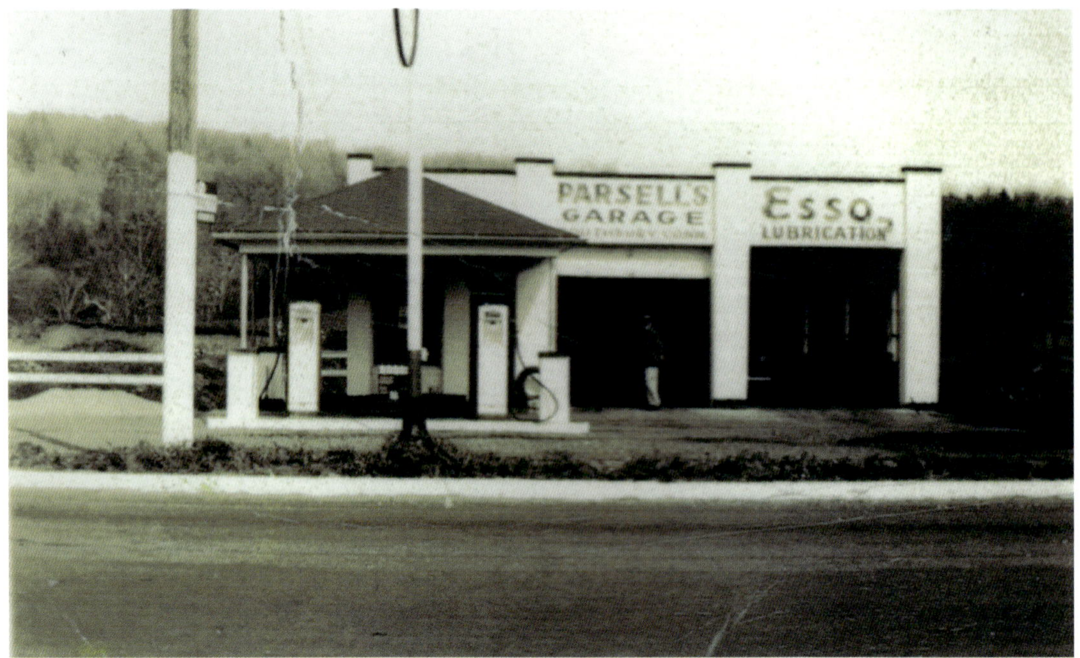

OLDEST BUSINESS: Wallace Parsell opened his Esso gas station on Main Street South in 1945 when Route 6, the main road from Danbury to Hartford, went right through town. The two-lane road sprouted many small gas stations along its route to take care of the traveler's needs. Parsell also ran a used car dealership, which sold cars made by Kaiser Frazier Motors and the Hudson Motor Car Company. The Hudsons are pictured here below. Even though the gas station and the used car shop have disappeared, you can still find the business being run by the fourth generation of the Parsell family, who continue to service and repairs cars. (Photographs courtesy of Dusty and Jim Parsell.)

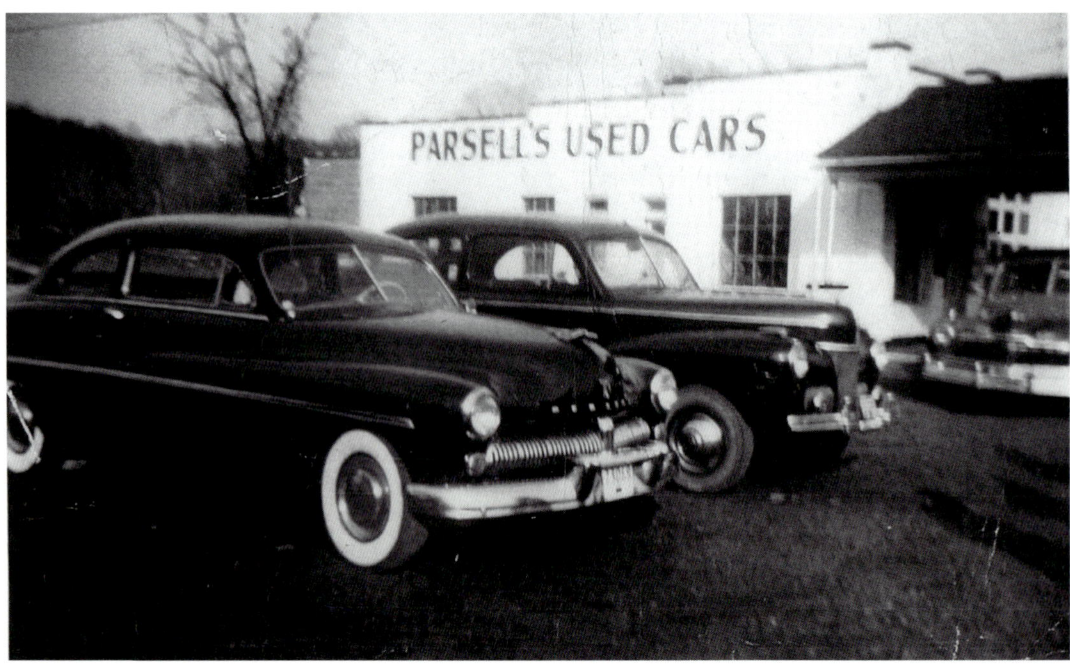

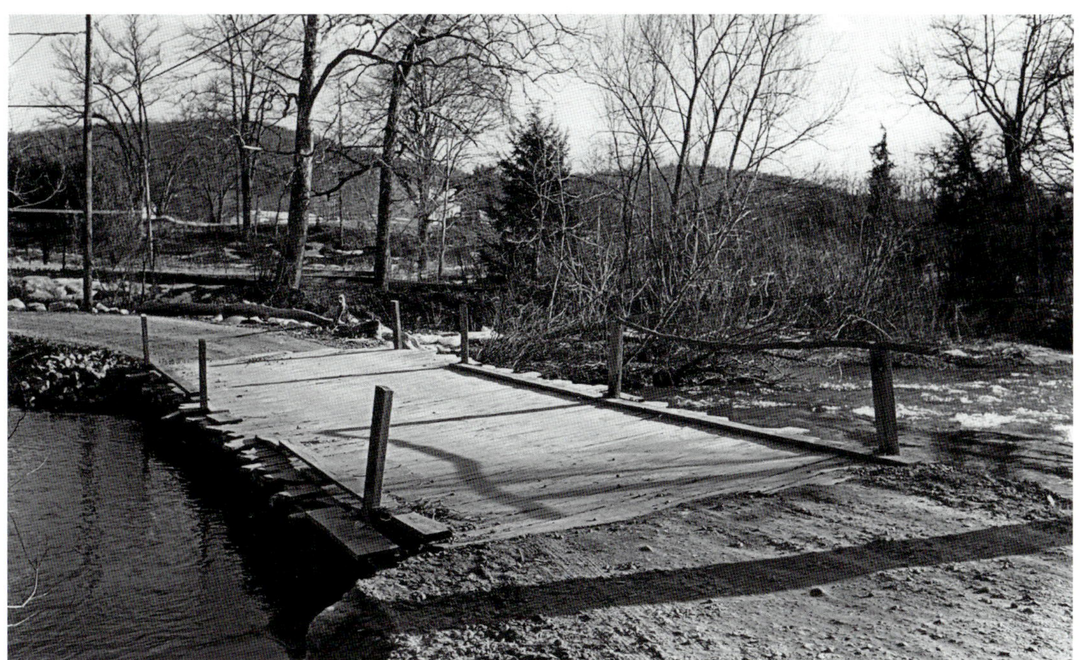

FLOOD BRIDGE: Early in the town's history, a southern route to South Britain was needed. The north route required a trip "over the mountain" according to early records, which was difficult to travel, especially in the winter. The decision was made that crossing the Pomperaug River at what is now called Flood Bridge was an easier route. Through the years, there have been many bridges that had to be replaced due to high waters, especially during the spring freshets or ice jams. The two photographs show views from different years. The old bridge was finally replaced with a higher, stronger, concrete structure that will likely withstand flooding for many years.

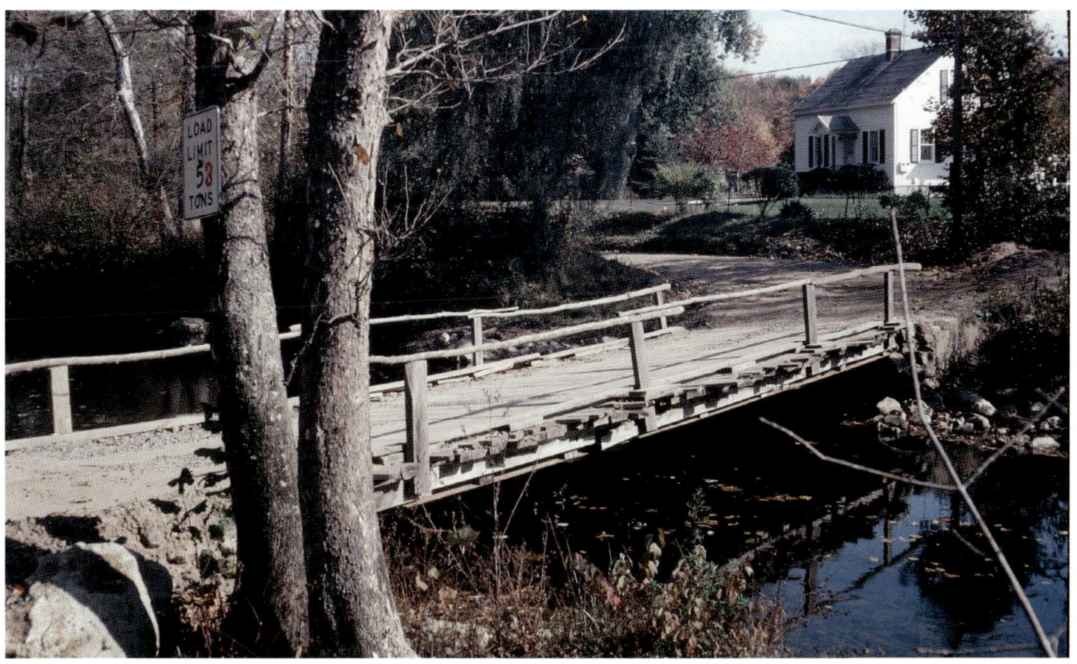

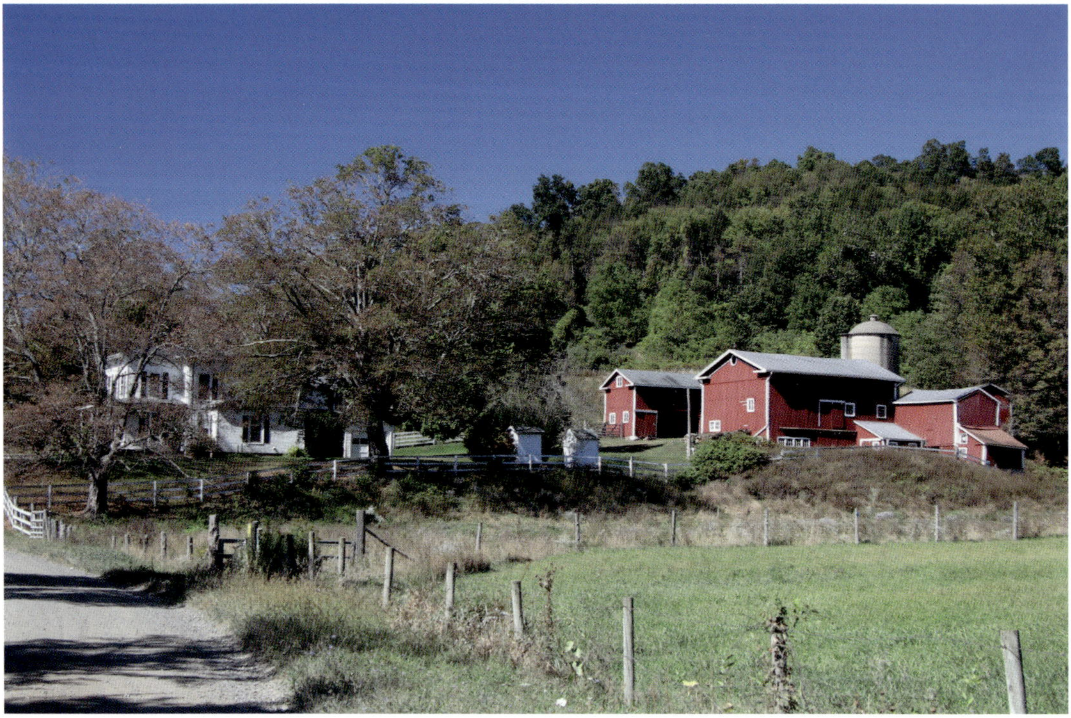

PLATT FARM: Following the route of Rochambeau troops, the Flood Bridge road leaves the narrow passage along the Pomperaug River and opens into a meadow with an idyllic farm and barns built around 1800. The farm was previously owned by the Mitchell family for generations, and sold to a relative, Willis Platt, in 1950. The Southbury Land Trust purchased almost 110 acres of the land in 2001 to be preserved as it is for future generations. Even though the two photographs look almost identical, they were actually taken forty years apart.

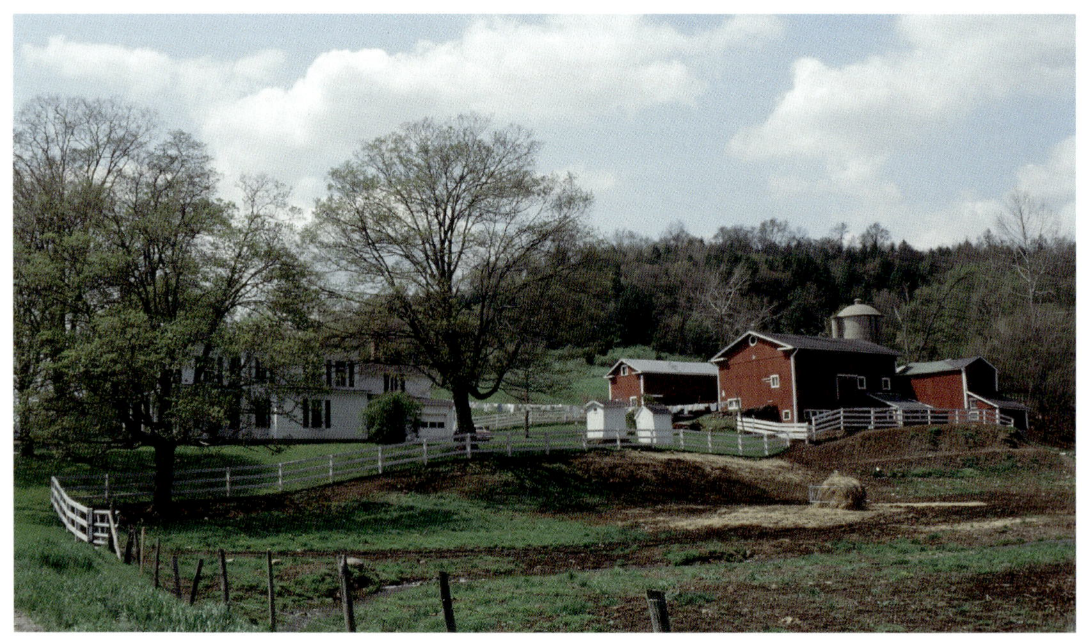

2
South Britain

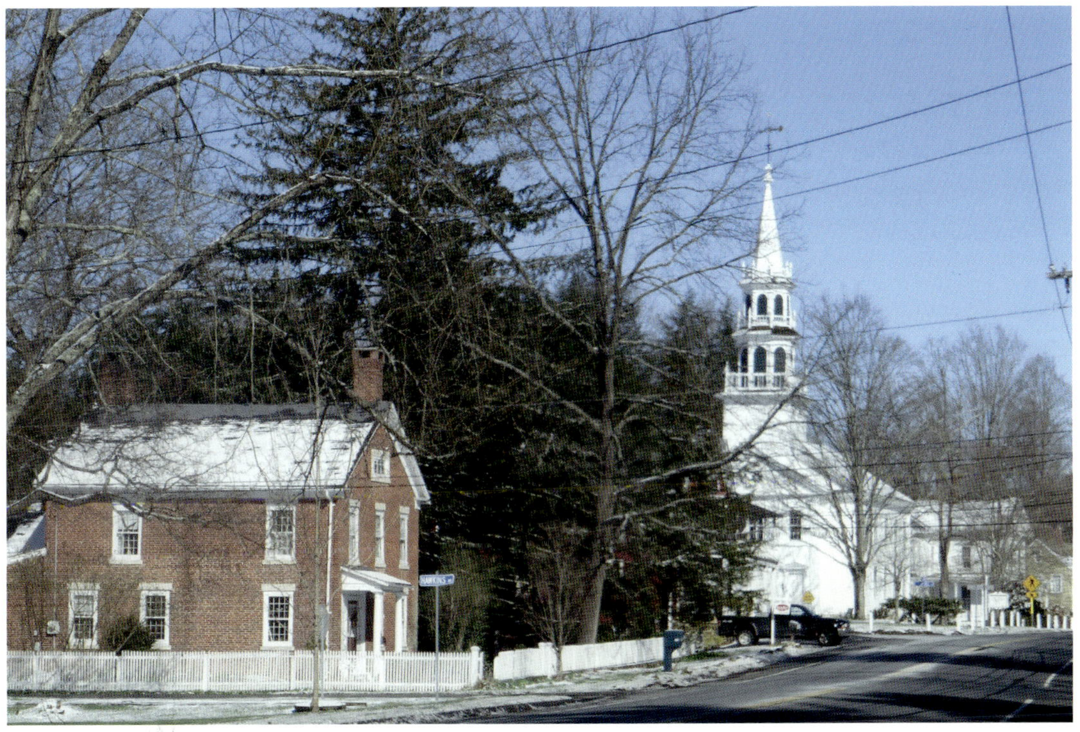

South Britain was physically separated from Main Street Southbury by the Pomperaug River and "the mountain," as the early settlers called the hills. Bridges across the river were often washed away and had to be reconstructed. In 1766, South Britain asked to be a separate Ecclesiastical Society so they would not be required to travel to the Southbury Meeting House every Sunday. Southbury, including South Britain, was incorporated as a town in 1787. It was only a generation later that South Britain petitioned to become their own separate town, but that was not approved by the General Assembly.

The Pomperaug River played a major role in the development of South Britain, where factories were able to harness the water flow. In spite of the active century of manufacturing, South Britain appears to be a village frozen in time.

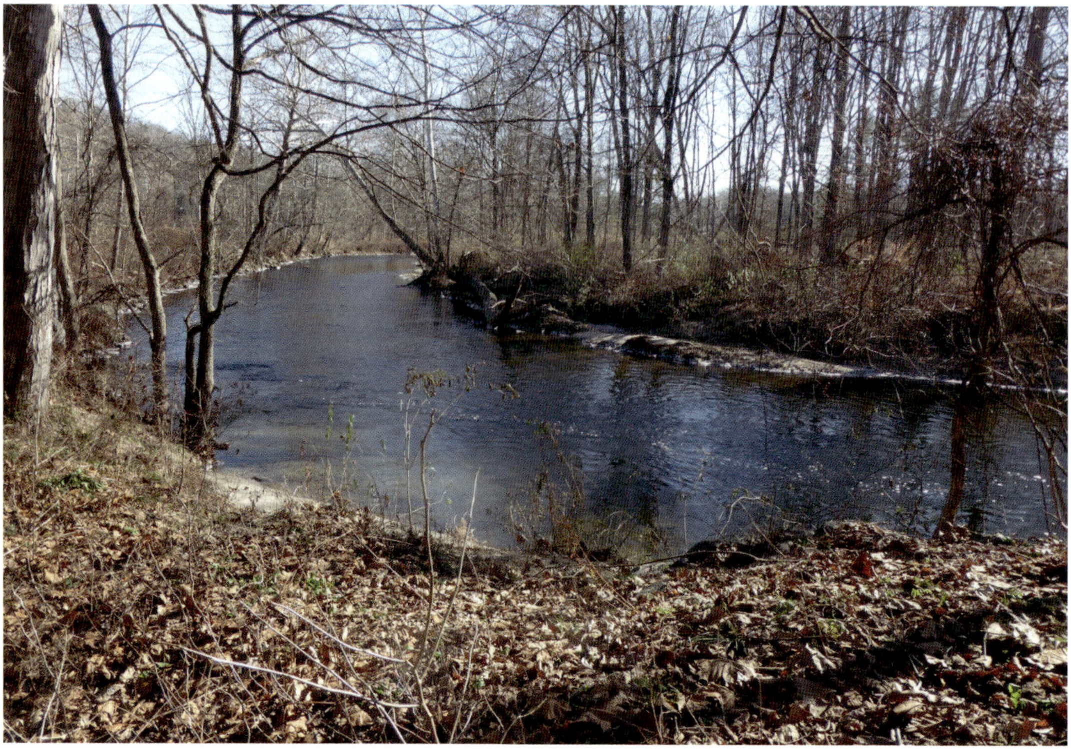

BENT OF THE RIVER: In South Britain, the Pomperaug River takes an interesting meandering route and at one point, making a severe turn. The natives used the turn or bend as a reference point. The early settlers called it "Ye Bent of ye River." The first people that settled in the area simply used "The Bent" as the name of the village long before it became South Britain. So far, no records have been found that give the source of the name of South Britain, even though some early deeds state the name as "Britain."

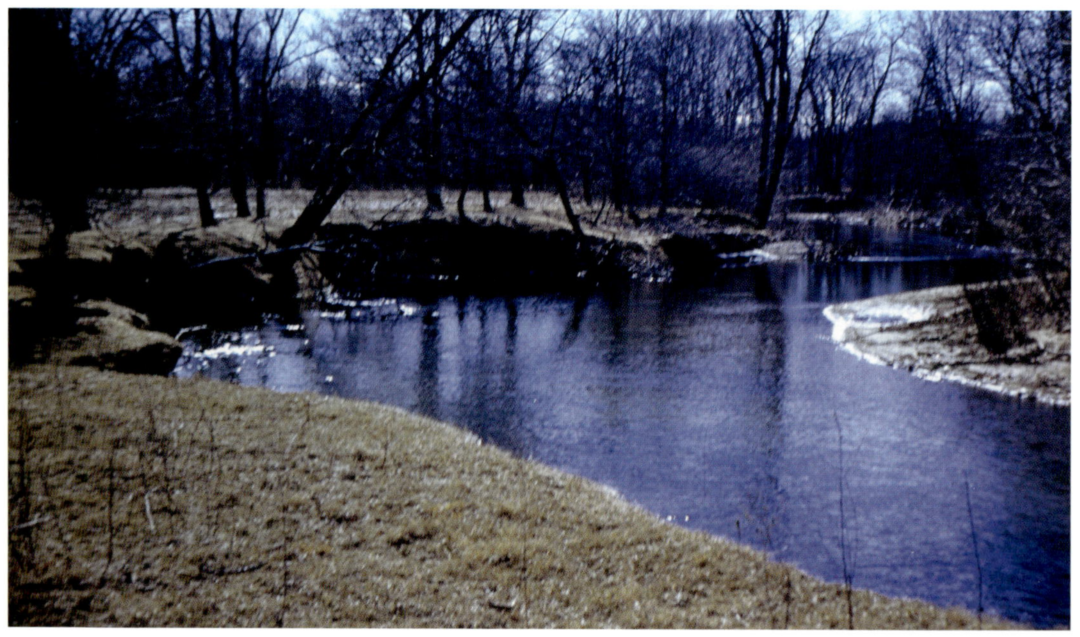

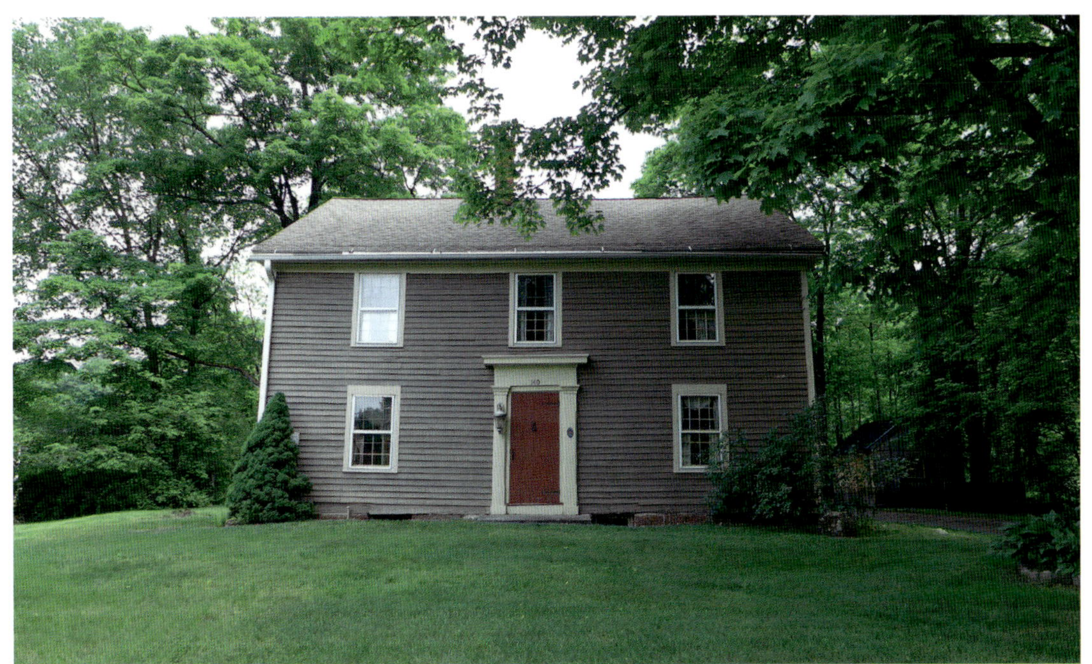

MOSES DOWNS HOUSE: Built by Moses Downs in the salt-box style around 1760, this house has an important place in South Britain history. The local residents met for winter services four months every winter starting in 1761, as it was too difficult to travel to the meeting house in Southbury. On June 5, 1766, the residents gathered in the Downs house and voted to establish their own Ecclesiastical church society, separate from Southbury. In September, they voted to build a meeting house in South Britain. Almost a hundred years later in October 1865, the Downs house was sold to the South Britain Methodist Church to be used as the parsonage for their ministers.

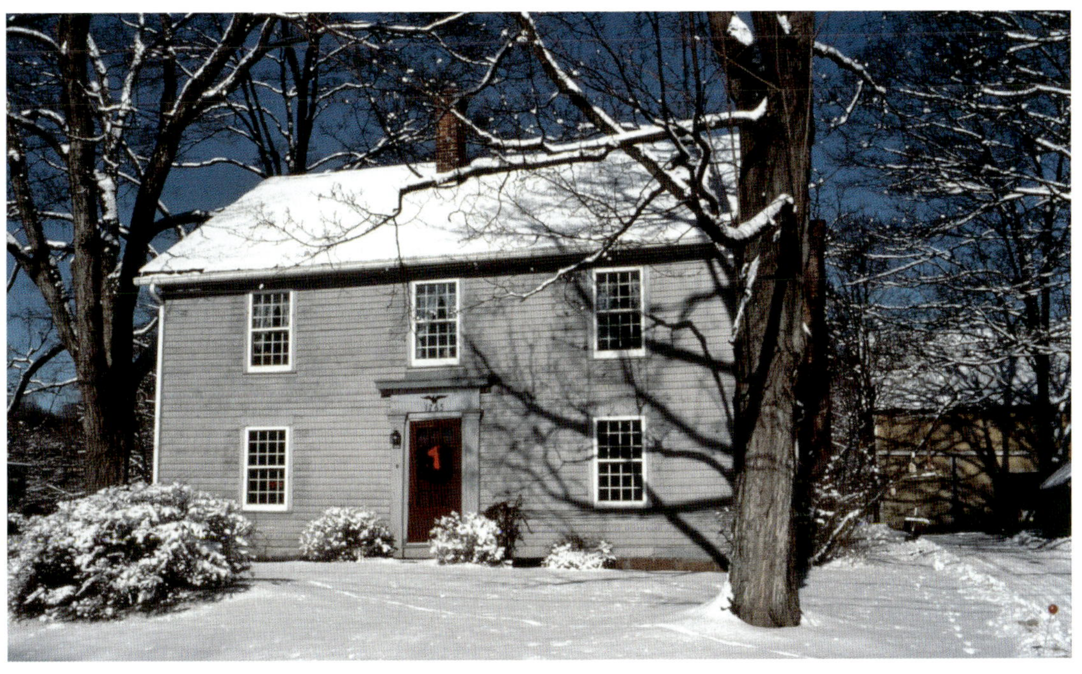

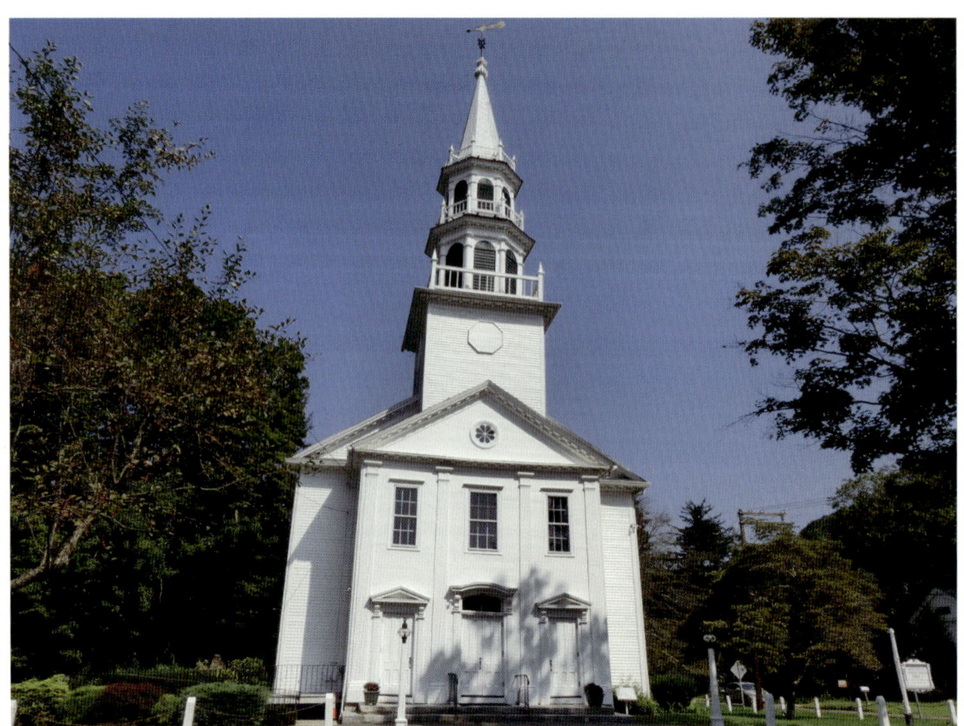

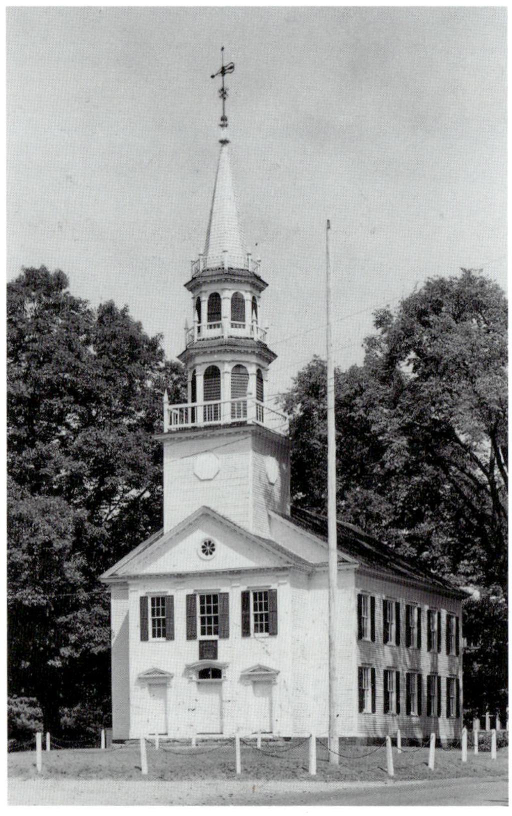

Meeting House: The first meeting house in South Britain was constructed in 1769, basically in front of the current church. In 1825, a new building was needed and Noah Smith donated the land north of the original building. The old meeting house was carefully dismantled and all salvageable pieces of wood were used for the new building. The meeting house, now the South Britain Congregational Church, is the oldest church building in the town of Southbury. Photographs of the building were spread all over the country after the church was used as the venue for a town meeting on November 23, 1937, to establish a zoning committee when the German American Bund decided to build a camp in the town.

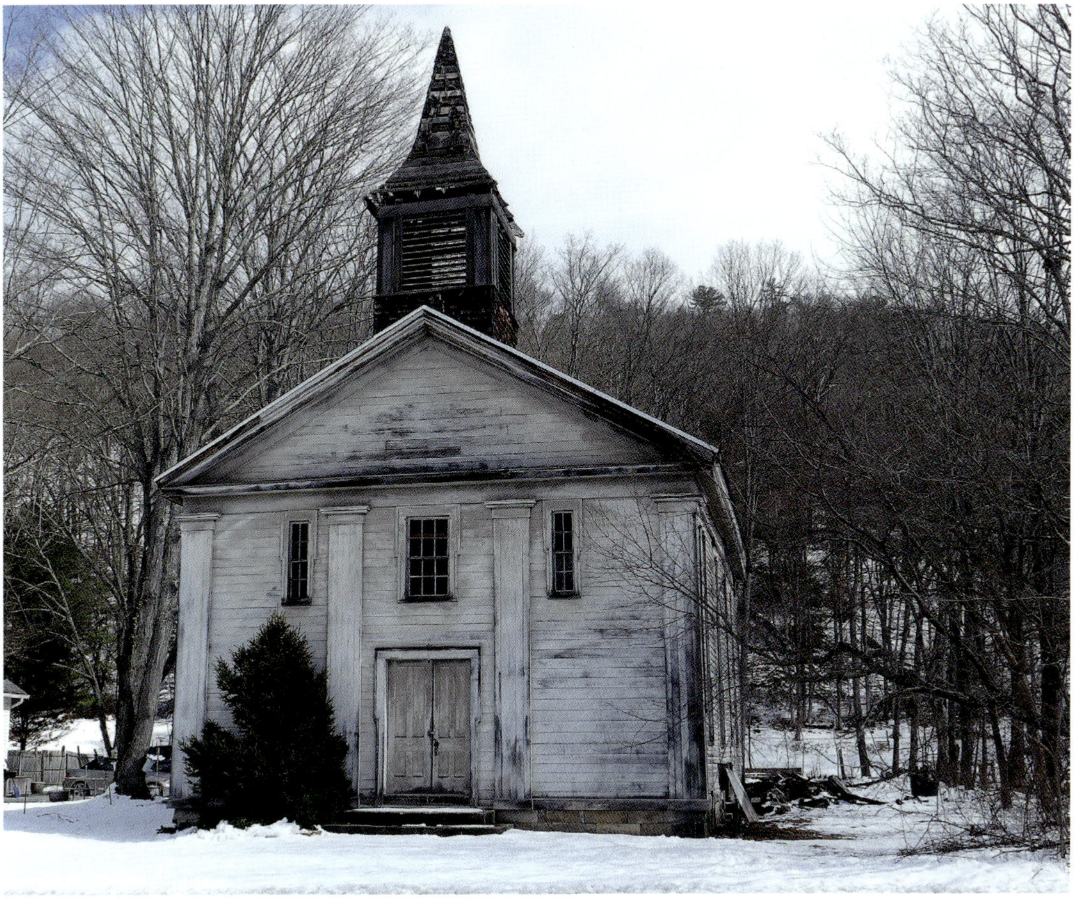

METHODIST: The South Britain Methodist Church was built in 1832 on land that was donated by member Erastus Pierce and paid for by member Judson Manville. The congregation had out-grown their previous building on Georges Hill Road, where they had met regularly since 1803. As the congregation continued to increase, the building was enlarged and improved in 1851. The church held services there until 1941, when the building was closed due to dwindling parishioners and sold to the McCarthy's, who lived on the adjacent property.

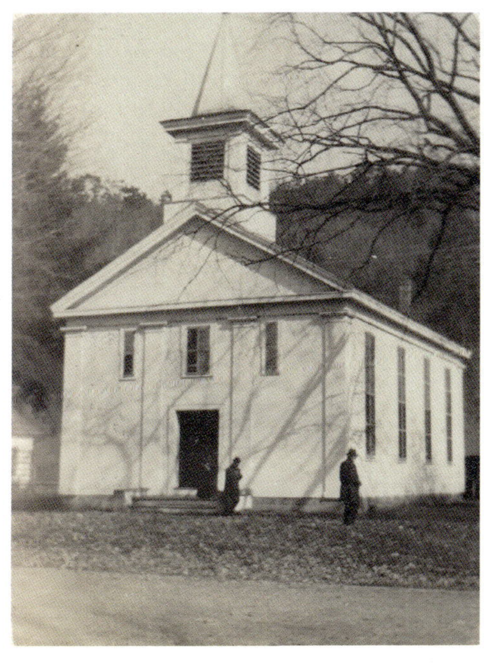

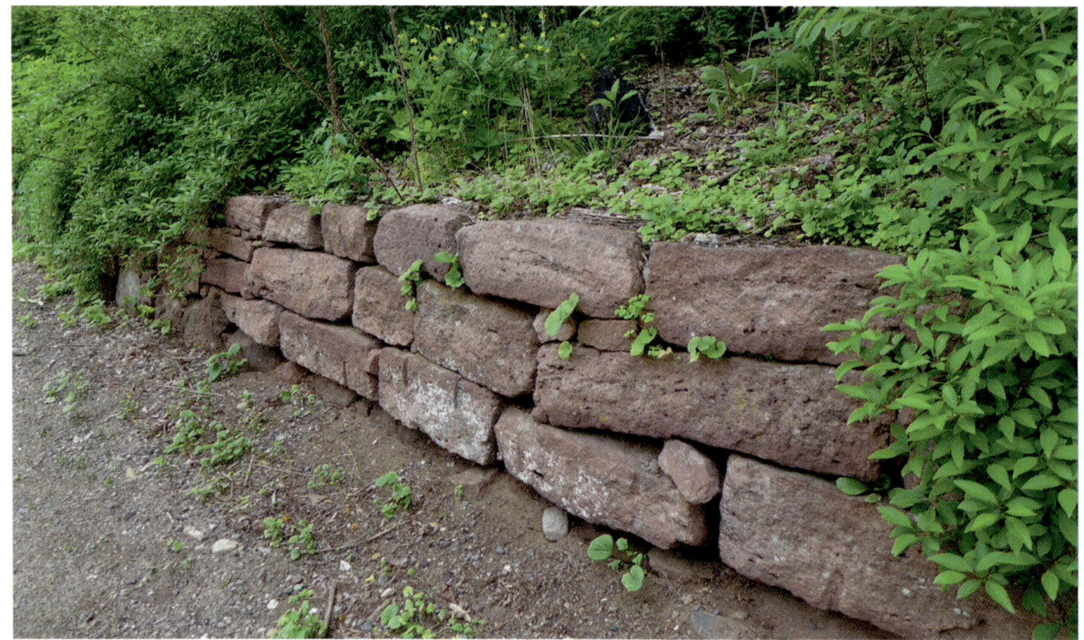

QUARRY: Hidden away in South Britain is an old red sandstone quarry which began operation as early as 1760. While you cannot see the quarry near the Pomperaug River, you can see the evidence of it all around the town in many building foundations, including the Bullet Hill School and the Old Town Hall Museum. The Middle Road in South Britain also has a large retaining wall of the red stone. Early settler and stonecutter, James Stanclift and his son, not only cut building blocks and steps of various sizes, but they also intricately carved the red sandstone gravestones that can found in the local cemeteries. The quarry is no longer used.

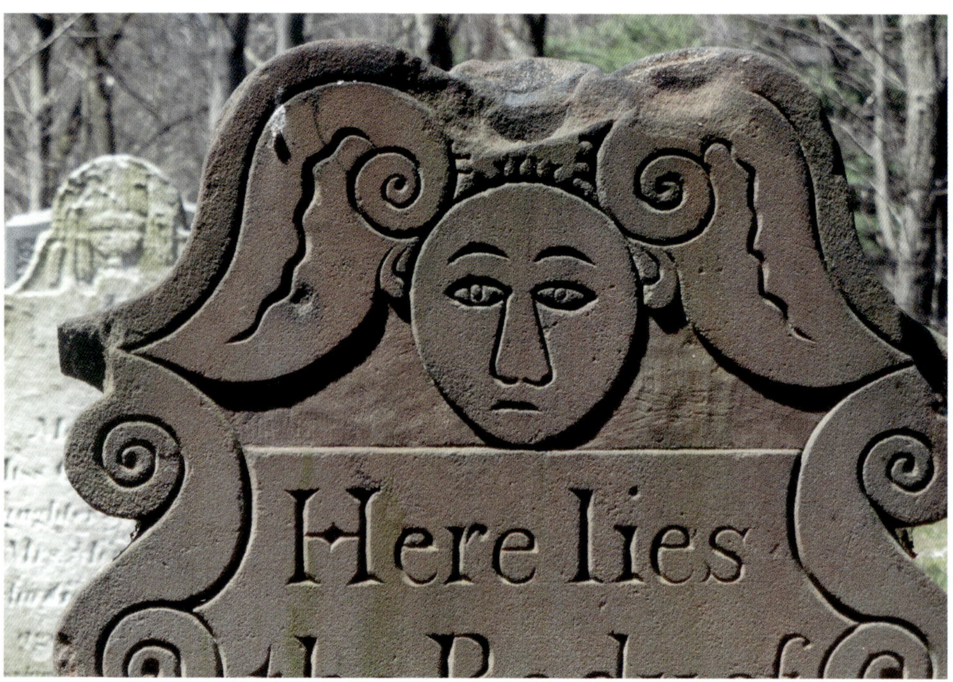

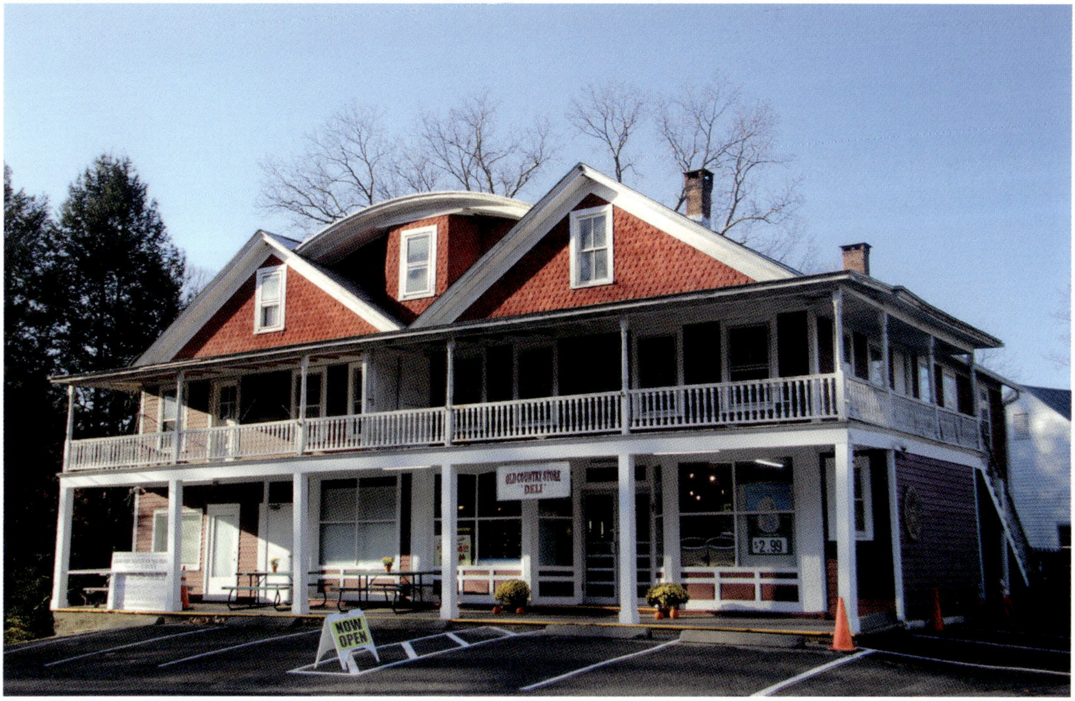

MITCHELL AND WILLIAMS: A small general store was opened by George W. Mitchell during the 1800s, conveniently located at the crossroad near the two churches. Mitchell's daughter married Charles Williams, who became co-proprietor in the business. The store burned down in 1903, and was immediately rebuilt bigger and better. While this building has undergone many changes through the years, it is still a stopping place for local residents. One of the old store signs is housed at the Old Town Hall Museum.

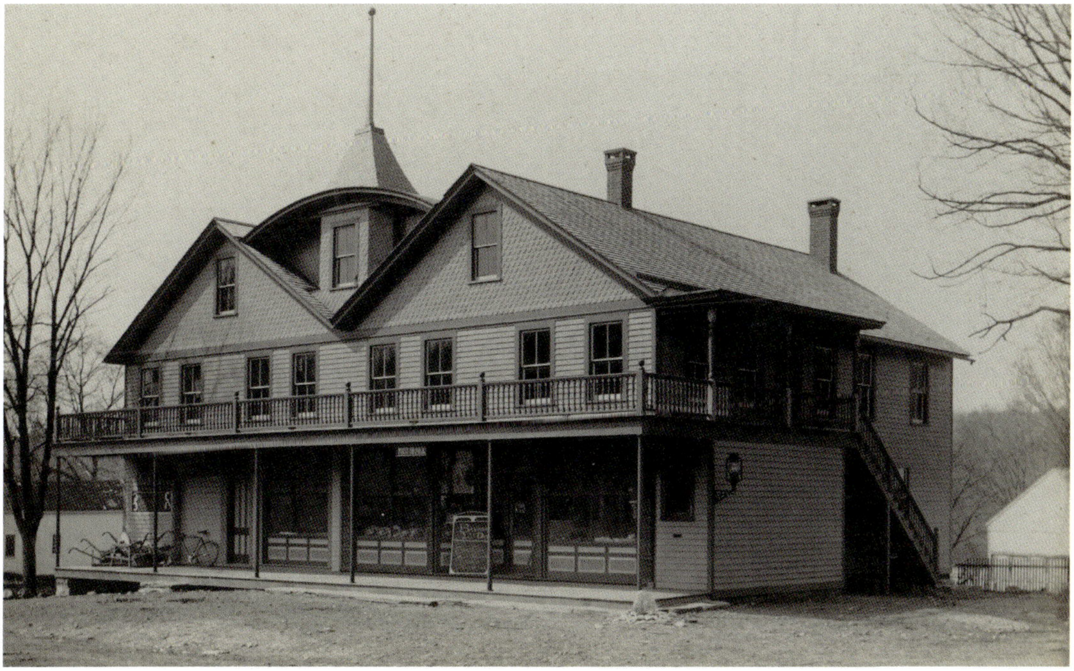

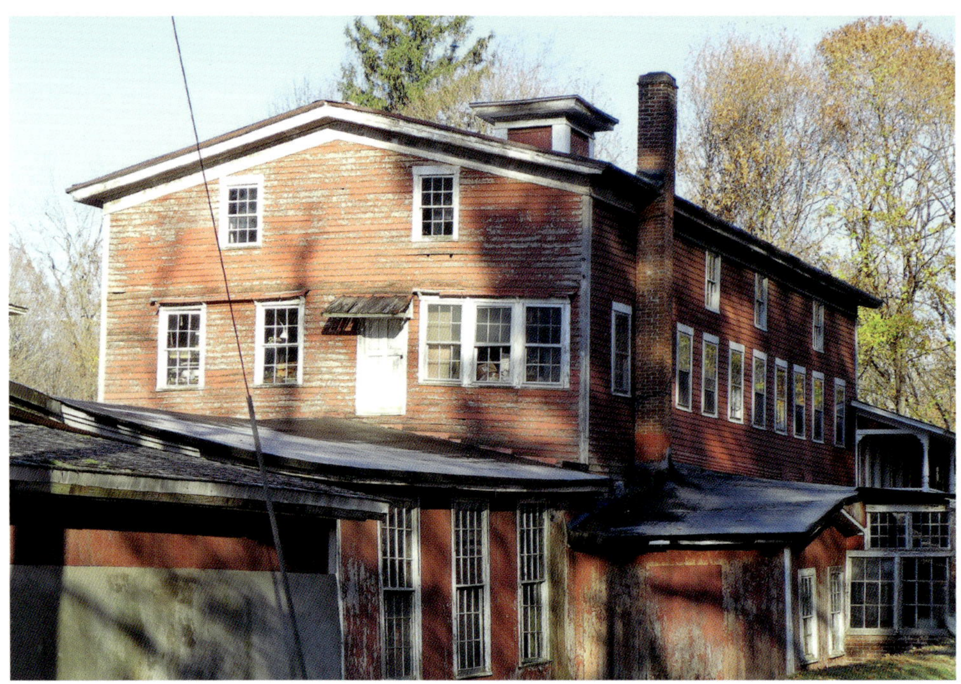

Bradley Factories: Fulling or woolen mills were located on the Pomperaug River as early as 1800, including the Curtiss Woolen Mill and the Bradley Satinet Factory. Satinet was a woven twill cloth made of cotton and wool that was used for trousers. While not as sturdy as wool fabric, the satinet was quickly provided to manufacturers for Civil War uniforms. After several mills had come and gone, Bradley, Hoyt & Company built a four-story woolens mill in 1866. The business was very successful and was known for high-quality fabrics. The photograph shows the Bradley, Hoyt & Company structure, and the Hawkins Factory built around it.

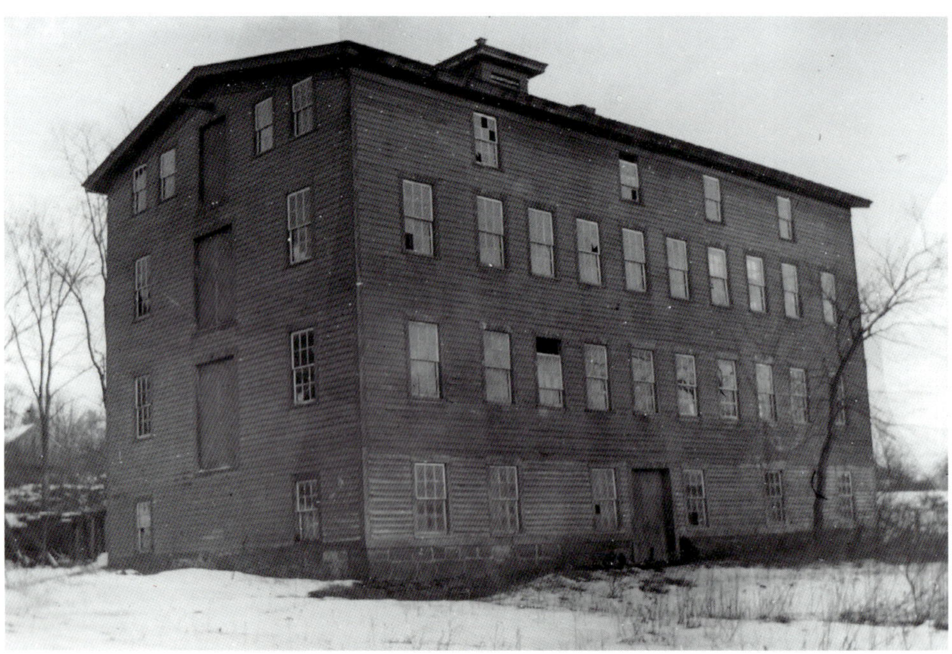

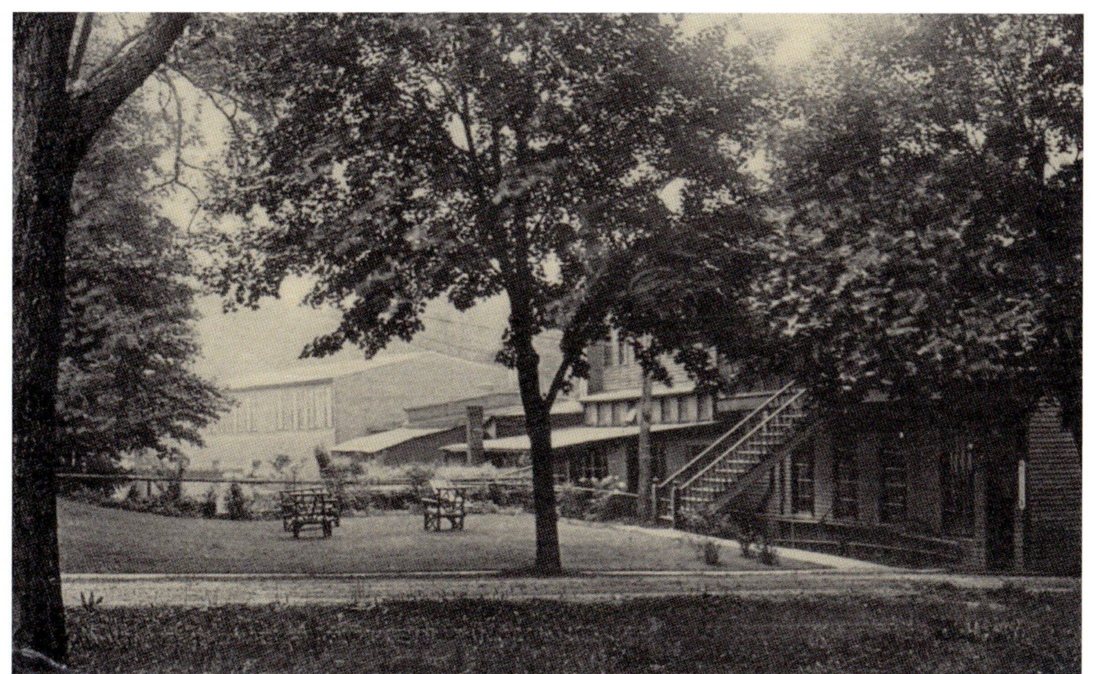

Hawkins Factory: The Bradley, Hoyt & Company factory shut down in 1892, when other factories started to make cheaper fabrics. Ira Hawkins purchased the building in 1901 and began building a complex series of additional workshops for metal products, specifically seamless tubing. Hawkins merged with Blake and Lamb Company to produce animal traps, which proved to be a very lucrative business serving the whole nation and Canada. Manufacturing continued along the Pomperaug River until the buildings became too outdated to be used in 1970. The site has been purchased by a private citizen who is restoring and renovating portions of the buildings.

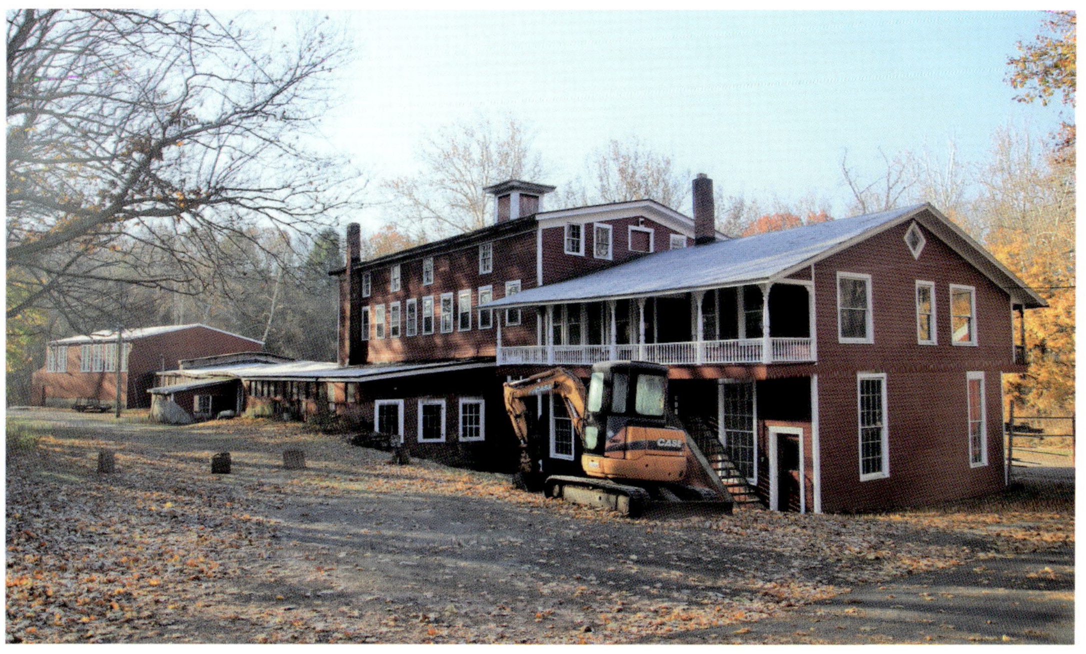

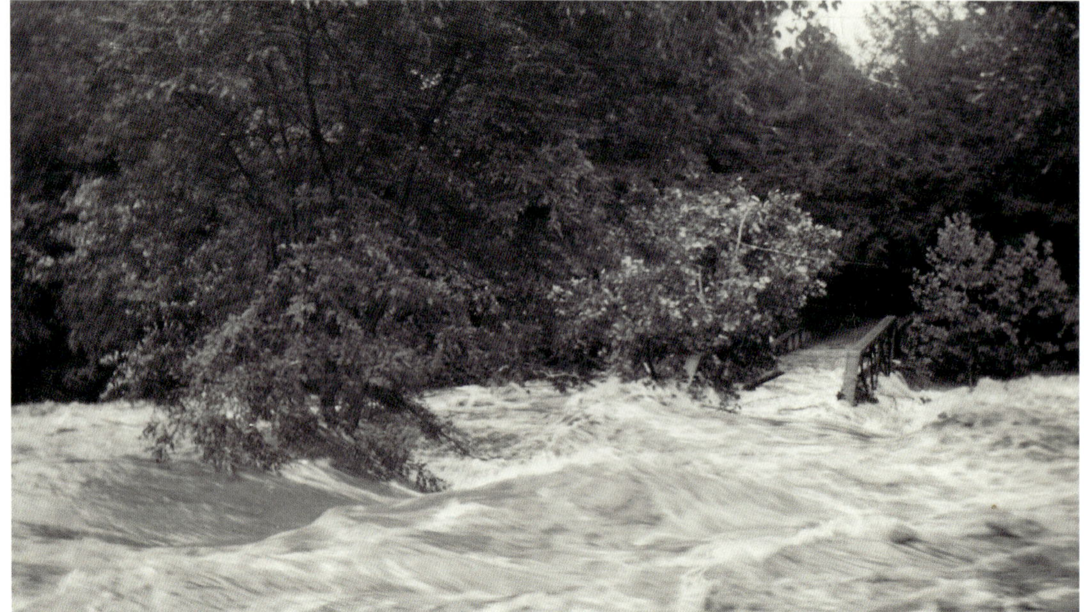

HAWKINS BRIDGE: In order to get across the Pomperaug River to additional factory buildings, Hawkins built a bridge at that same place where a much-earlier structure once stood. Stone carver, James Stanclift, had a covered bridge that he struggled to keep standing throughout the late eighteenth century. However, floods and ice destroyed it. The Hawkins Bridge was built on high foundations and later with steel girders. As you can tell in the upper photograph, the bridge was no match for the 1955 flood. It is hard to image that the water could be so high. Today, only one pillar remains along with the last steel section.

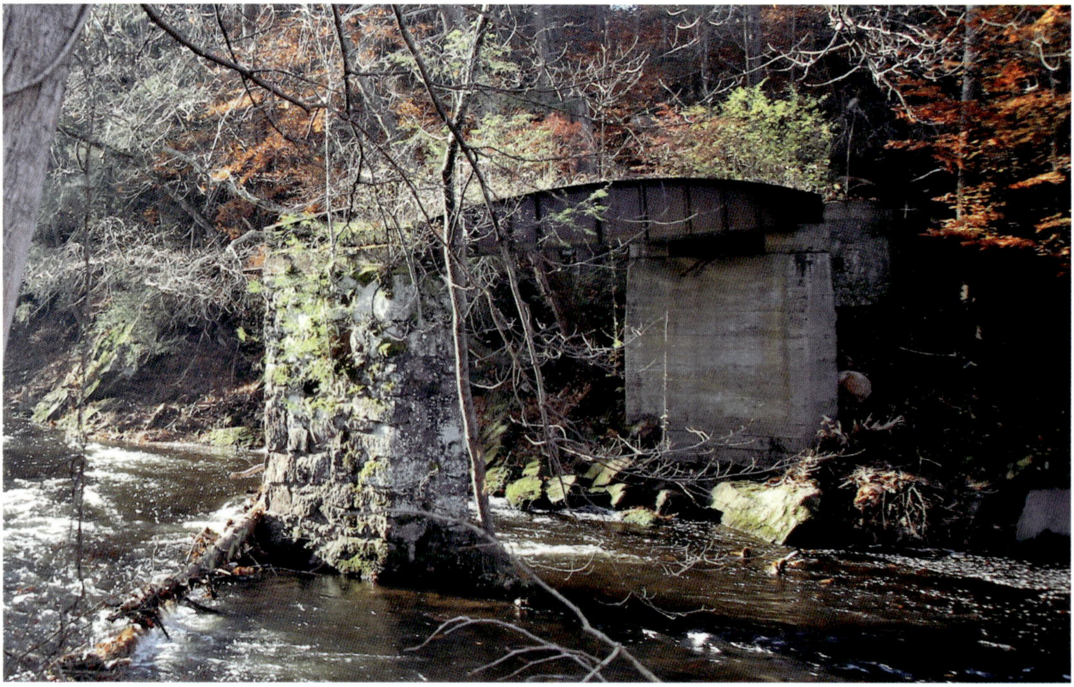

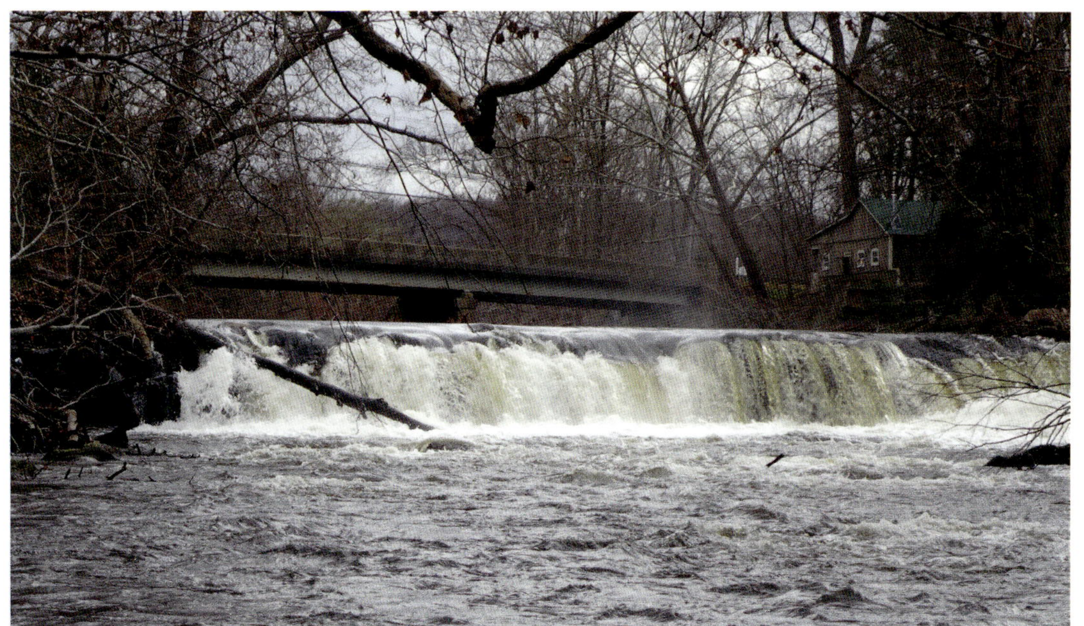

BRADLEY MILL DAM: During the 1800s, factories lined both sides of the Pomperaug River through South Britain. The once-called Bradley Dam, or South Britain Falls, is a hidden treasure, even though the upper side of the falls is only steps away from Route 172. In order to harness the water power for his factory, Bradley had the dam constructed of wooden logs, and a part of the water was diverted along a canal, or race, to the factories. At some later point, concrete was put in front of the wooden dam to stabilize the structure.

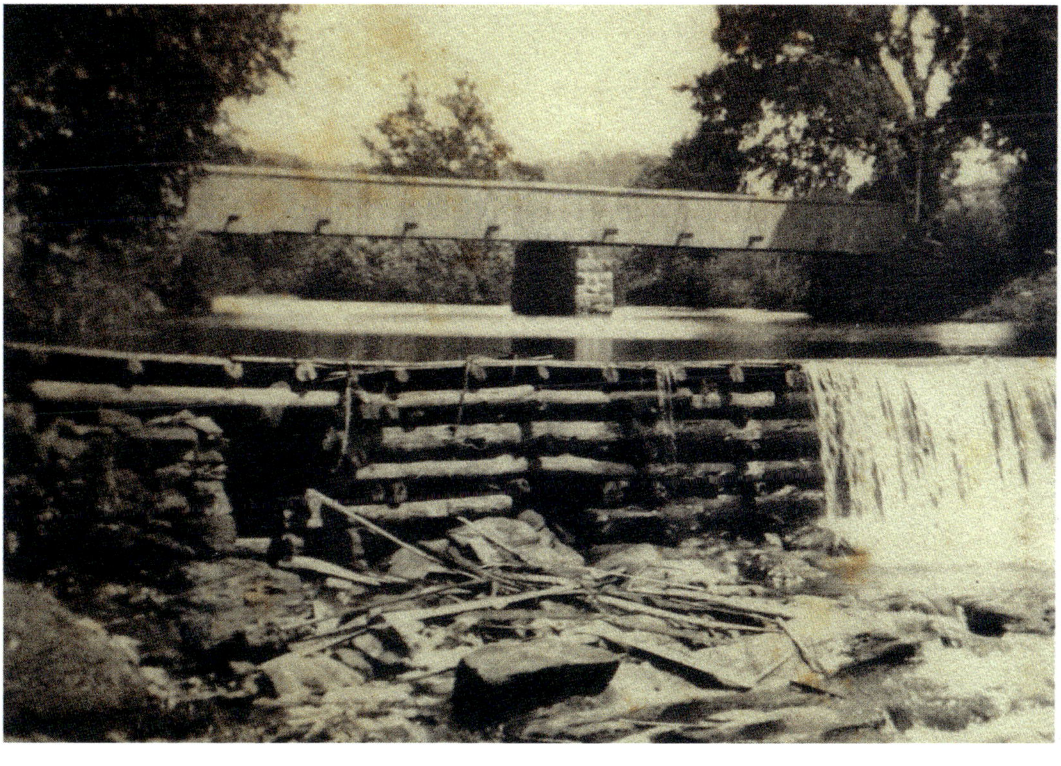

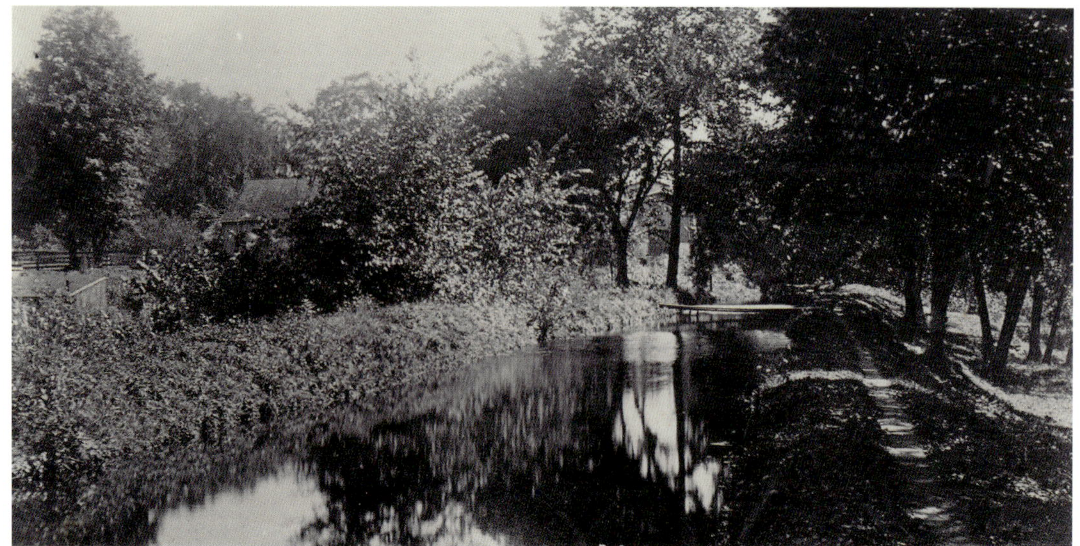

HAWKINS CANAL: Lover's Lane in South Britain was actually the path along the canal near Hawkins Factory. Much of the canal system was destroyed in the Flood of 1955. Water still sat in the canal for many years, making it a popular place for little boys to hunt tadpoles. In the photo below, the old canal on the left side is filled in with debris and fallen trees. The Pomperaug River can be seen to the right. Even though the trail might not be wide enough for two lovers to walk side by side now, the path still allows a nice stroll with beautiful views.

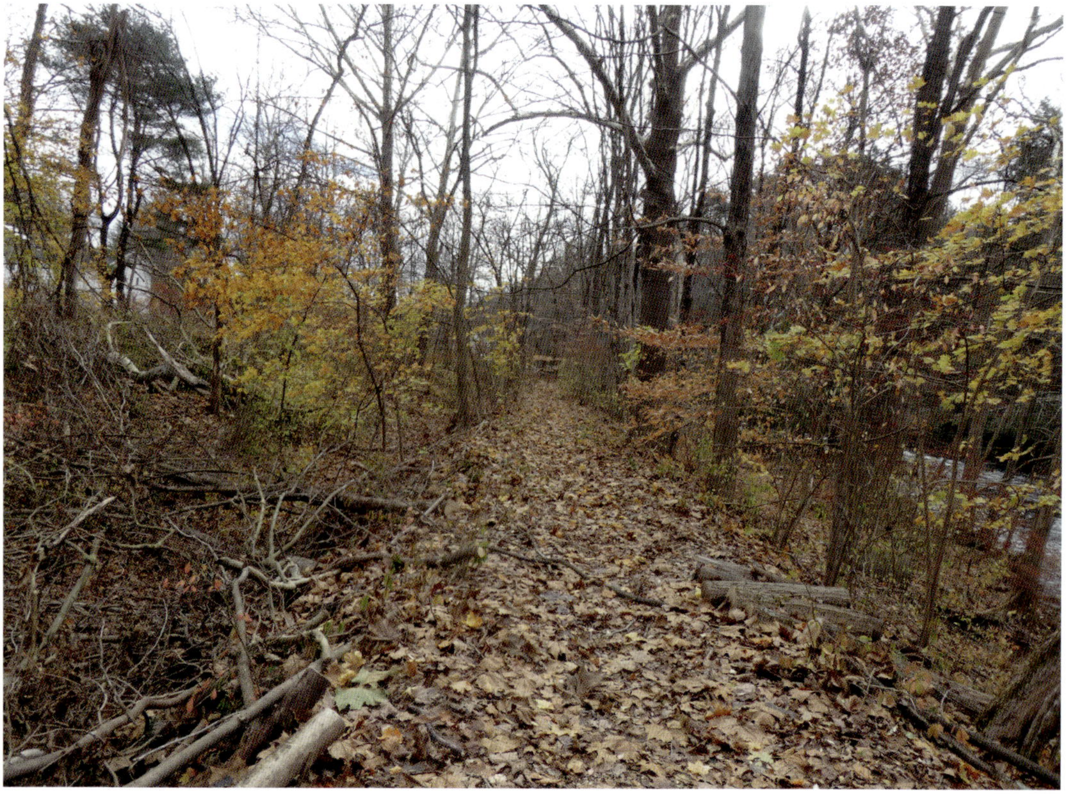

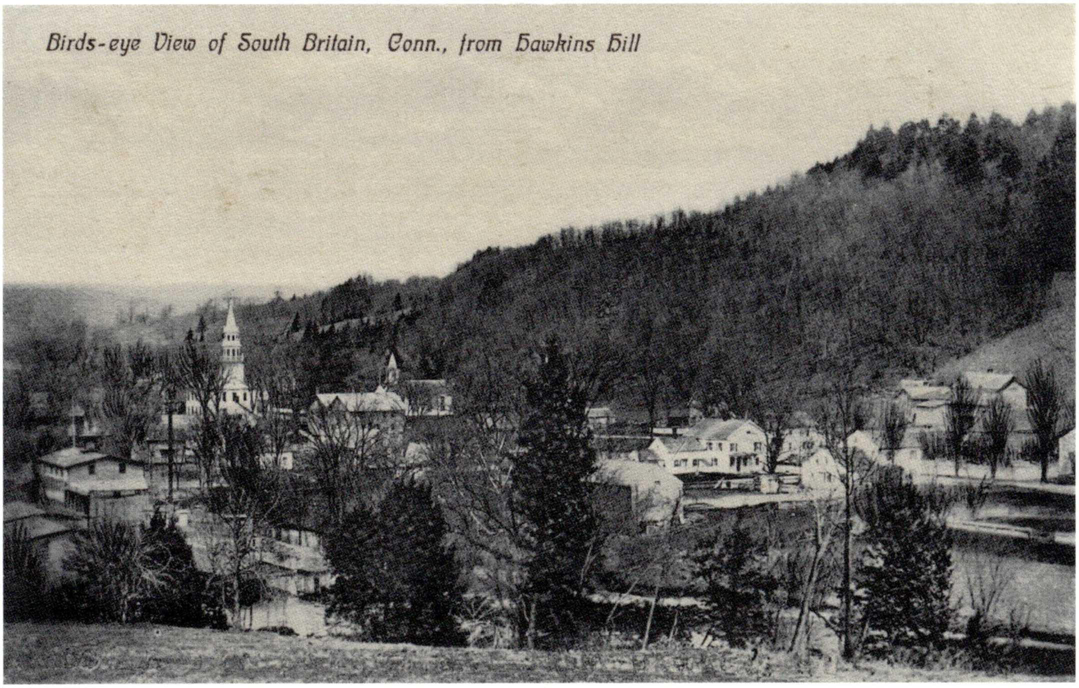

Birds-eye View of South Britain, Conn., from Hawkins Hill

RARE VIEWS: The scene above is taken from Hawkins Hill, which is on the peninsula in the Bent of the River. Starting from the left is the Hawkins Factory and canal. The white church steeples are visible of both the Congregational Church and the Methodist Church, with the Mitchell Store in between. On the far right is a large building that was the Creamery. The Congregational Church Parsonage is in the middle. The bottom photograph is looking north on South Britain Road, starting with the Methodist Church slightly showing on the right. Up the road to the left is the South Britain Cemetery.

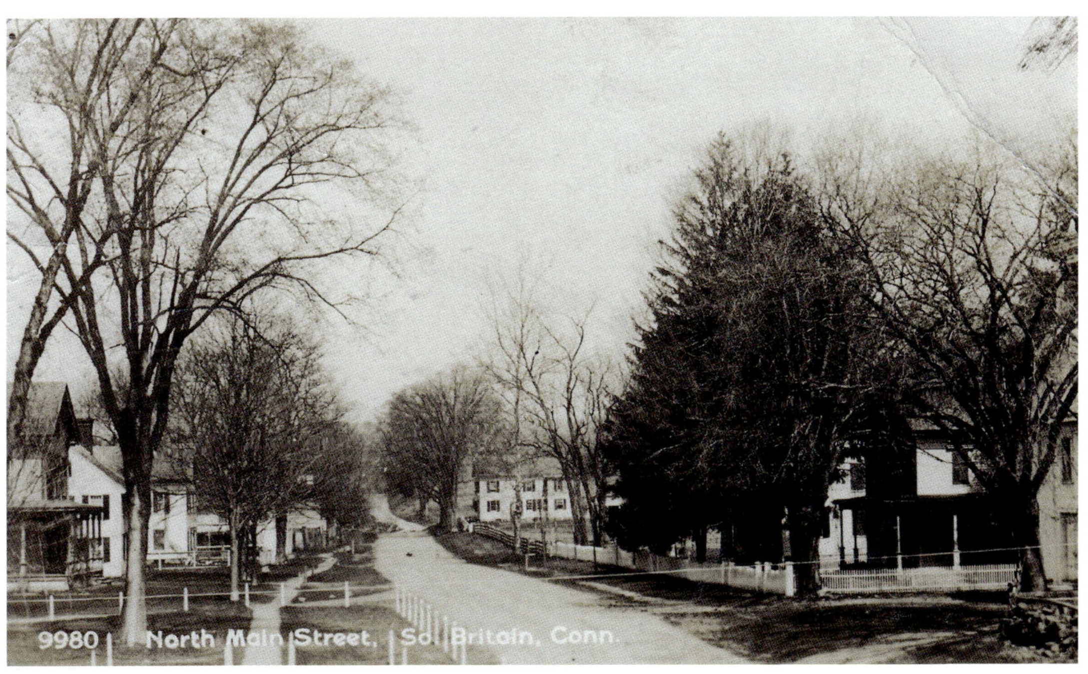

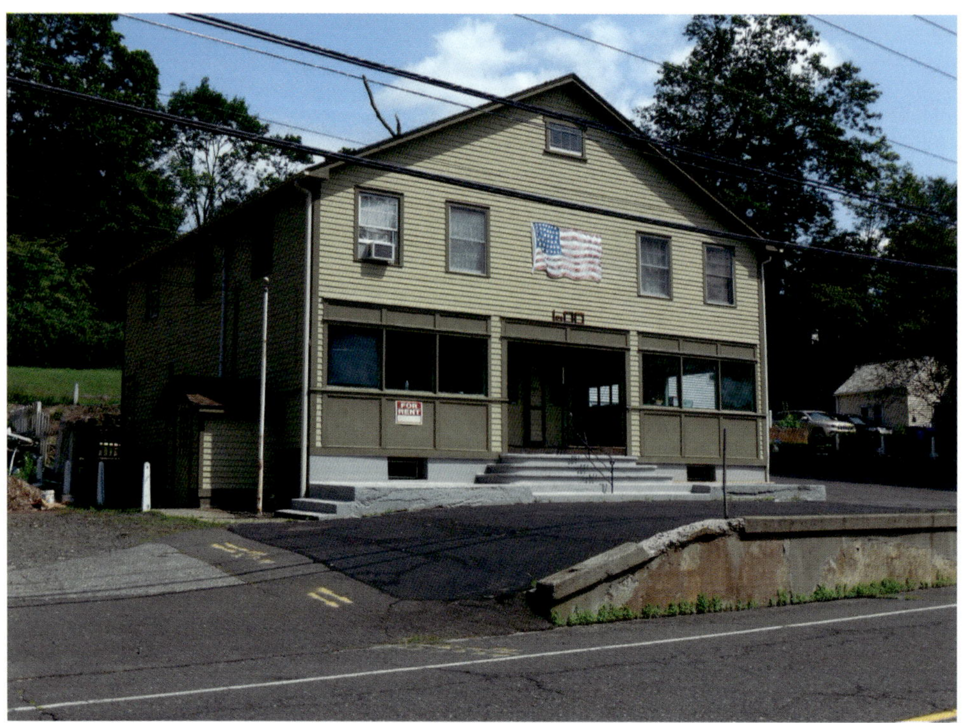

CONDON STORE: Condon's Store was a busy place to visit. David Condon was a butcher by trade, starting out with John H. Cassidy. In 1930, Condon made an agreement with Standard Oil to sell gas at the store. In the old photograph below, you can see the small gas pump to the right of the building. For a while, Henry McCarthy and David Condon worked together, but McCarthy decided to open a store across the street. The South Britain residents could pick up their mail there at the Condon Store until the boxes were moved to the Southbury Post Office in the late twentieth century.

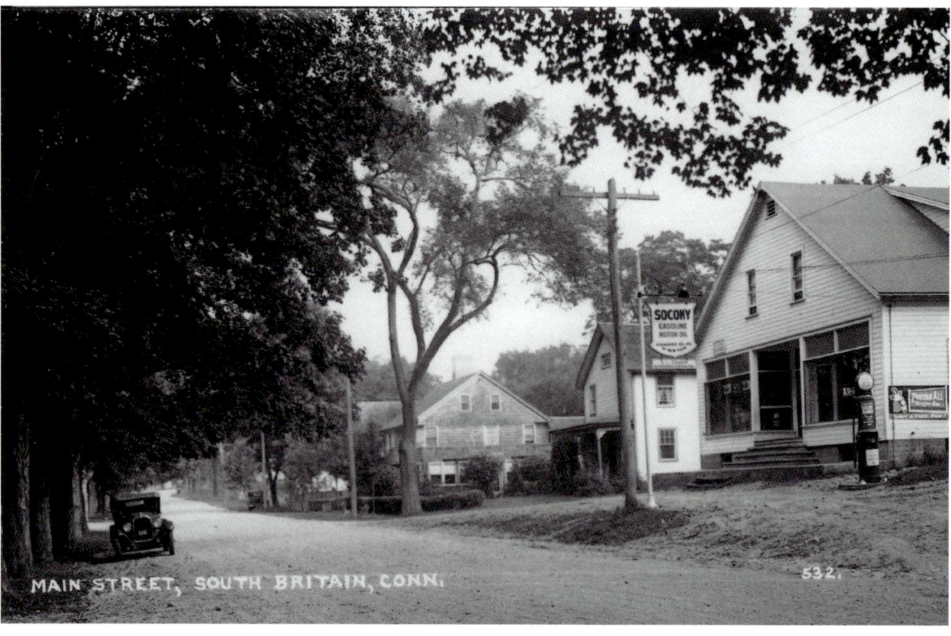

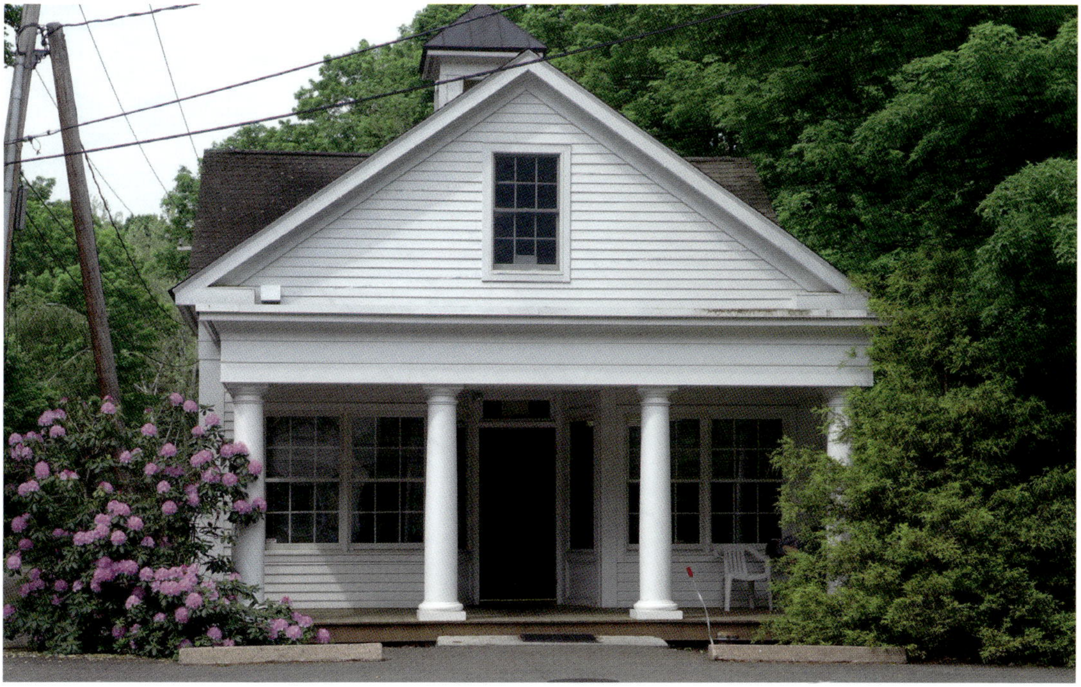

McCarthy Store: Henry McCarthy built this store in 1928 specifically to sell groceries and dry goods, allowing the Condon Store to specialize in meats, and the post office duties. In 1937, members of the German American Bund stopped by his store to order future supplies for the people working on clearing land for a camp. McCarthy said that he would think about it and alerted the first selectman immediately. He kept the shop until his death in 1950. The building burned at some point, and a modern structure of the same size and style was put in its place.

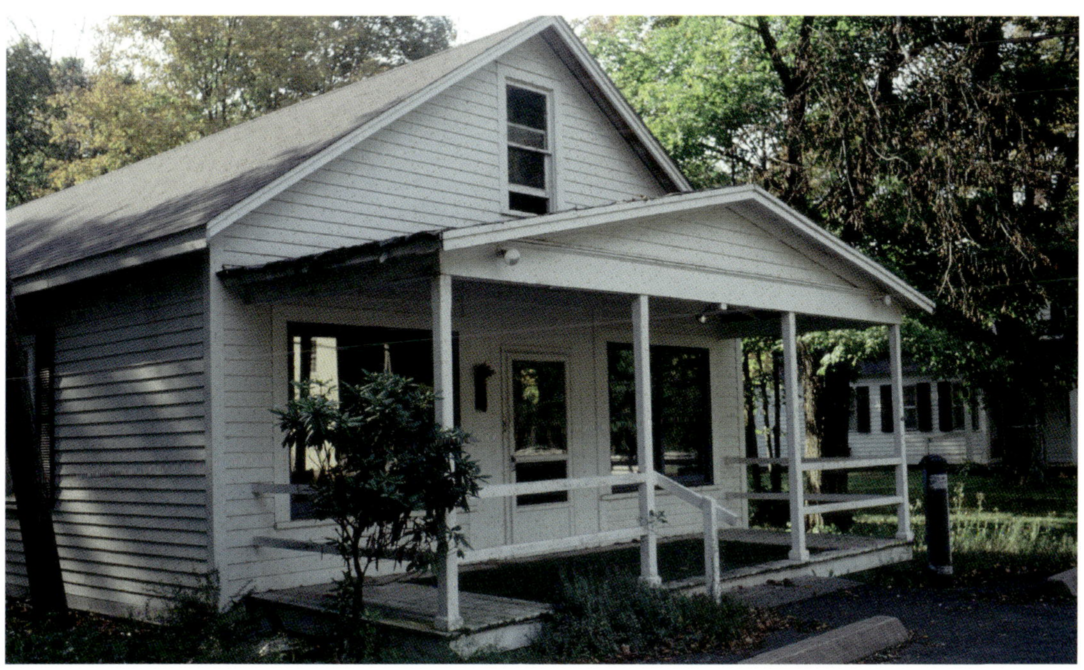

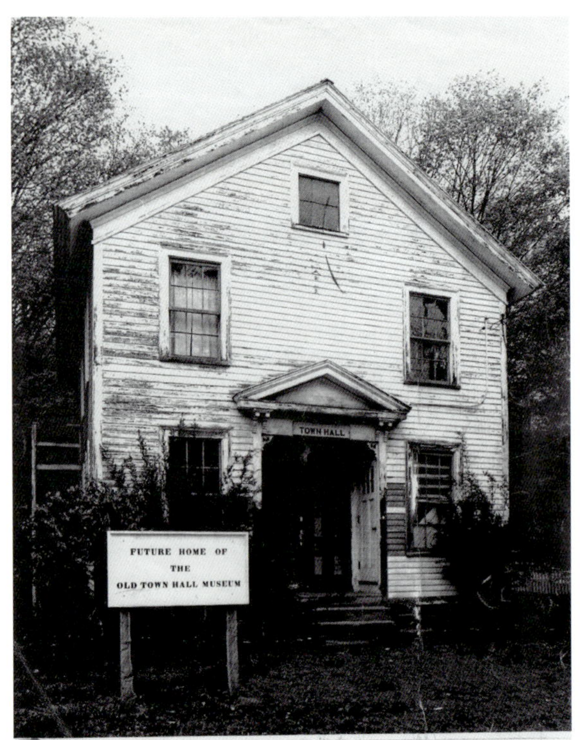

TOWN HALL: In 1873, Southbury's first designated town hall was built in South Britain, where much of the town's industry and businesses were located at the time. Scheduled to be a one-story building, the ladies of the South Britain Congregational Church raised funds to make a second floor. The town hall was used through December 31, 1963, when the new town hall was opened on Main Street. After several years of deterioration, the Southbury Historical Society brought the building back to life by making it into a museum. Many interesting local history items can be found there, along with the original vault now used to store the society's archives.

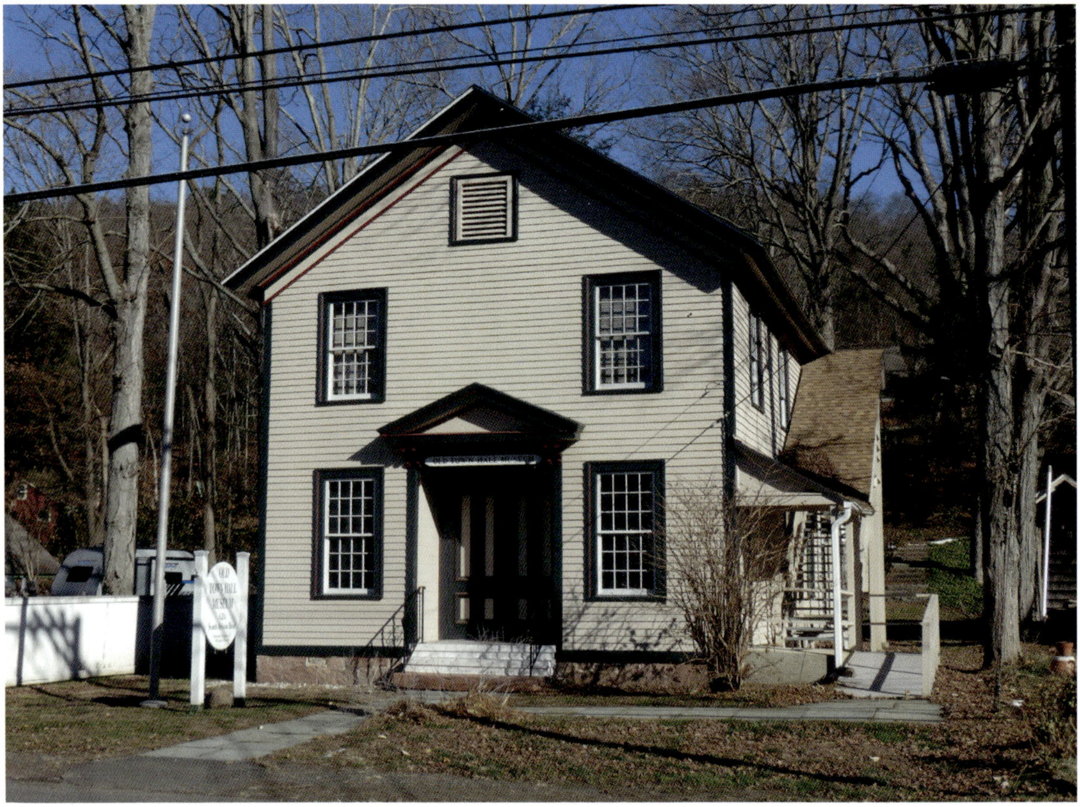

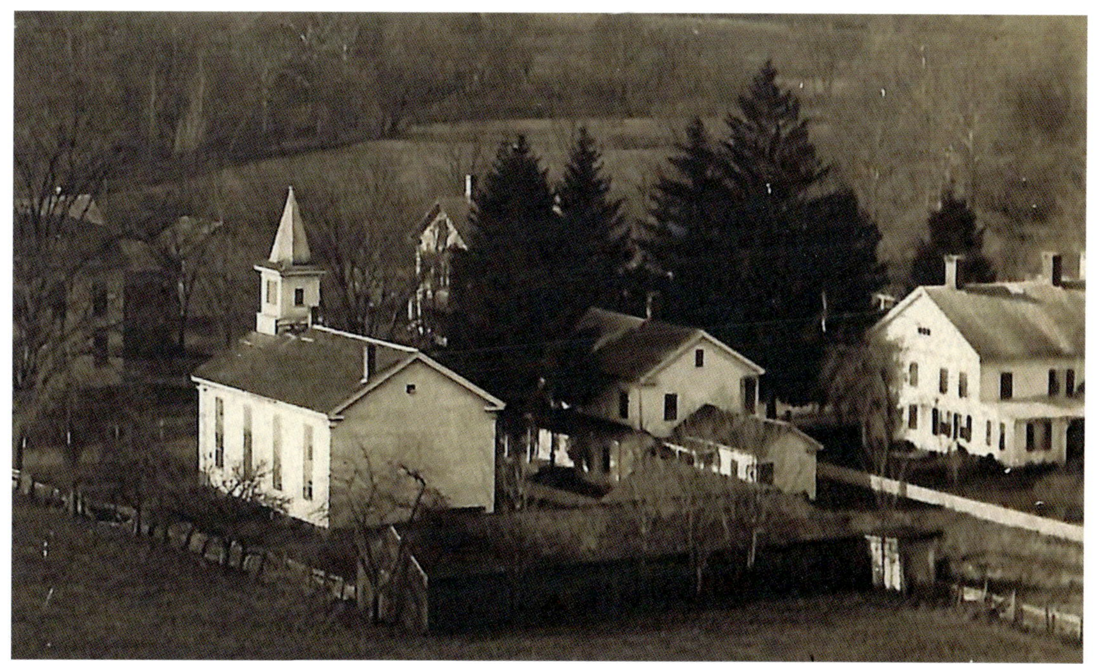

Victorian Privy: No one knows exactly how long the "convenience facility" stood behind the horse sheds of the South Britain Methodist Church, as seen as the small white building on the right side of this old photograph. The building was thought to be Victorian and some experts believed it could have once been part of a steeple from a local church. In 1993, the owner, Mrs. Catherine McCarthy, offered the small building to the town of Southbury as a historical building. The offer was accepted, and the privy was moved to the back yard of the Old Town Hall Museum, where it was restored and can still be viewed by visitors.

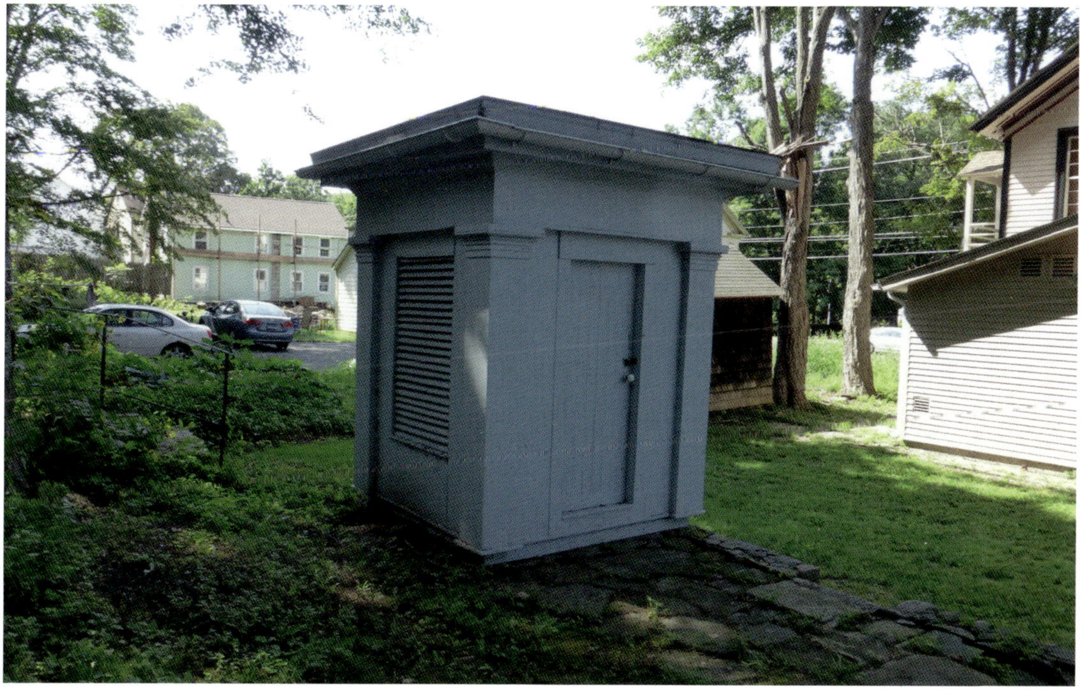

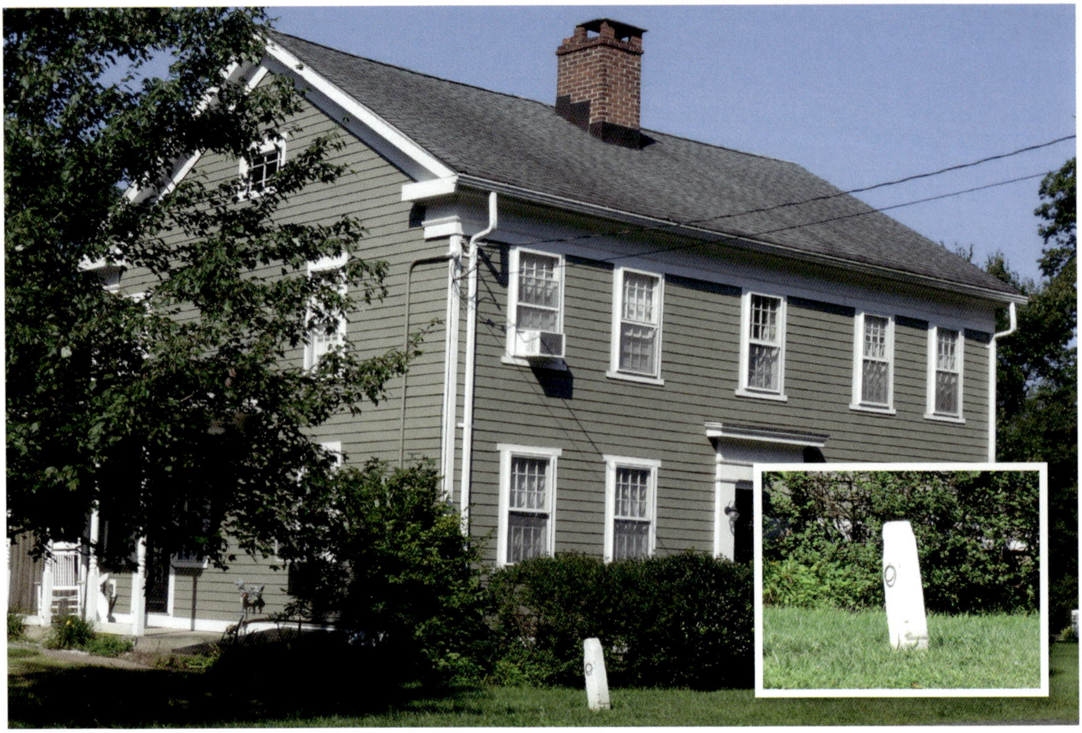

HITCHING POST: The building known as "The Parsonage" was constructed in 1785 by Moses Downs. The house was used as a home for the South Britain Congregational pastors for many years. The hitching post, a rare remnant of Southbury's past, remains standing in front of the building. Visitors to the parsonage would tie their horse's reigns to the post, knowing that the horses would be there when they returned. Hitching posts were once a common sight in town, even after the horses were replaced with automobiles. A large number of the hitching posts were removed due the road-improvement projects, with the roads being widened for modern traffic. (Bottom photograph Courtesy of SBCC Archives)

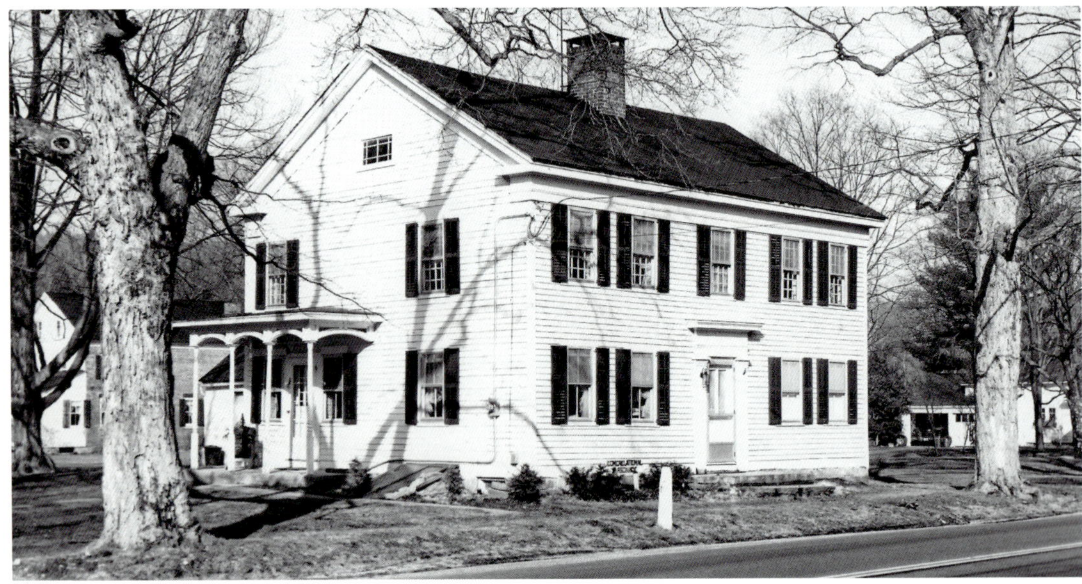

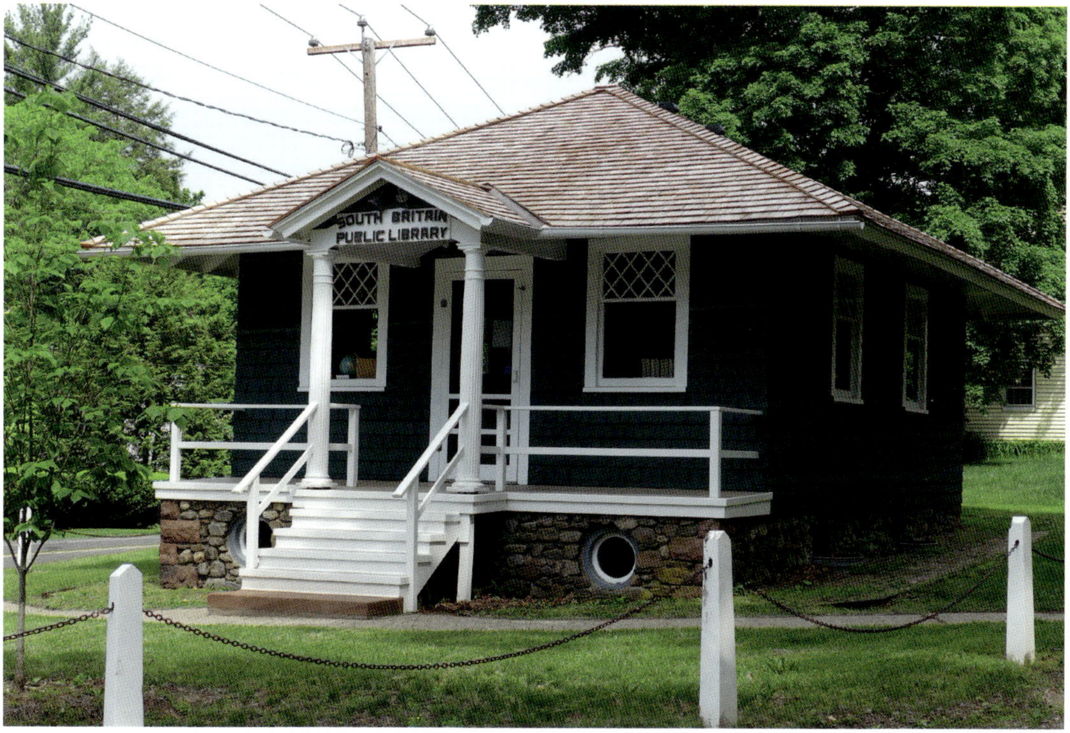

FIRST LIBRARY: According to a log book in the Southbury Historical Society's vault, lending libraries were kept in various houses throughout the village. In 1904, Southbury's first library building was a small one-room structure built by Axel Harry Wilson, a master carpenter from Finland who settled in South Britain with his family. The library continued as the only town library until 1969, when the new one opened on Main Street South. Ira Hawkins was a major sponsor of the library. At the South Britain Library is an original nineteenth-century "box library," an old book-filled wooden crate that traveled through town to provide books for those who couldn't go to the library.

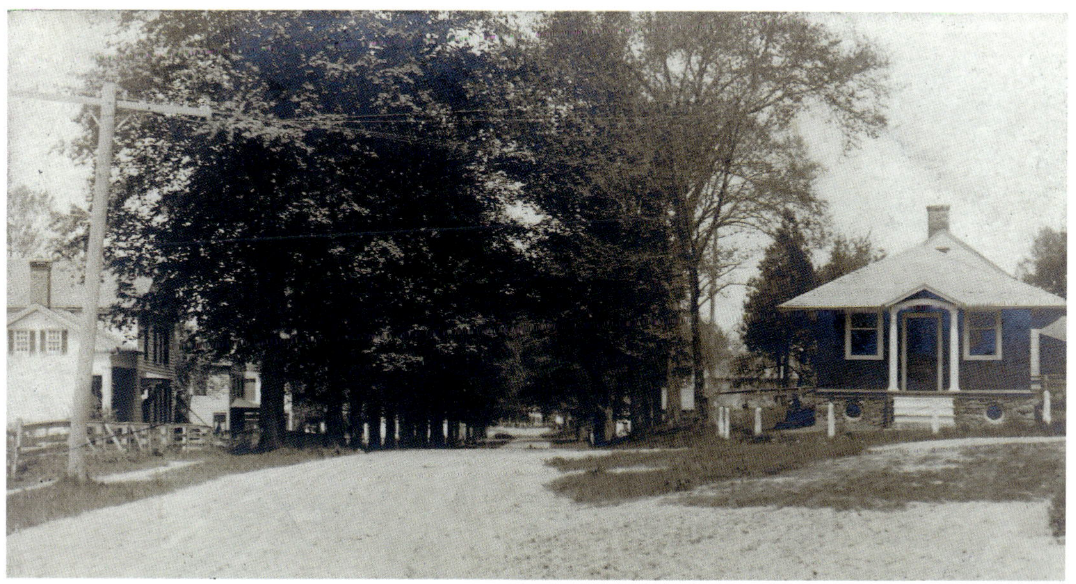

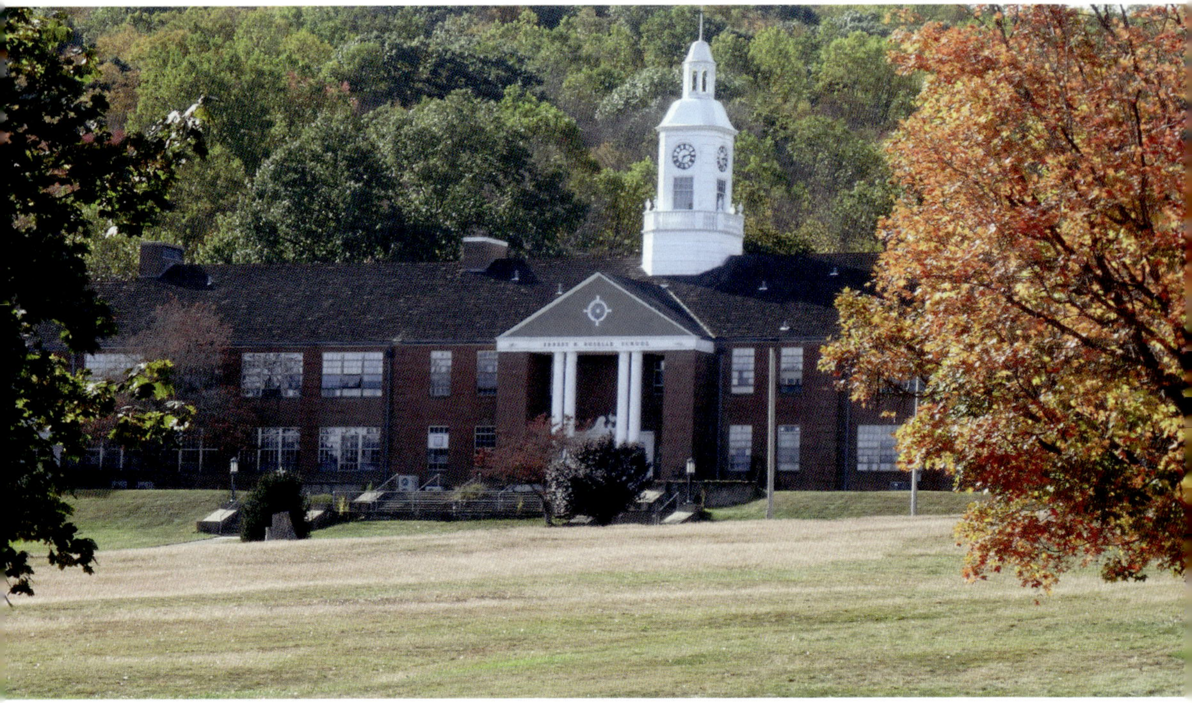

TRAINING SCHOOL: The State of Connecticut chose Southbury to be the site for the Southbury Training School, purchasing 1,600 acres of land and building 125 structures. Many farms and local residents were relocated, along with the Pierce Hollow School. The training school provided education and job skills for the children and adults with developmental difficulties in a residential setting. There was also a working farm, complete with orchards, fields, and animals. The school is no longer taking new residents and may be closed within the next decade. The old photo was taken during the construction.

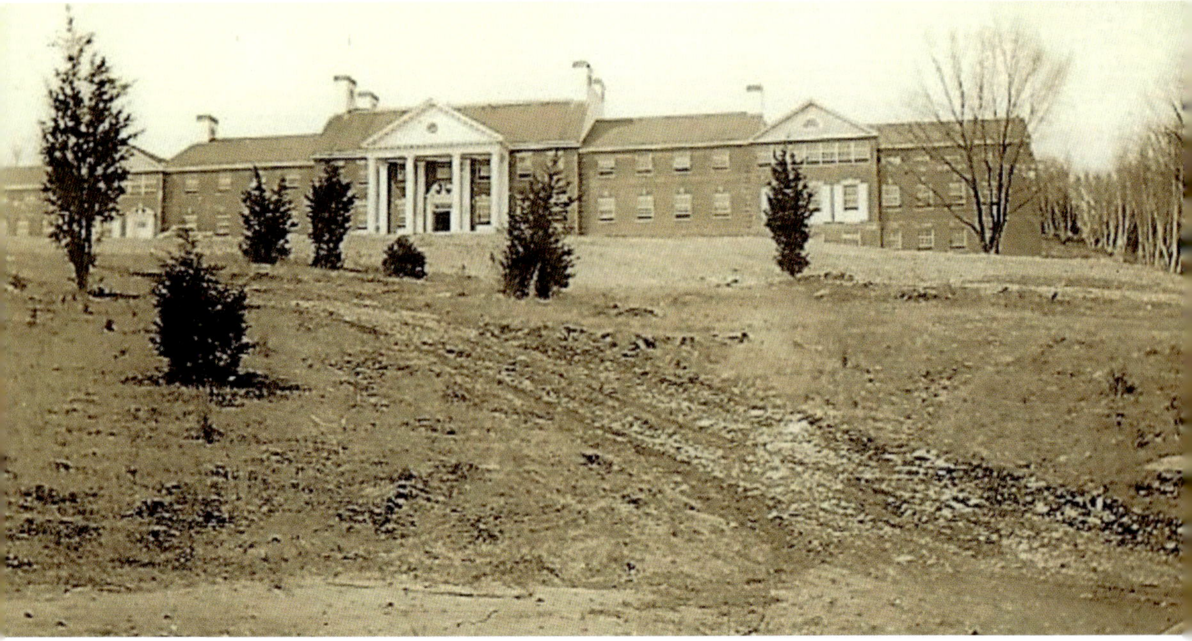

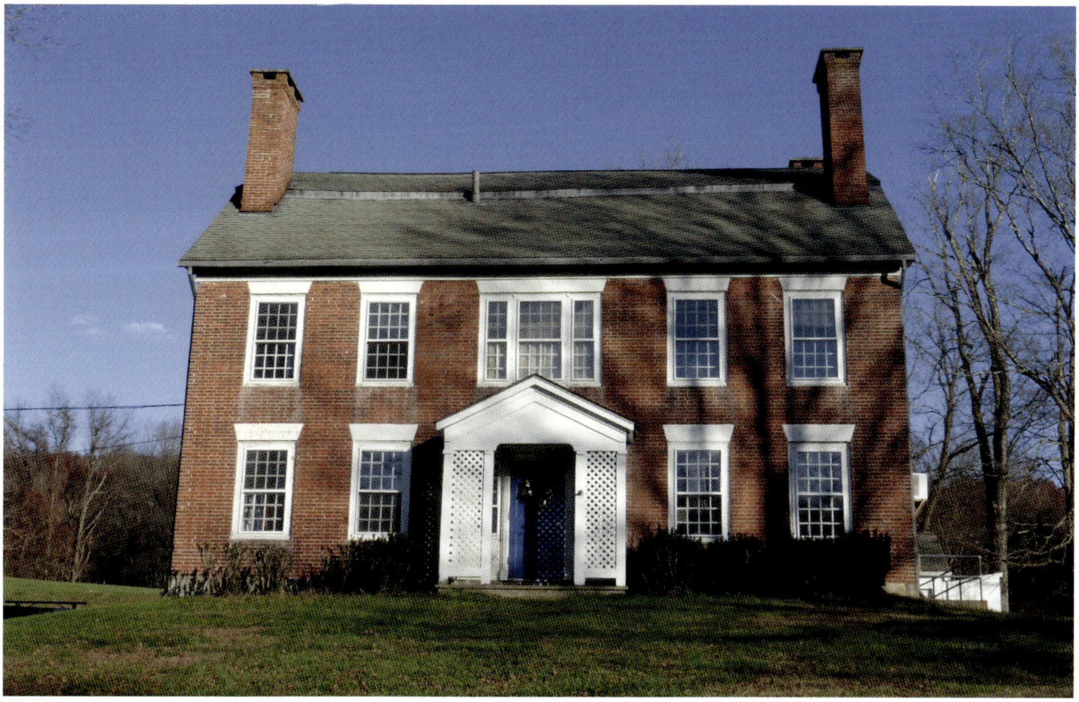

THRIFT SHOP: The Joel Pierce House, built in 1811, has been owned by the Southbury Training School since 1952 for staff housing. It is now used as the thrift shop. The Pierce House is a stately brick building with a gambrel roof and four large chimneys, two on each end of the building. The Pierce (Pearce) family settled much of the area, beginning in the late 1780s, owning many farms and beautiful houses. The Pierce Hollow Cemetery is across the street from the Joel Pierce house, with the entrance partially hidden in the undergrowth.

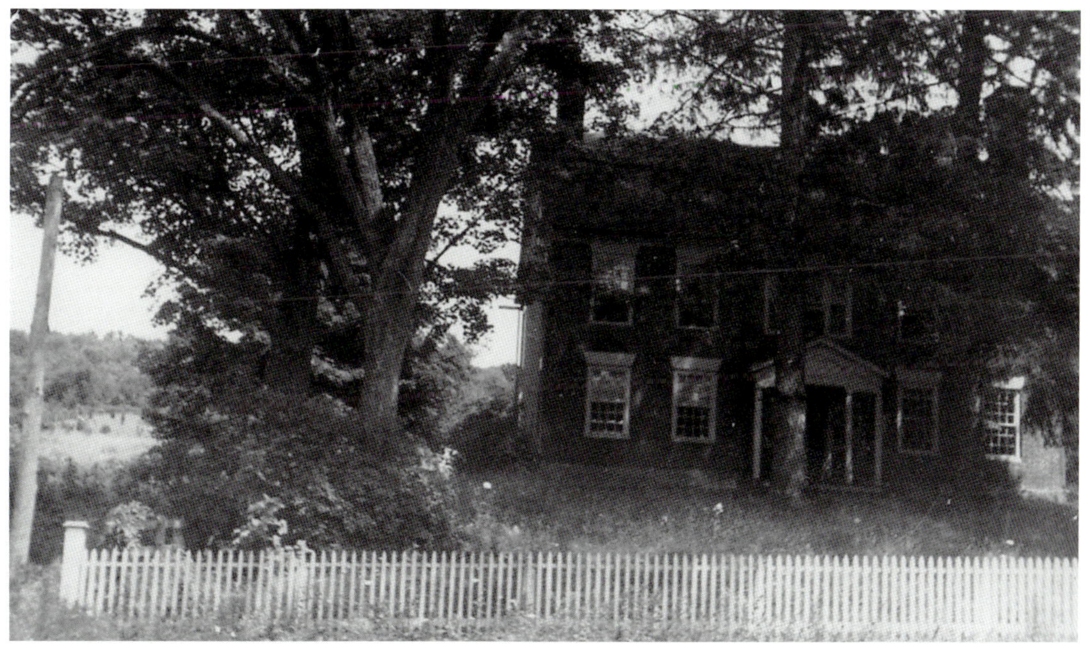

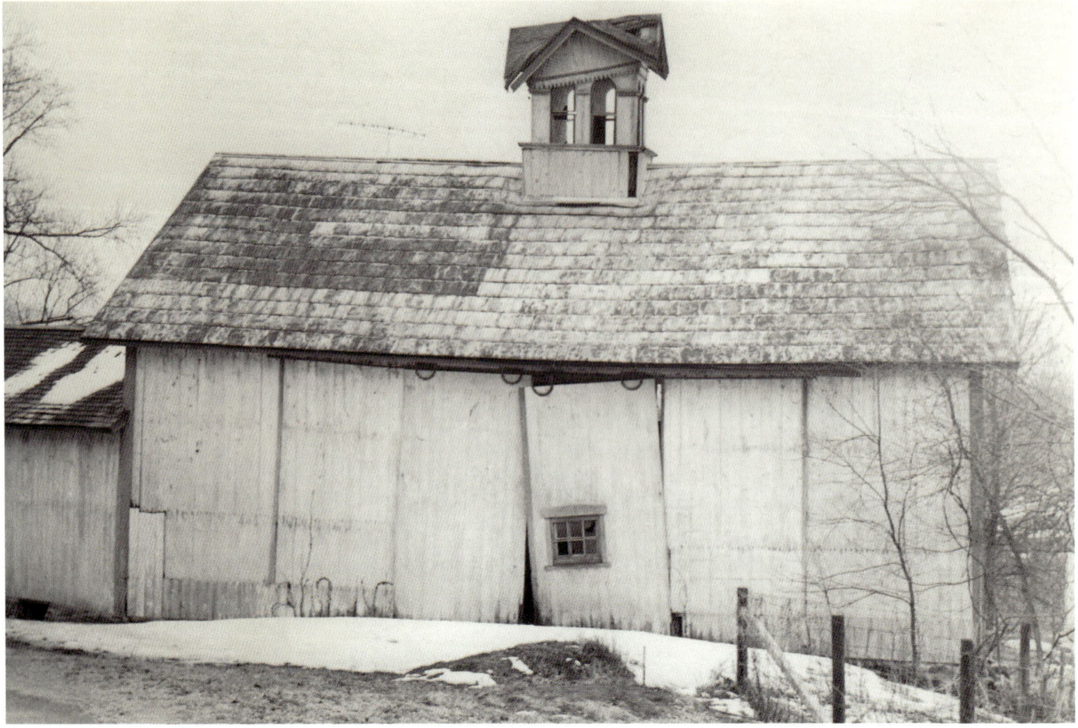

Dairy Barn: The charming nineteenth-century barn was once part of the dairy farm owned by Robert Platt, and was once Pierce land. The dairy farm was in operation until 1960. The cupola from the barn has disappeared, but one like it still remains on an adjoining barn. Dairy farms were very prevalent in the Southbury for much of the twentieth century. During the early 1900s, the fresh milk would be carted to the large creamery in South Britain or to the train station and shipped to Waterbury for processing. Today, only a couple of dairies are in operation in Southbury.

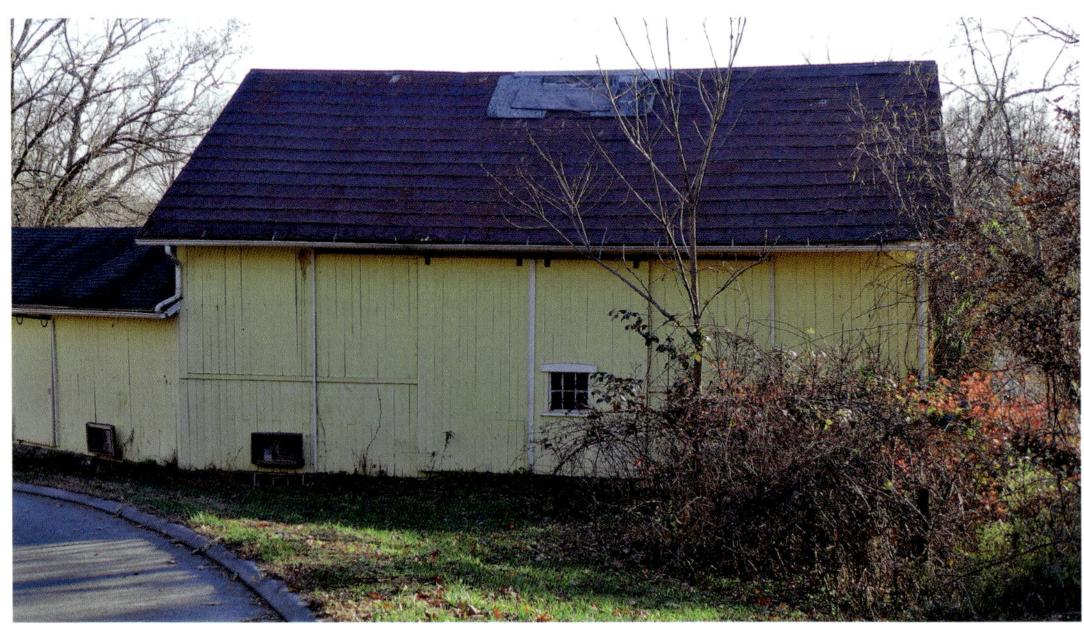

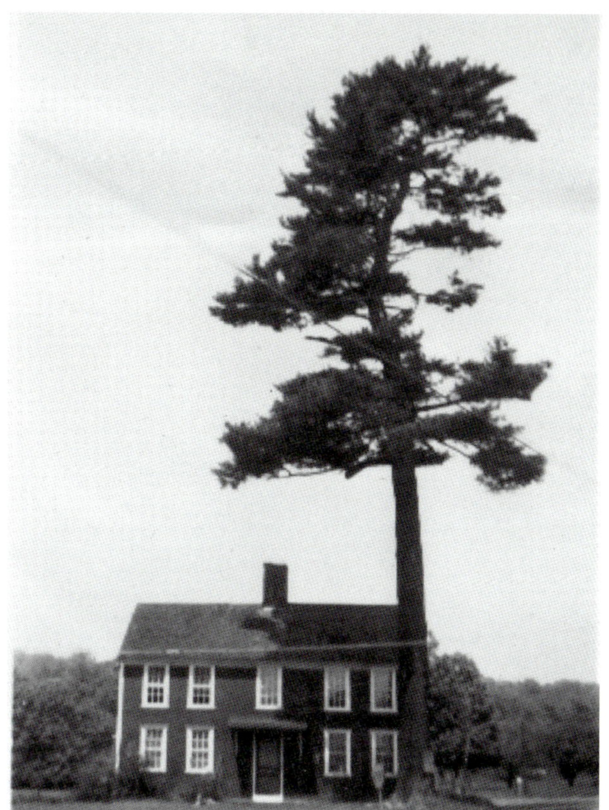

TALL PINE TREE: Pine Tree Corner was named after an extremely tall pine tree near an intersection. The home was built around 1750. The over 80-foot tall tree came down during a storm in 1938, shortly after this photograph was taken. Whenever there was a major crossroads, you could usually find a general store, and later, a gas station. The intersection at Routes 172 and 67 was just the same. Now, the old Pine Tree House shares the intersection with Christ the Savior Orthodox Church, The Church of Jesus Christ of Latter-day Saints, and another private residence.

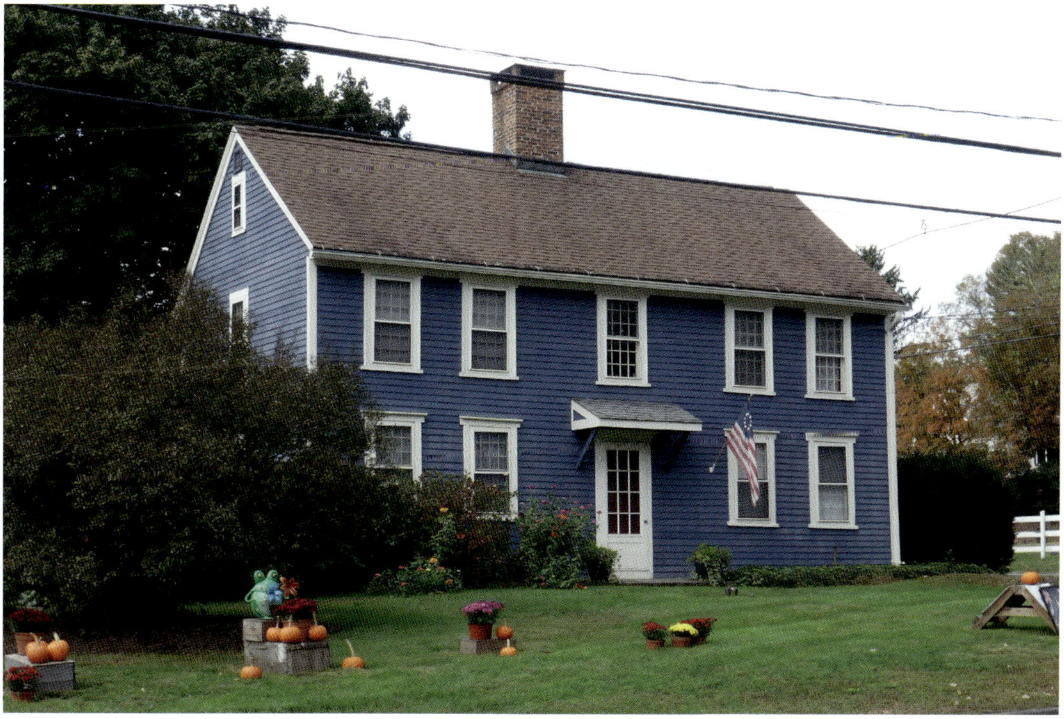

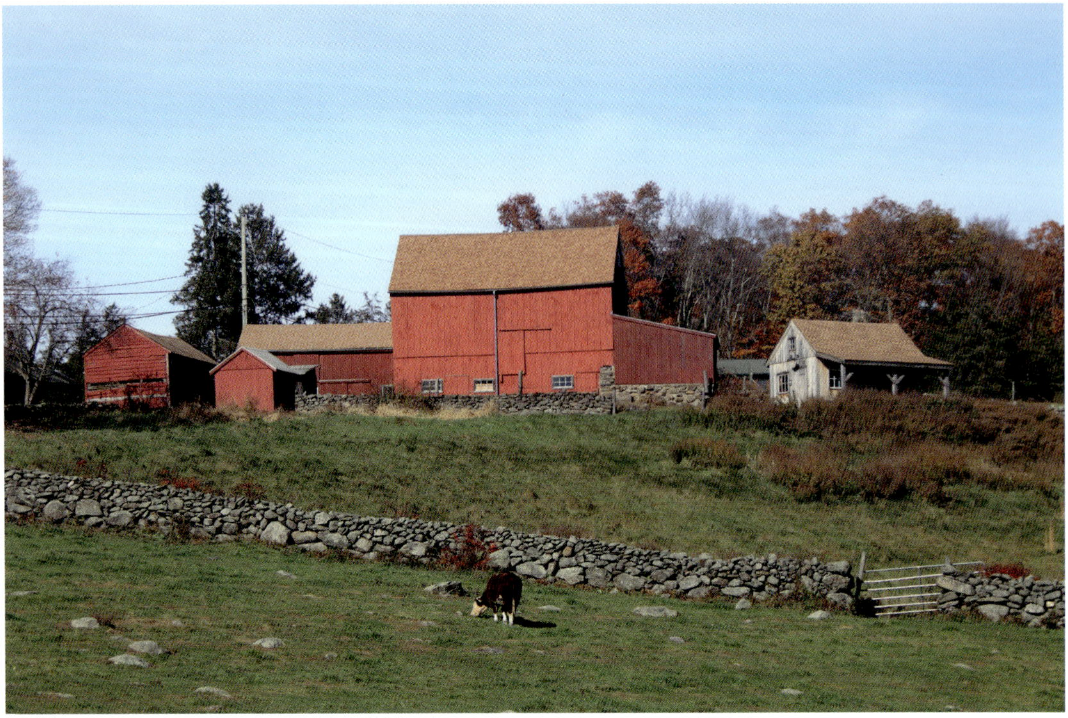

LUDORF BARN: The farm now known as the Ludorf Farm has its beginnings in the early nineteenth century. The old barn was built about 1820. Anson and Julius Ludorf purchased the land in 1886 and the Ludorf family still own portions of the original farm. Located at the end of the road until the 1960s when the road was extended to Roxbury, the farm was left undisturbed and still appears very much as it has for generations. The barn was donated to the Southbury Historical Society in 2009, whose goal is to make it into a farm heritage museum.

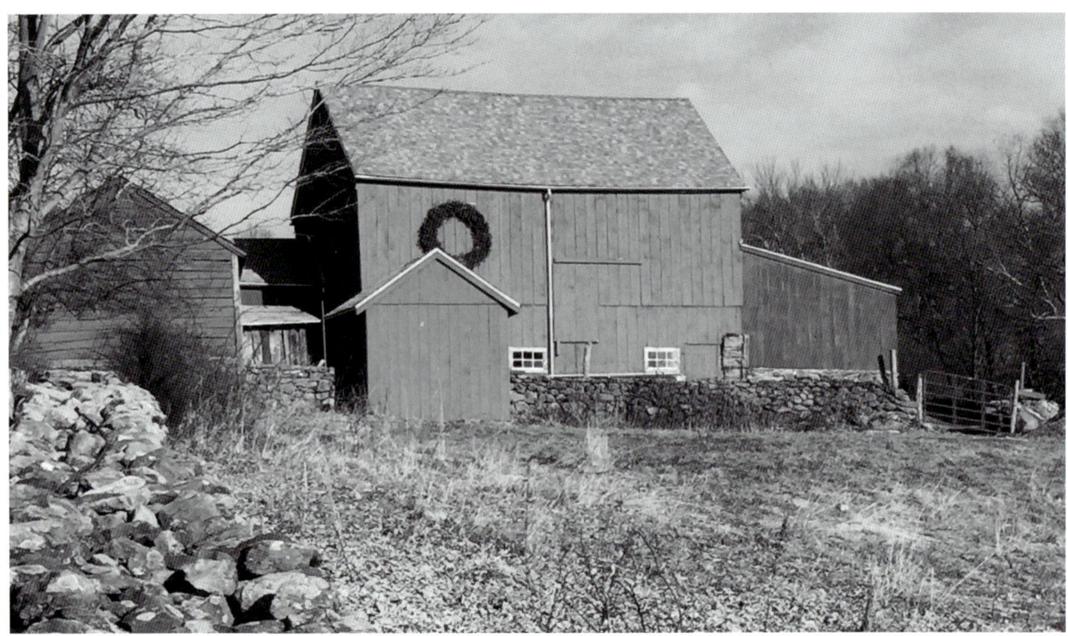

3

Points In Between

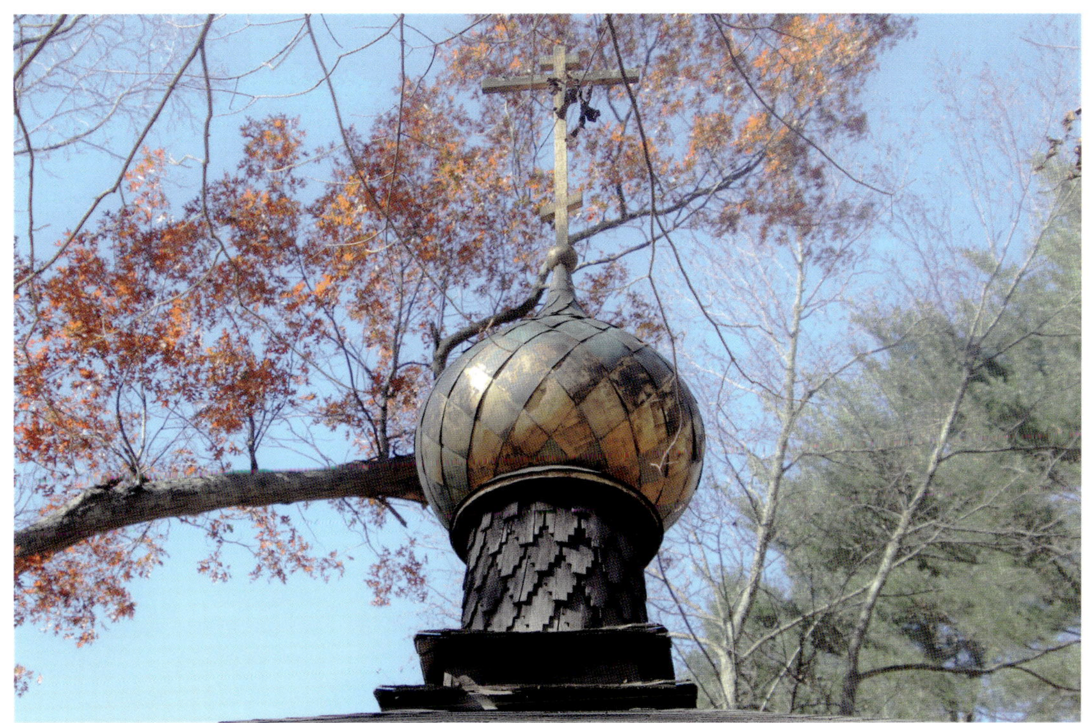

This chapter takes us from the Housatonic River crossing at the Silver Bridge, following the river for a short while and along the path of the old railroad tracks toward Southford.

The primary road between Danbury and Hartford once went right through Southbury, following Main Street North and South. The railroad tracks were just south of Main Street South, bisecting the town until Kettletown Road. When Interstate 84 was first discussed, the plans called for the highway to go directly down the Main Street South after passing Ichabod Road. Town officials protested, and the state decided to follow the basic path of the railway instead, leaving the town roads intact, and forming a dramatic curve on the interstate.

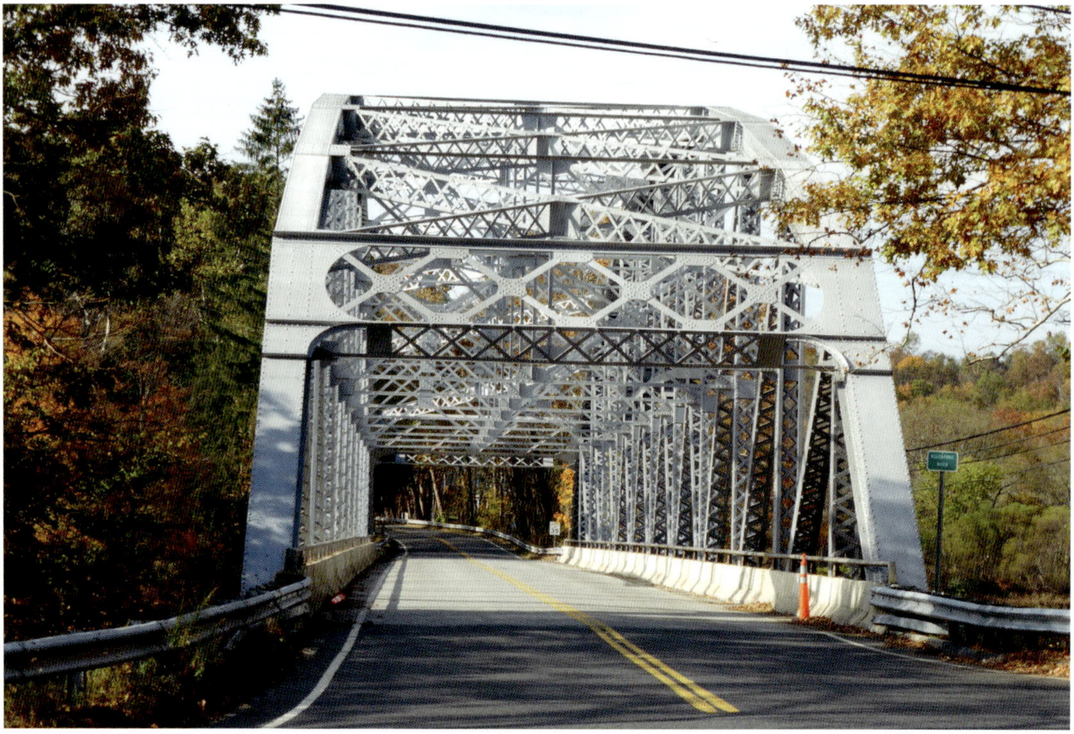

BRIDGE OVER HOUSATONIC: Long known locally as the Silver Bridge, the structure over the Housatonic was the main road into Southbury from Sandy Hook since it was built in 1934, replacing a lovely, but antiquated bridge. Another long-time bridge, the Bennett Bridge, a mile down the river, was removed in 1919 when Lake Zoar was created and the water levels rose. The Silver Bridge was the only Southbury Housatonic crossing until the Rochambeau Bridge was built in 1952. It went through a variety of colors through the years, including a pale blue and a rusty color. Recently, the structure was spruced up with new pavement, restored steel, and a paint job, bringing it back to its original silver color.

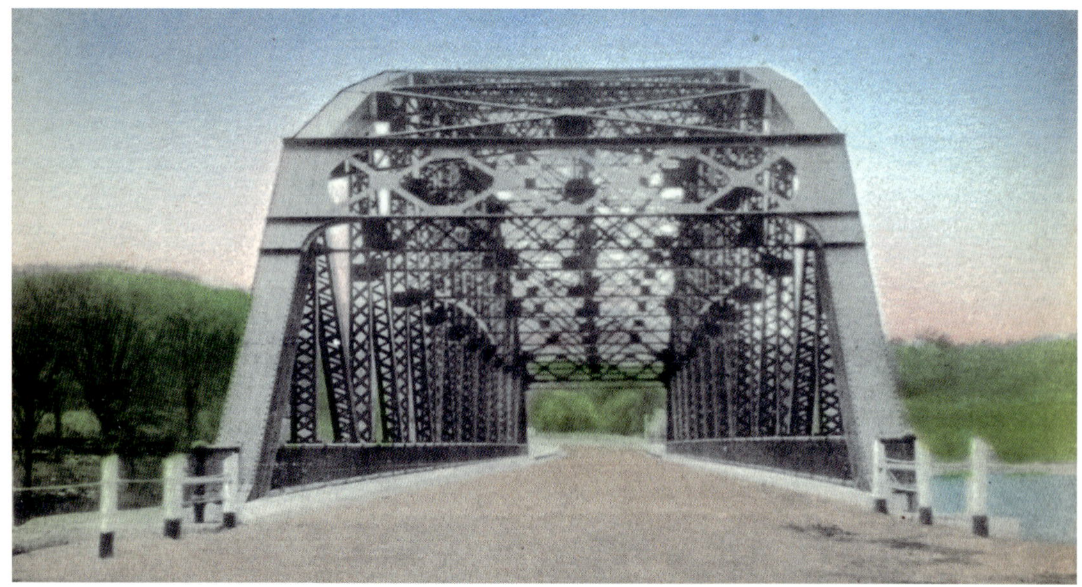

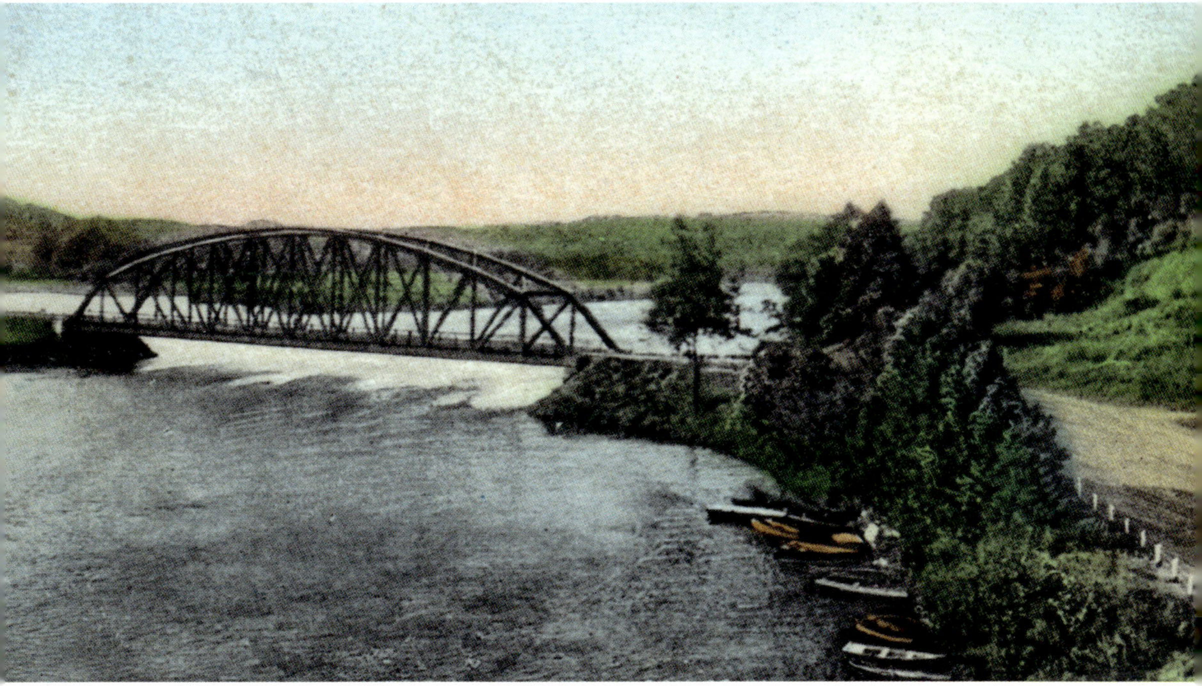

ROAD ALONG LAKE ZOAR: A birds-eye view of the Silver Bridge allows you to see the surrounding area. Besides the growth of the trees, very little has changed since the bridge was built. On the right side is the approach to the bridge from Southbury. The bottom photograph is a short distance from the bridge, following closely to the edge of Lake Zoar. The guard rails were a necessary boundary along the steep curve. Sandy Hook is across the lake on the right side of the photograph.

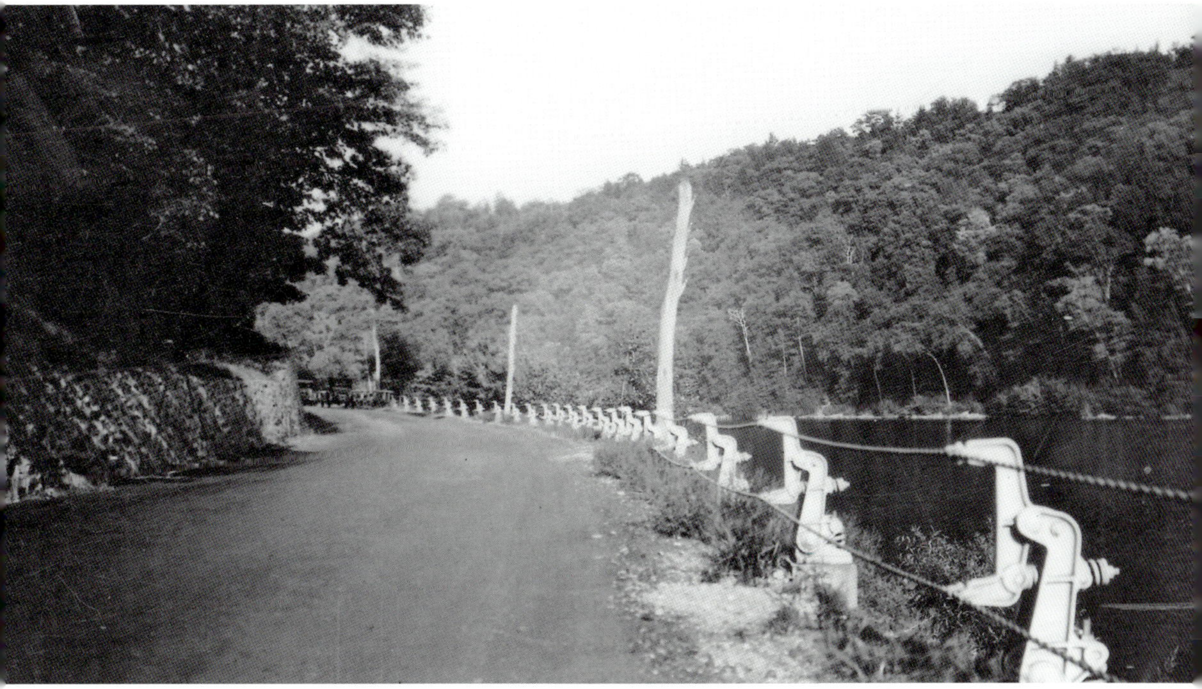

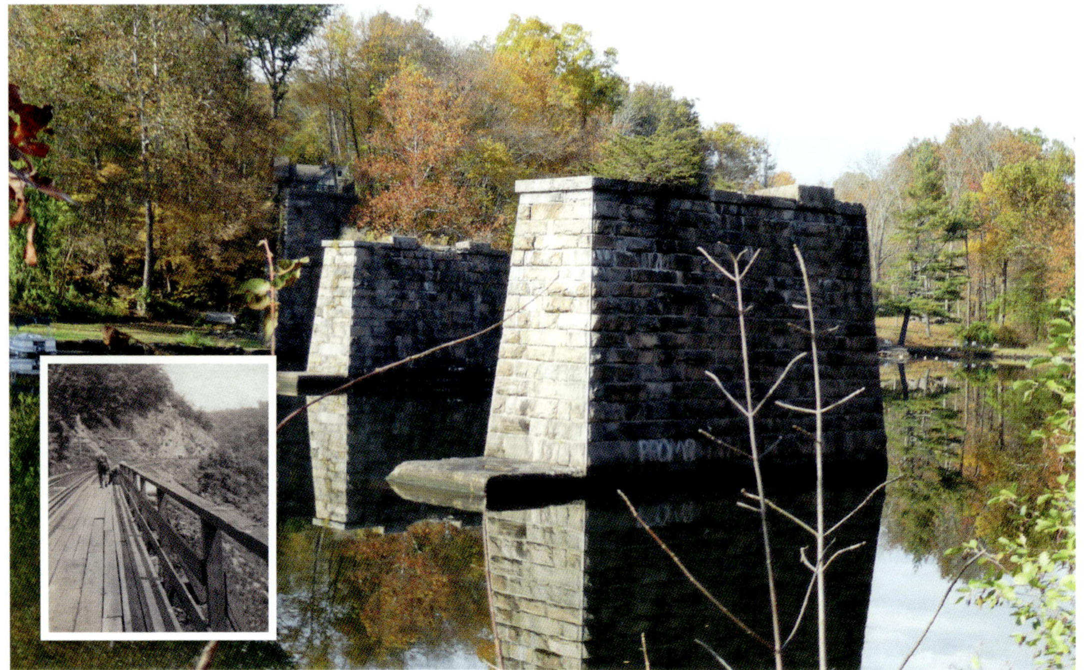

Housatonic Trestle: The first survey to determine where railroad tracks would be placed through Southbury was completed in the fall of 1845 when the New York and New England (NY&NE) Railroad planned to have a direct route from New York to Boston. Tracks through Southbury were completed between 1866 and 1880. The train trestle over the Housatonic River from Sandy Hook to Southbury was first constructed of wood. The wooden bridge was destroyed by fire in 1905, and was replaced with a steel structure that was used until 1948, when the railroad was no longer needed. The stone pilings still in the river remain a strong reminder of the railroad days.

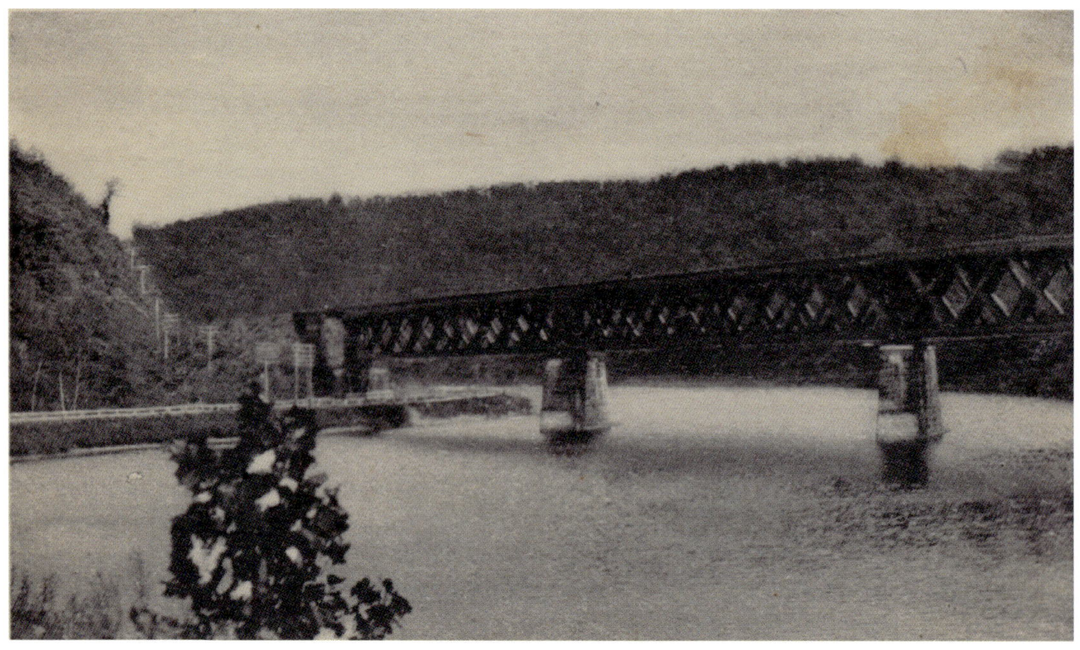

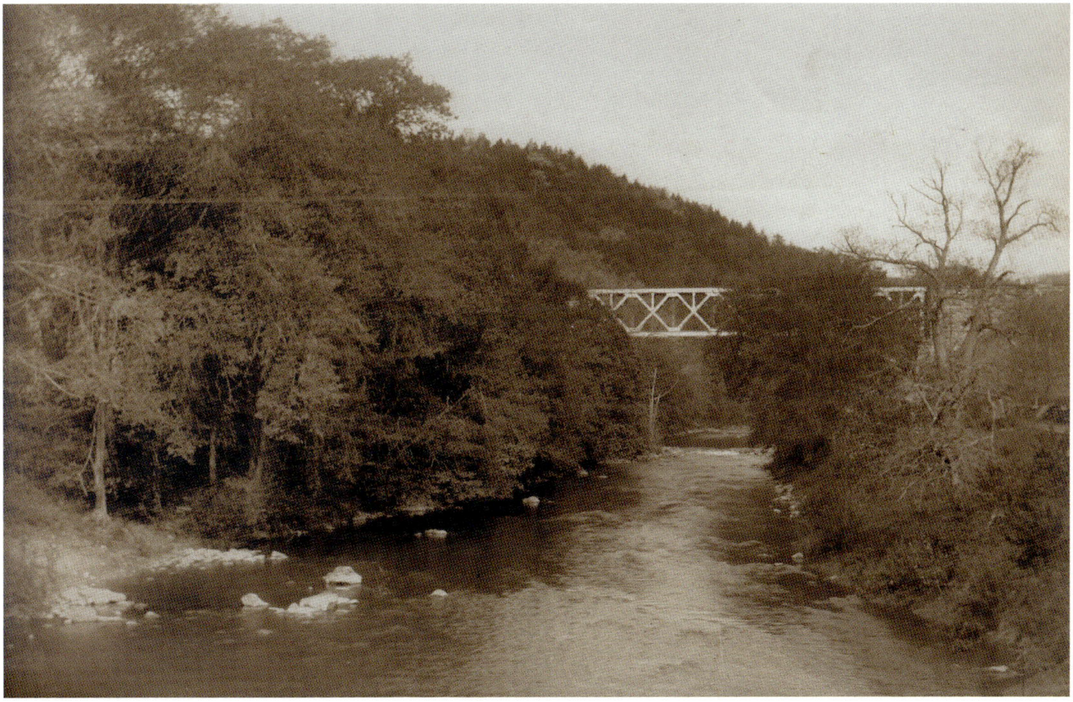

POMPERAUG TRESTLE: After crossing the Housatonic River, the train tracks start climbing along the hillside. By the time the train reached the Pomperaug River, the trestle was high above the river's surface. The abutments on both sides of the river are standing and best viewed during the winter when the leaves are gone. The tracks continued uphill, basically following the route of what is now I-84, pausing briefly at the South Britain stop near Ichabod Road and continuing on a demanding climb until it reached the Southbury station. Extra engines were required to pull the trains up the steep grades.

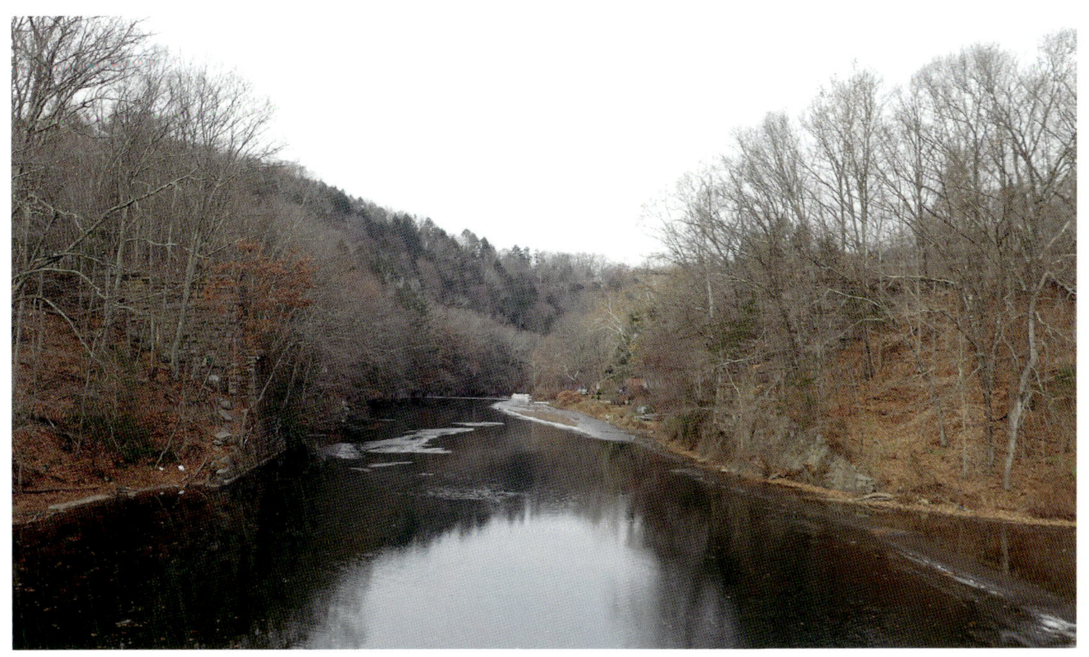

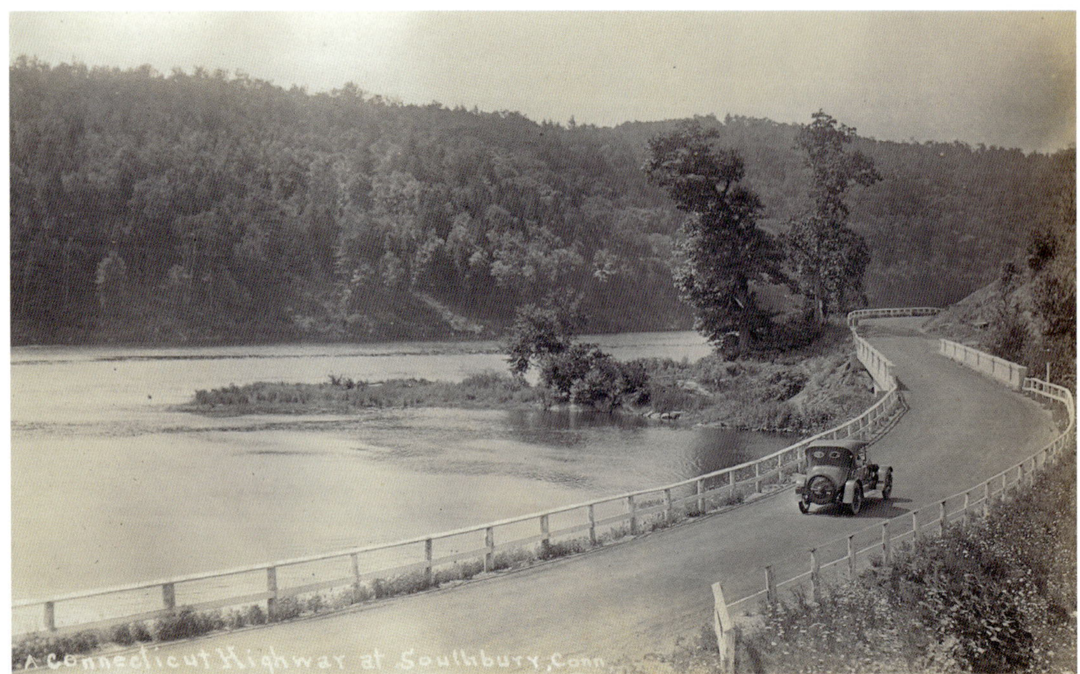

POMPERAUG RIVER BRIDGE: When the Stevenson Dam was built across the Housatonic River in Oxford and Monroe, it created Lake Zoar in 1919, but also caused problems in Southbury. The river valley flooded, and new roads and bridges had to be built higher and above the lake. The long-time Bennetts Bridge was removed over the Housatonic, forcing all the traffic to go across the old bridge onto Glen Road in Sandy Hook. A new white concrete bridge was built over the Pomperaug River in a modern style and allowed exciting views of the new lake.

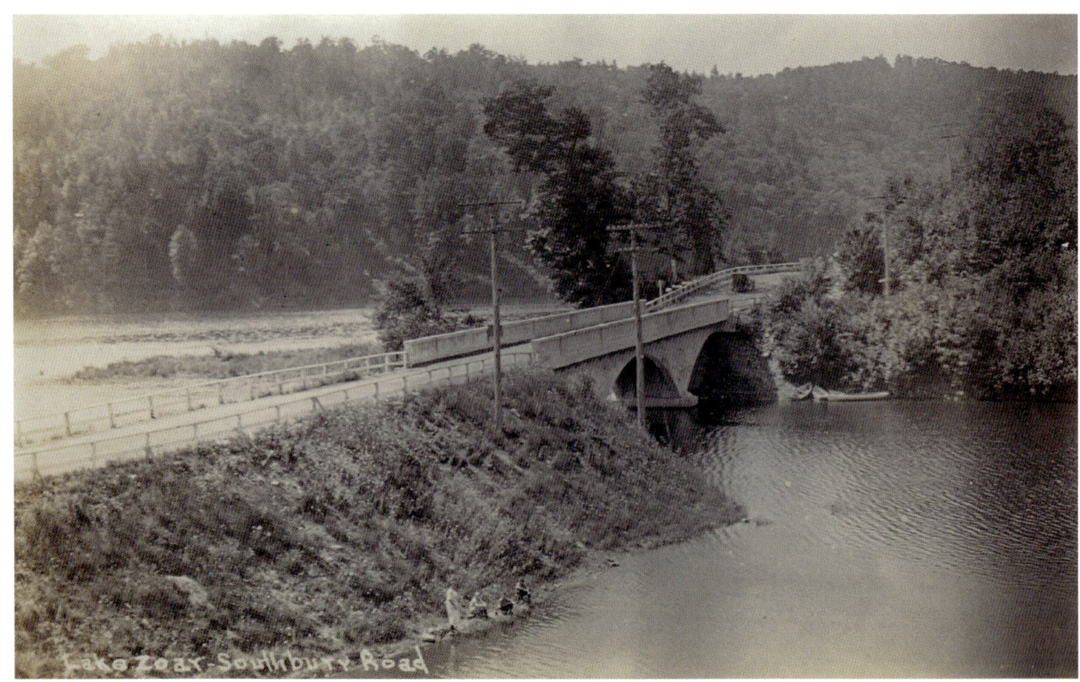

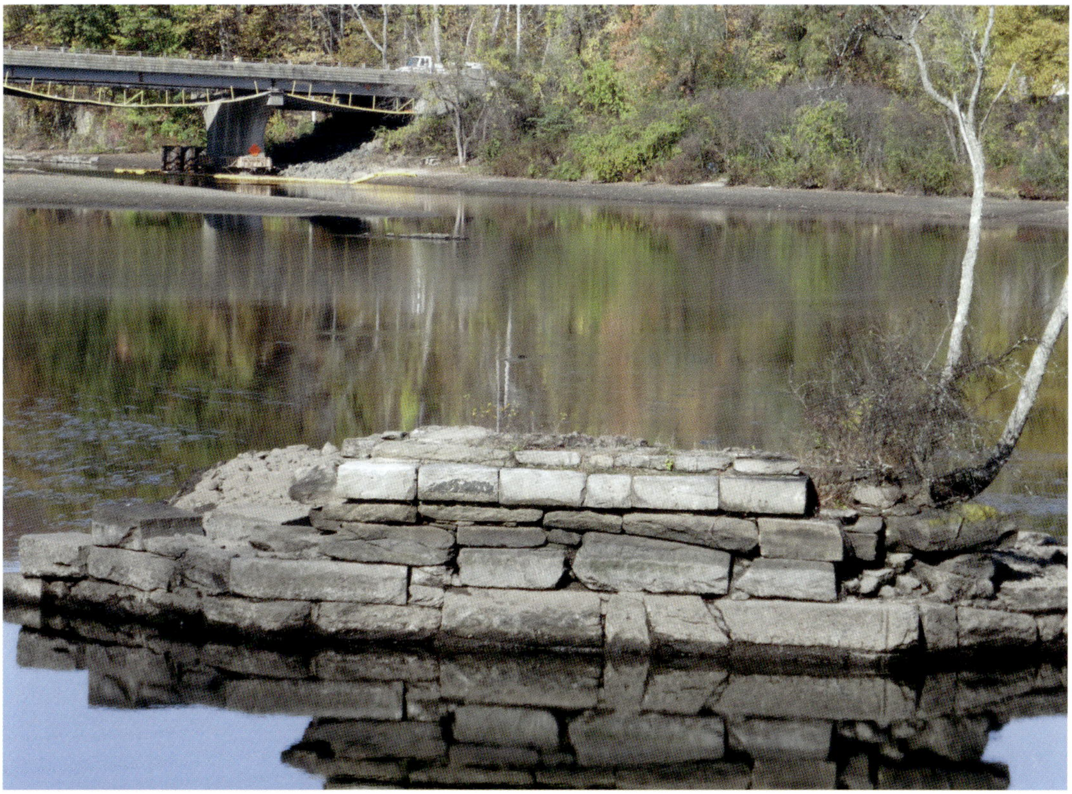

BRIDGE TAKEN DOWN: Bennett's Bridge over the Housatonic River was named after the brothers who had the rights to build a bridge in the nineteenth century and to charge tolls. The Bennett Brothers had previously conducted a ferry service in the same area. The bridge was constructed in two sections across the river, with a small island in the middle. The damming of the river brought the demise of the bridge when Lake Zoar was created. One stone piling is still visible most of the time near the Sandy Hook shore, and another piling can be seen near the Pomperaug River Bridge when the water is reduced by the power company twice a year.

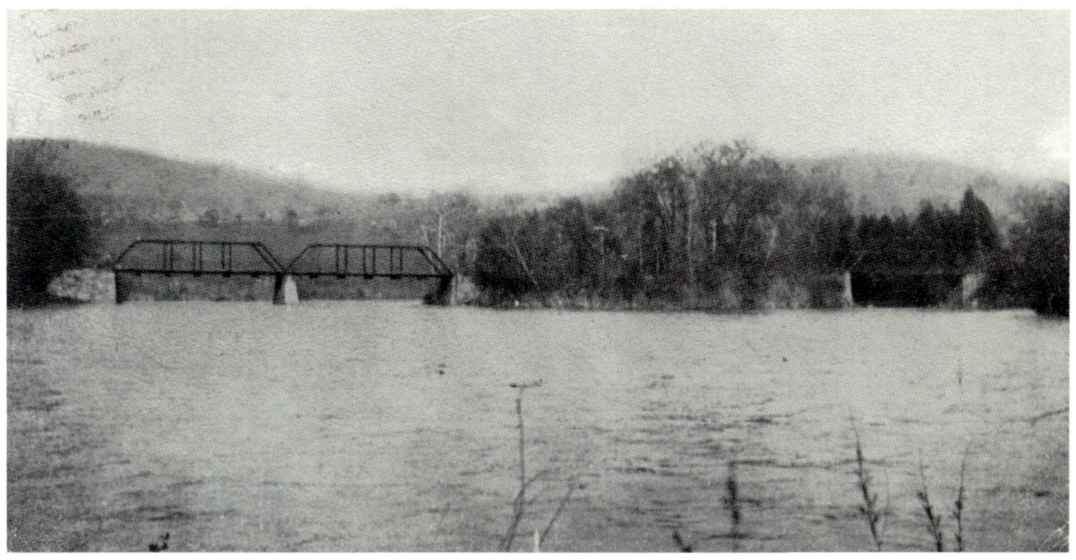

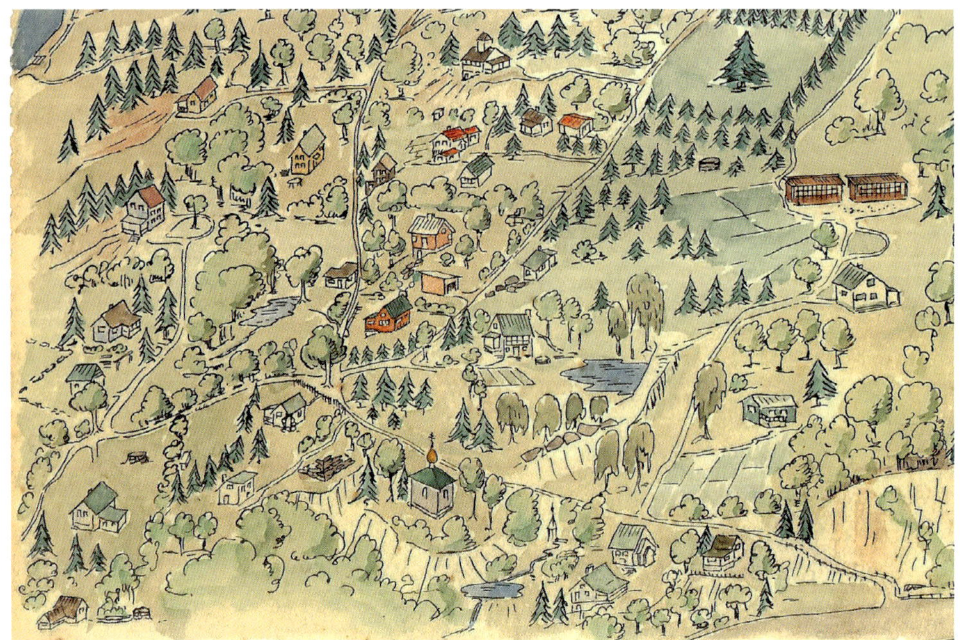

RUSSIAN VILLAGE: In the 1920s, Count Ilya Tolstoy discovered a beautiful section of Southbury and decided it would be a great place for a summer residence. Author George Grebenstichikoff organized the area as a Russian artisan community, encouraging other Russians to build cottages. They named the community Churaevka, after a Siberian village in one of Grabenstichikoff's books. The above photograph is from a watercolor map made by Vladimir Tchistiakov in 1961. In the photograph below is the typewriter that belonged to George Grebenstchikoff, who once said, "When I'm gone, Churaevla might not last for long. In fifty years, it might be deserted and overgrown with grass." Fortunately, he was wrong.

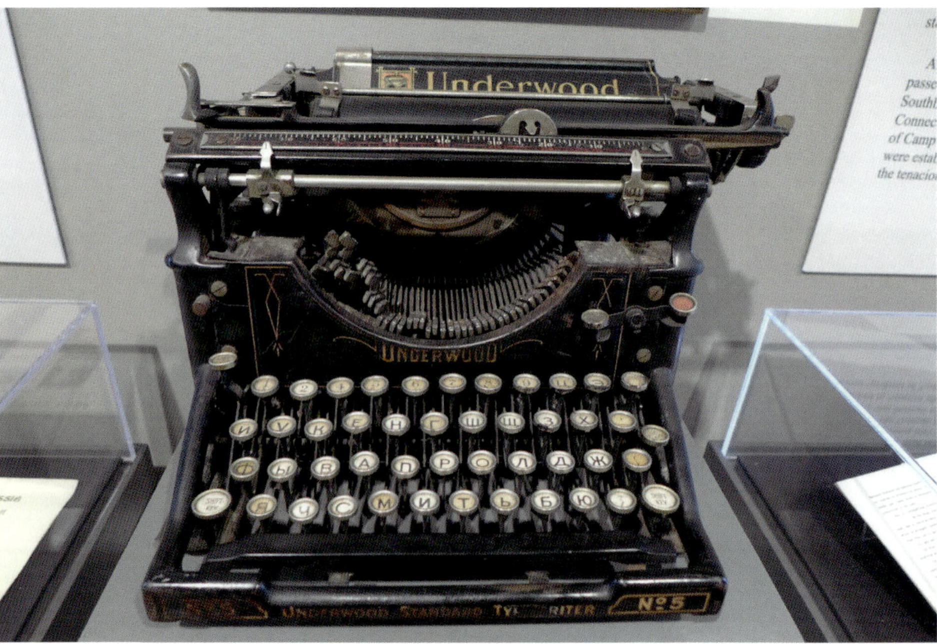

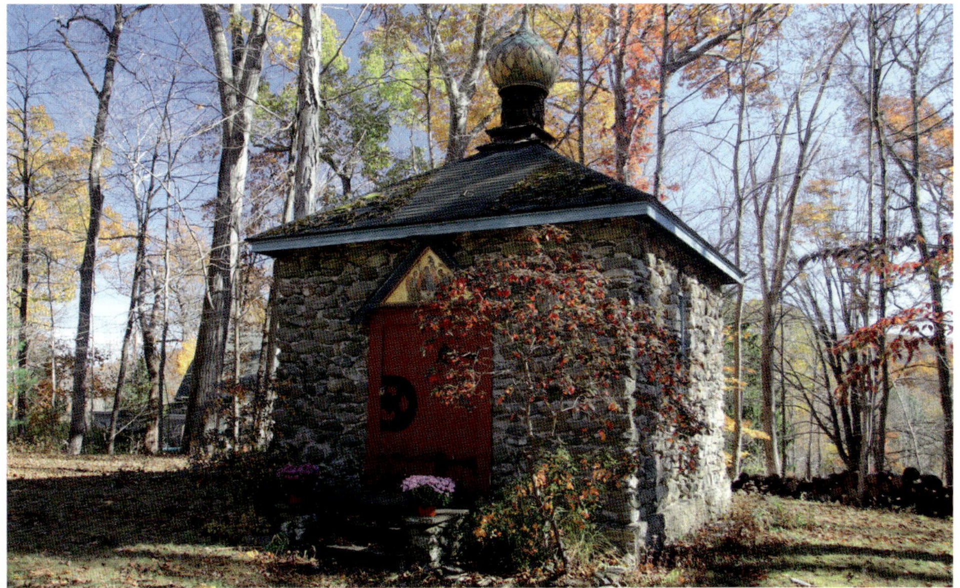

RUSSIAN CHAPEL: An unexpected treasure in Southbury can be found in Russian Village. The charming stone chapel is visible shortly after entering the village. It was built in 1931 by residents under the direction of Ivan Wassil, based on the plans of Nicholas Roersch, who was a philosopher and painter. The chapel was designed with Saint Sergius in mind; the Saint who blessed the Russian armies. The dome is covered with gold leaf and glows in the sunshine. The interior is covered with gilded, hand-painted icons of Russian saints. A small amphitheater along the hillside is the perfect place to sit and have a quiet moment.

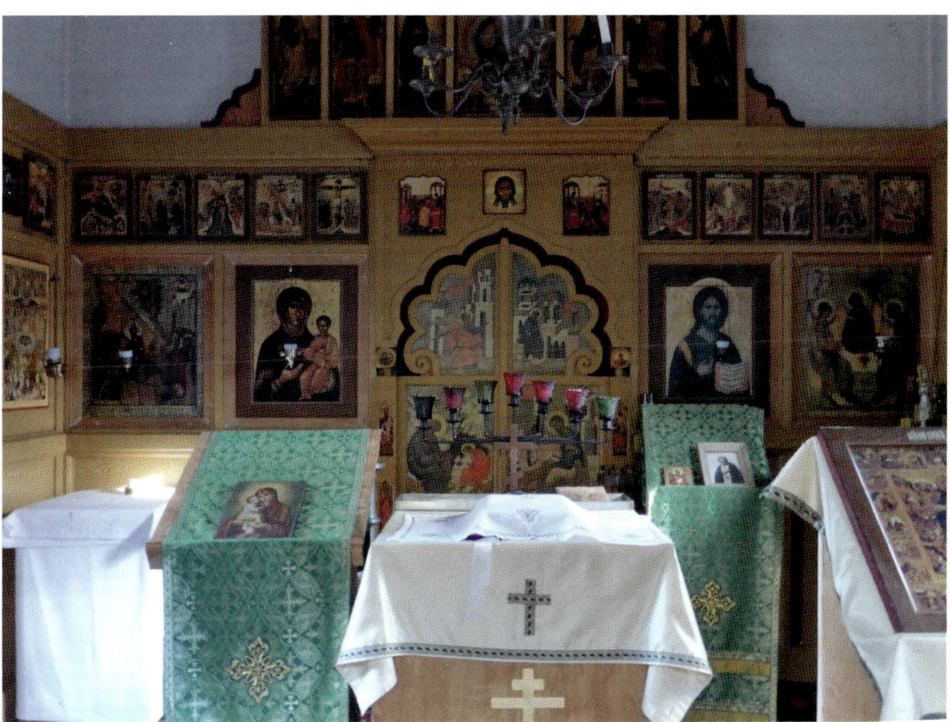

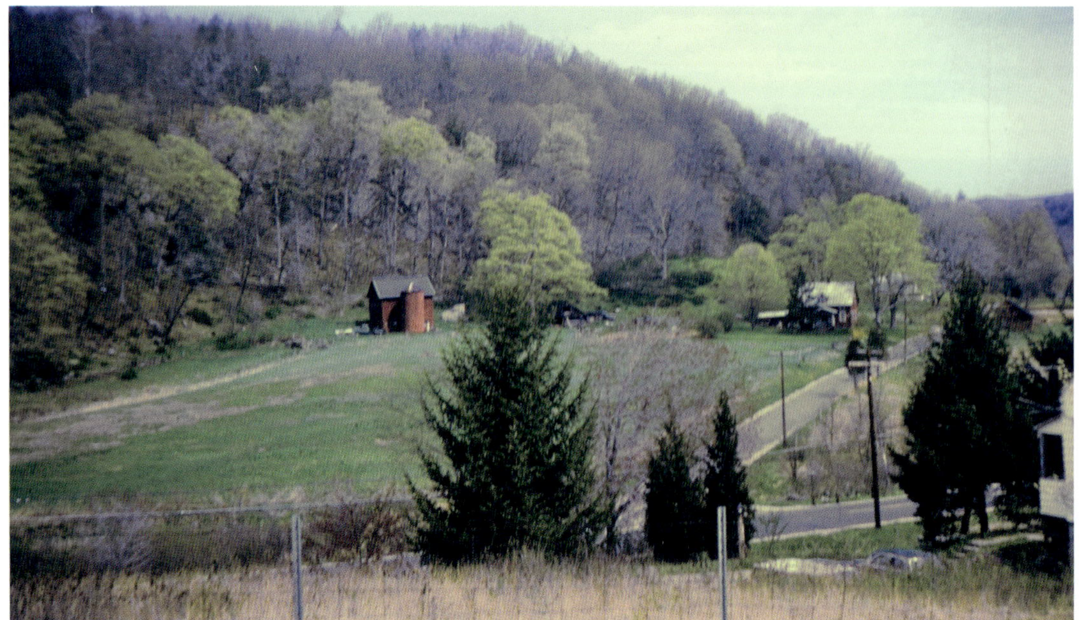

Barn at Hollow Swamp: In the old property deeds for Russian Village, they clearly state that the entrance to Russian Village was a bridge over the railroad track and that the buyer should cross at their own risk. The South Britain whistle stop station was near the corner of Ichabod and Fish Rock Roads. The train tracks basically followed the path where I-84 is now located until exit 15. Views from the train would have included the old barn and silo on Hollow Swamp Road. The above photo was taken from I-84 before the traffic was allowed on the road. The photo below is what is left of the barn, fifty years later. (KSL)

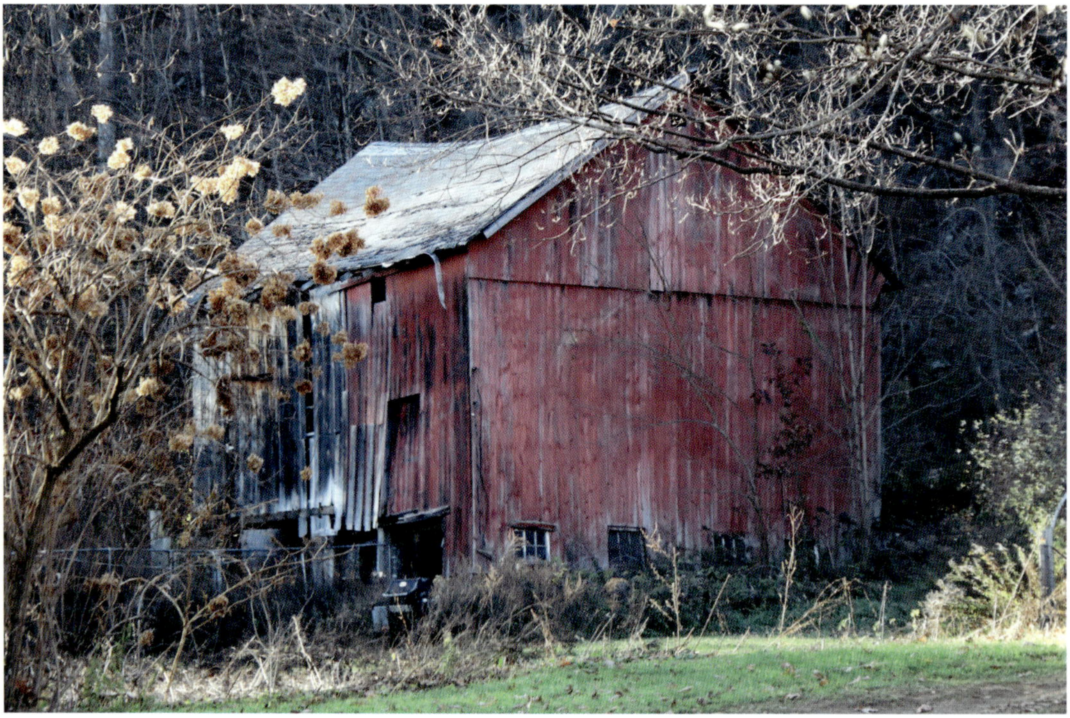

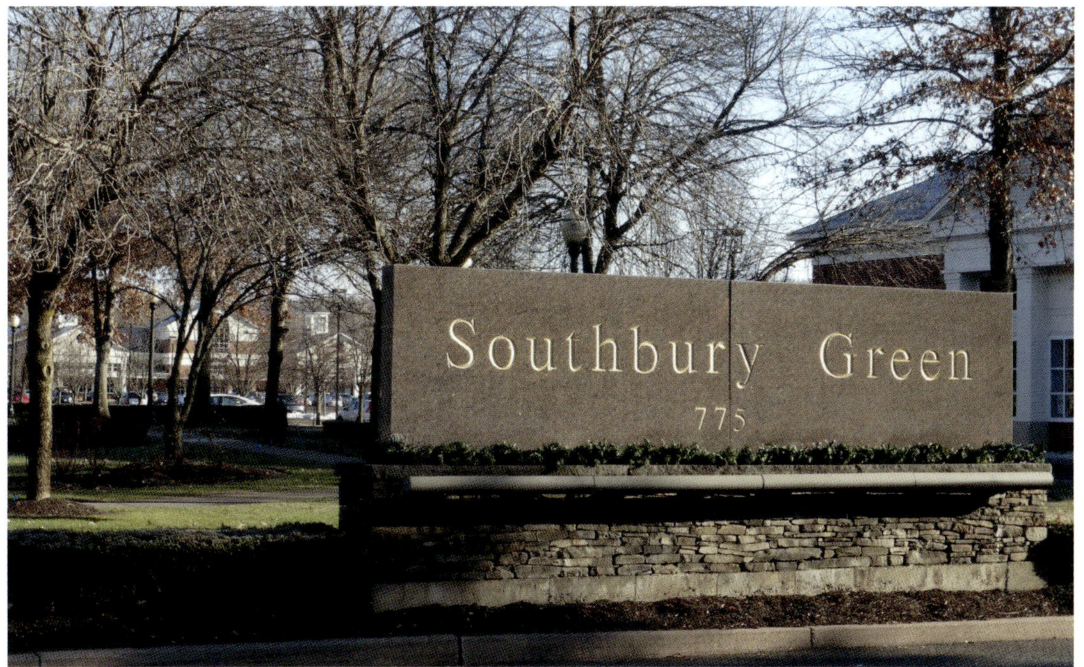

PUMPKIN PATCH: The Southbury Green shopping center has had a lot to offer the community since it came to town over two decades ago. The land was once used for another purpose. For many years, Brinley's corn field along Main Street South magically changed in the autumn to a field of orange orbs. A trip to the pumpkin patch was a fall tradition for all the local children on field trips, where they could be seen running happily through the field to find the very best pumpkin to take home. The students would return with their families to the pumpkin patch later to take a hay ride around the field and drink apple cider.

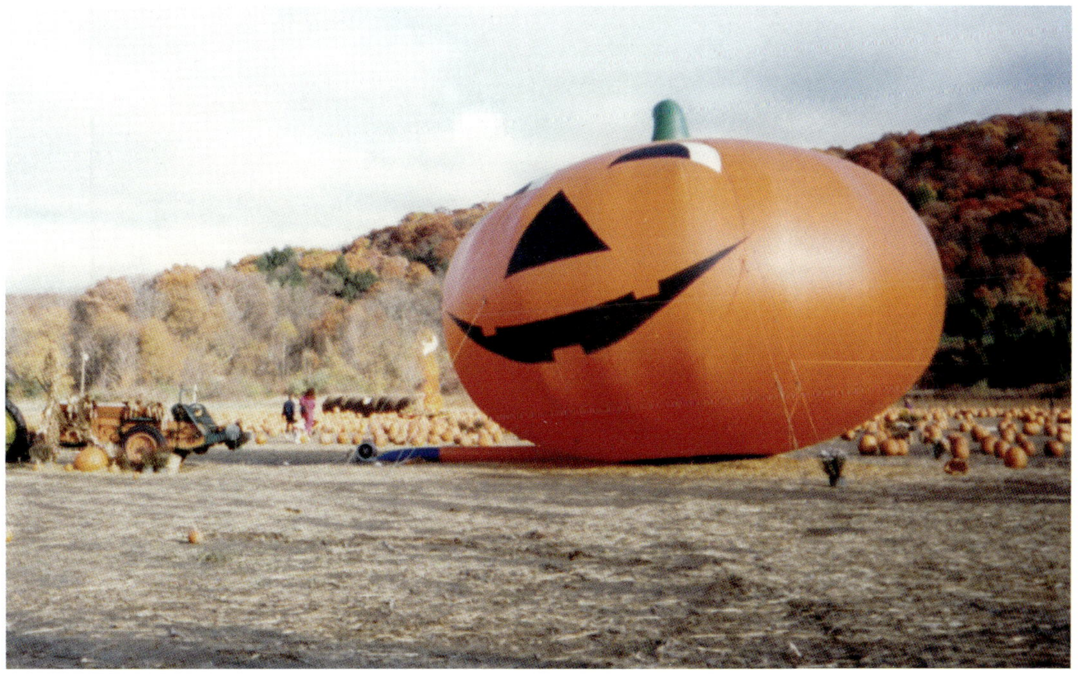

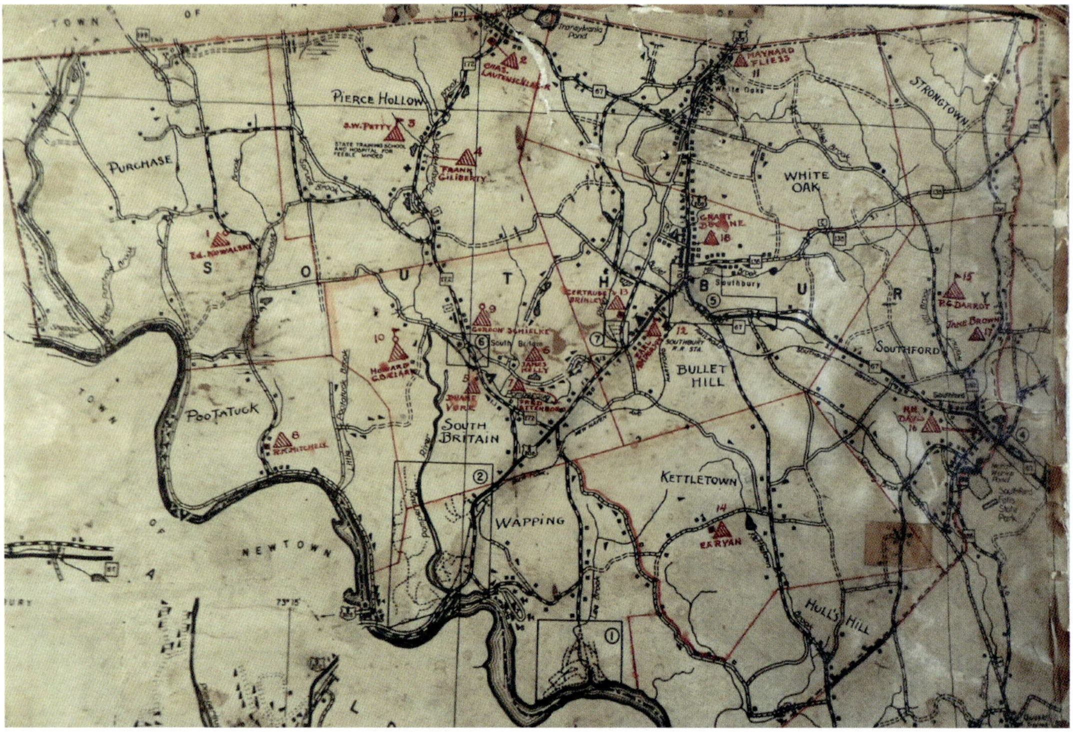

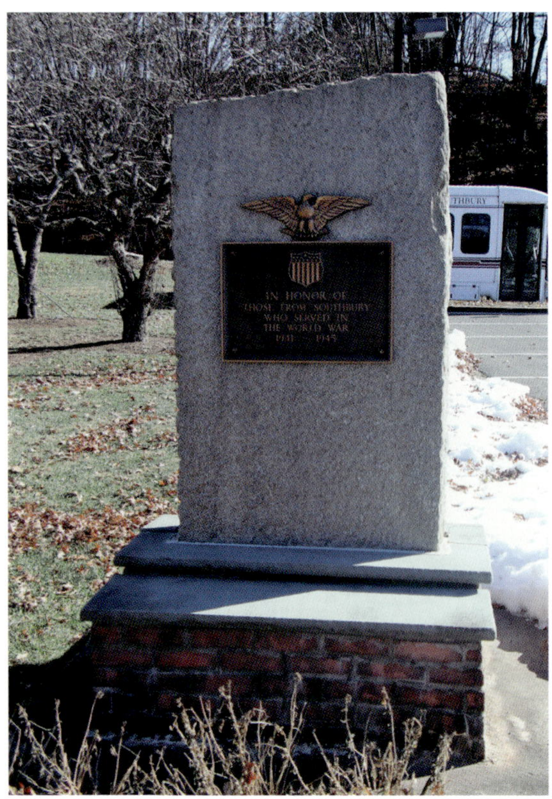

CIVIL DEFENSE: At the beginning of World War II, many residents were quick to organize the town Civil Defense team of Air Raid Wardens. Above is an Air Patrol map that shows the air raid warden districts within the red lines, with the red triangles representing each warden's name and home base. The warden's goal was to prepare his district for a possible air invasion by making sure the area could be totally blacked out, and drilling the residents on safety procedures. The bottom photograph shows our World War II monument in Veteran's Green.

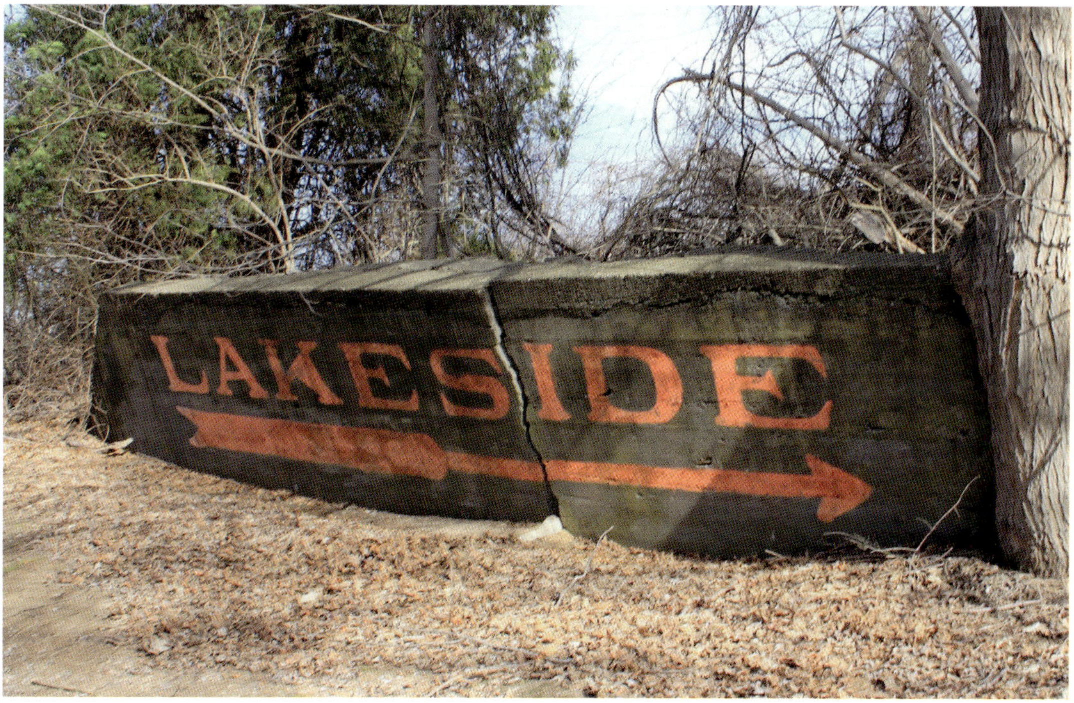

MISSING SIGN: For many years, a concrete slab with red printing with an arrow directing the way to the Lakeside summer community was located near the commuter parking lot at exit 14. Through the years, the sign area was cleaned of underbrush and repainted. Then one day, it was gone. Deemed a safety hazard, the town needed to act quickly to remove it. In the photo below is the restaurant and the real estate offices for the Lakeside community that once stood at the same location. If you look carefully, you can see the concrete wall protruding on both sides of the building. The Lakeside sign was painted on the concrete wall when Good Food eatery was pulled down.

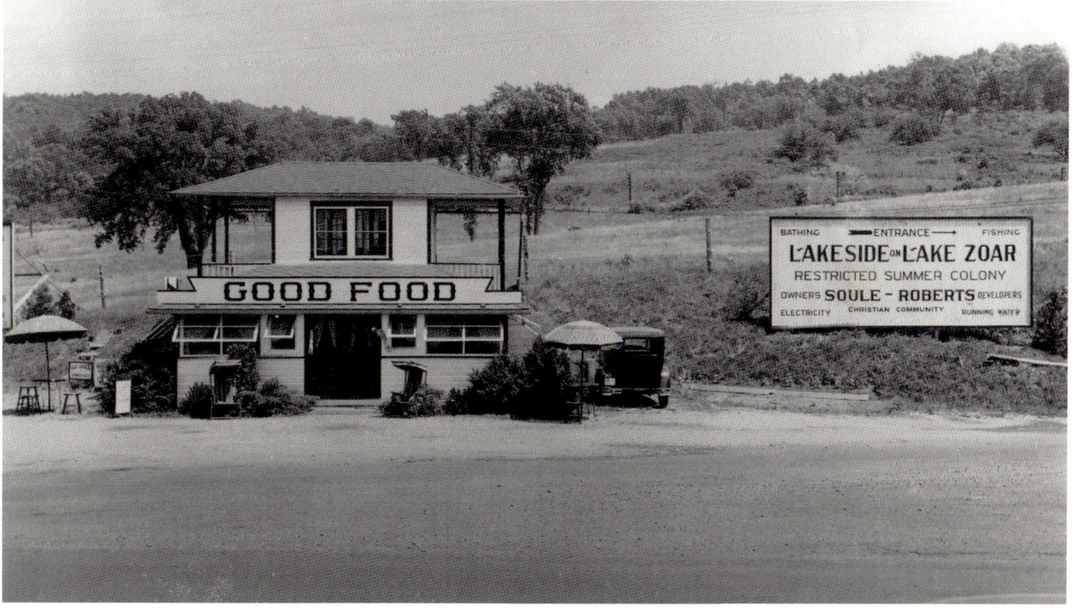

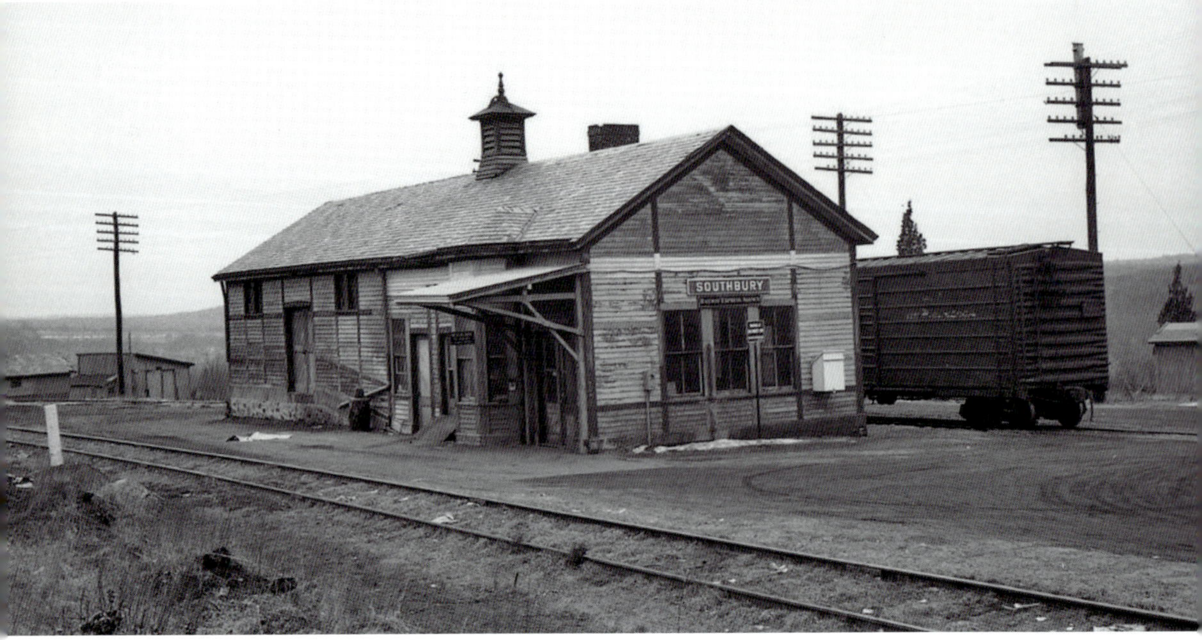

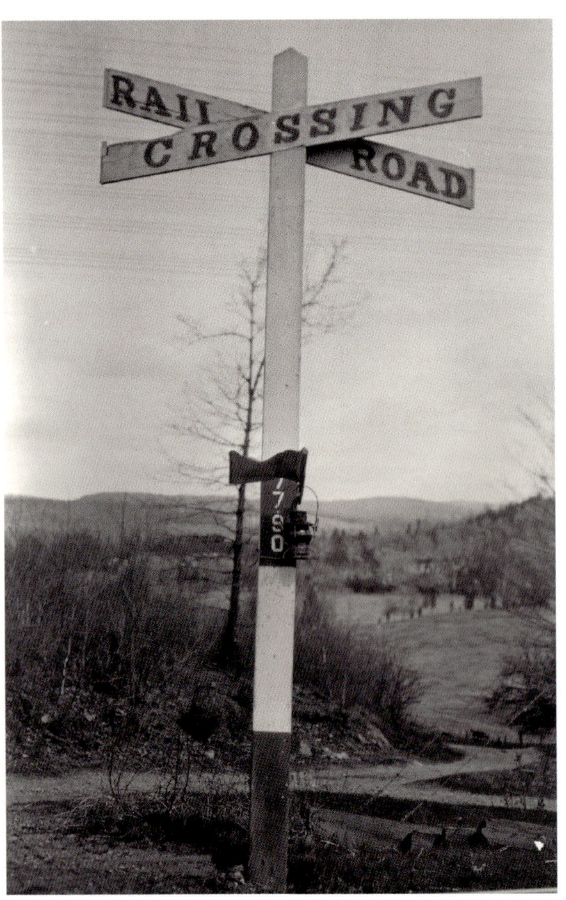

RAILROAD CROSSING AND DEPOT: As the railroad made its way through town, it needed to cross several roads. The tracks were south of Main Street, so they did not disturb the everyday traffic. The photograph from 1929 shows the railroad crossing over Peter Road, with views looking toward town. There is a lantern hanging from the post. The Southbury Depot sat on the hill overlooking the Pomperaug Valley. By the time it was decided to close the railroad line, the passenger service was already suspended, and the depots were falling apart. Freight trains continued to arrive and depart for several more years.

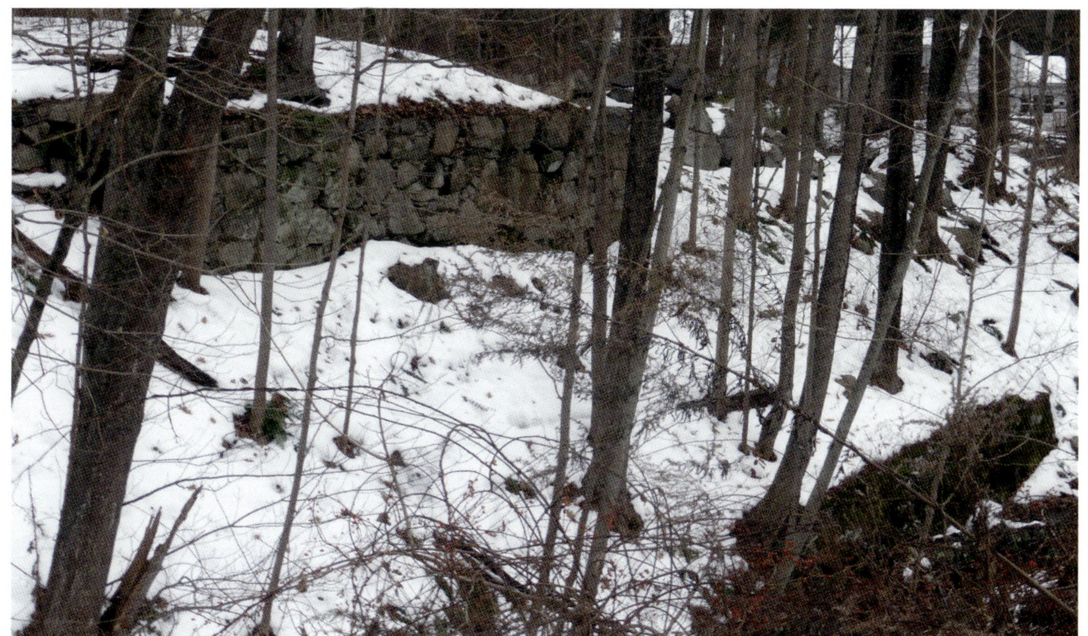

LARKIN STATE PARK TRAIL: Leaving Depot Hill area, the railroad traveled loosely parallel to Route 67 toward Southford. Near Curt Smith Road, the tracks went underneath the road, the Oxford Turnpike. The stone foundations of the bridge are still visible near the marked pedestrian crossing. In 1943, Dr. Charles Larkin purchased almost 11 miles of the railbed and gave it to the state to be used as a bridal trail. There are 2.4 miles of trail in Southbury between Kettletown Road and Route 188 where the Southford Depot once stood. (Bridge photograph courtesy of John Dwyer.)

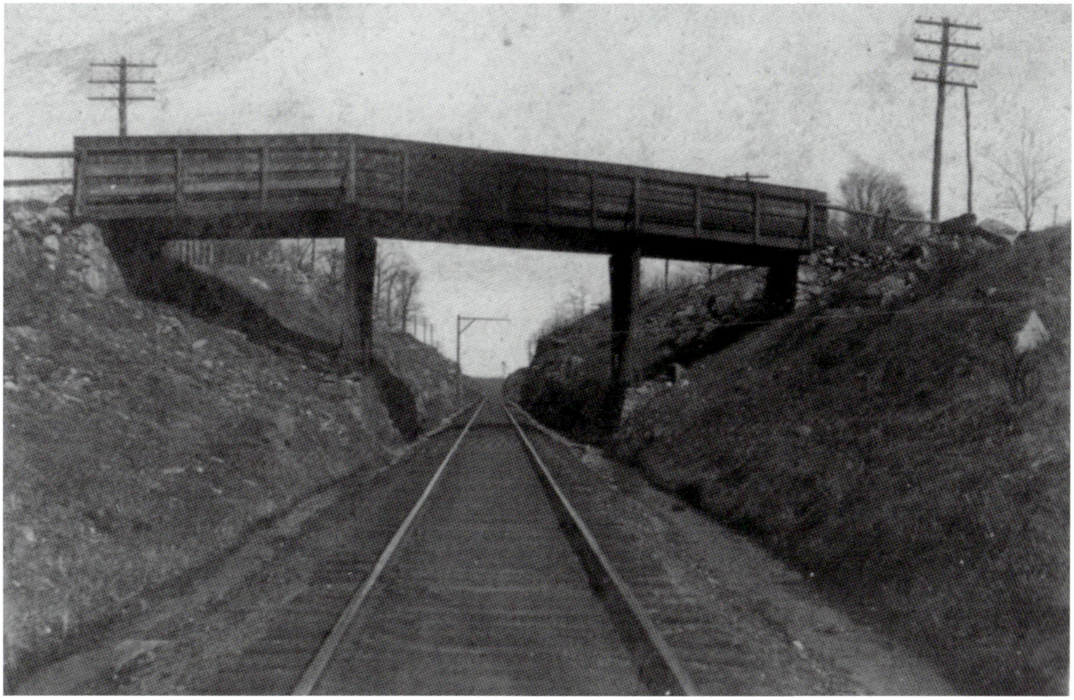

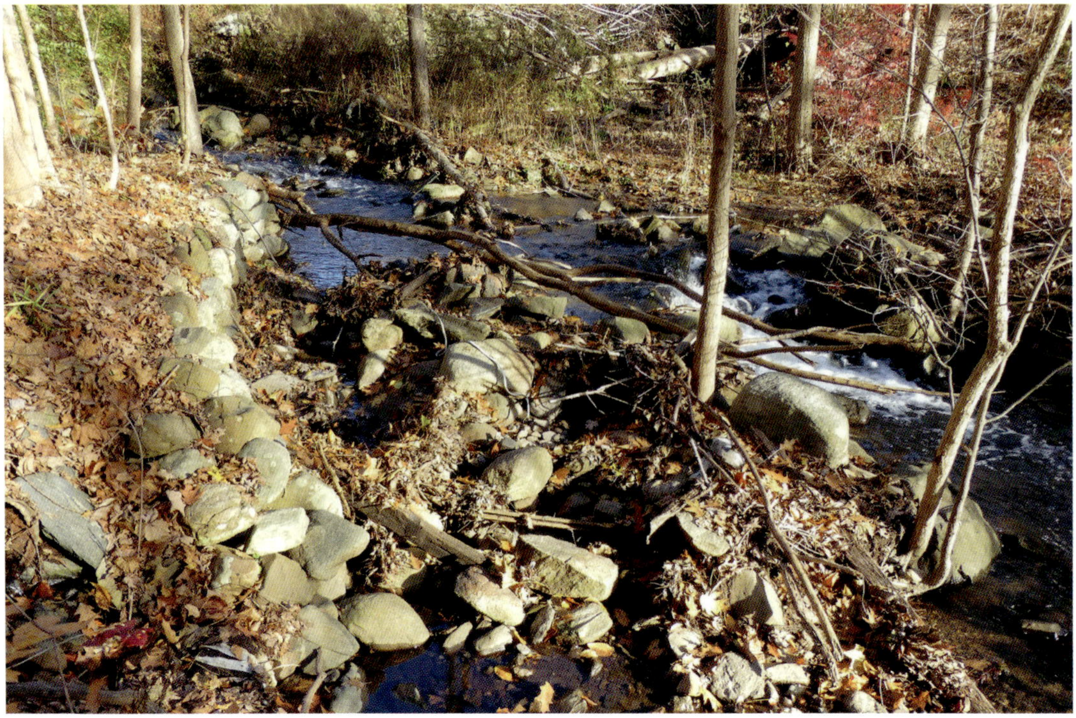

Smitties Mill: A short distance downstream from the Wakelee Mill was a smaller dam and a small grist mill. Known as the Smitties Mill, it was barely large enough to hold a grind stone. Thirty years ago, this small red building still sat along the stream, with yellow forsythia framing it in the spring. The structure was falling apart, and the mill stone was halfway submerged in the mud. Little remains of the little grist mill now. In its place are a few strips of lumber and a pile of stones, providing just a remnant of our past.

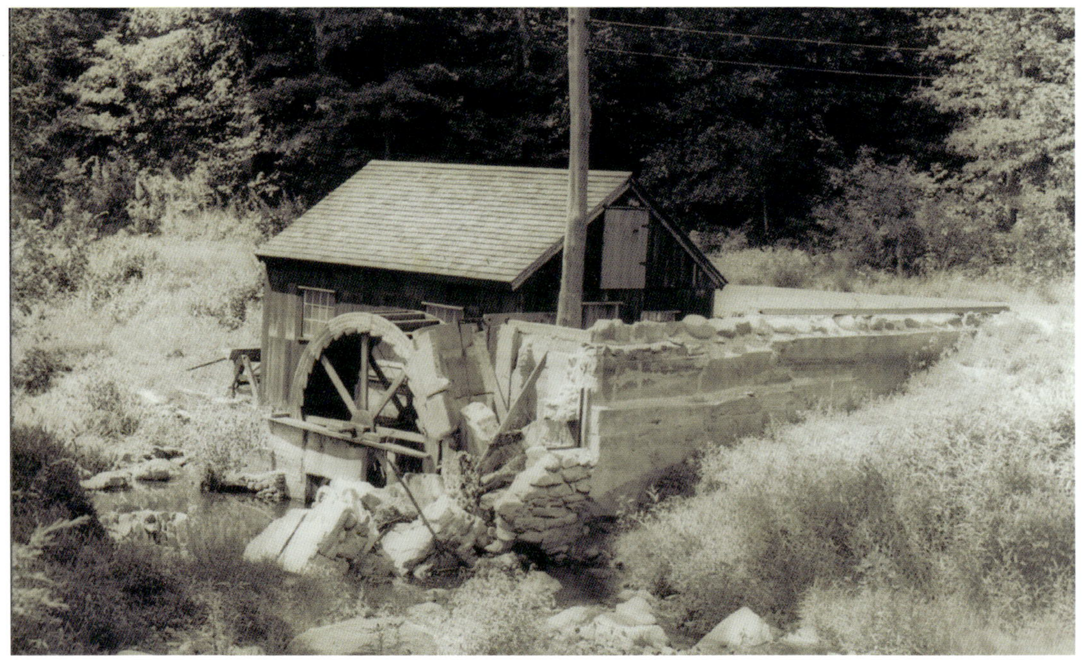

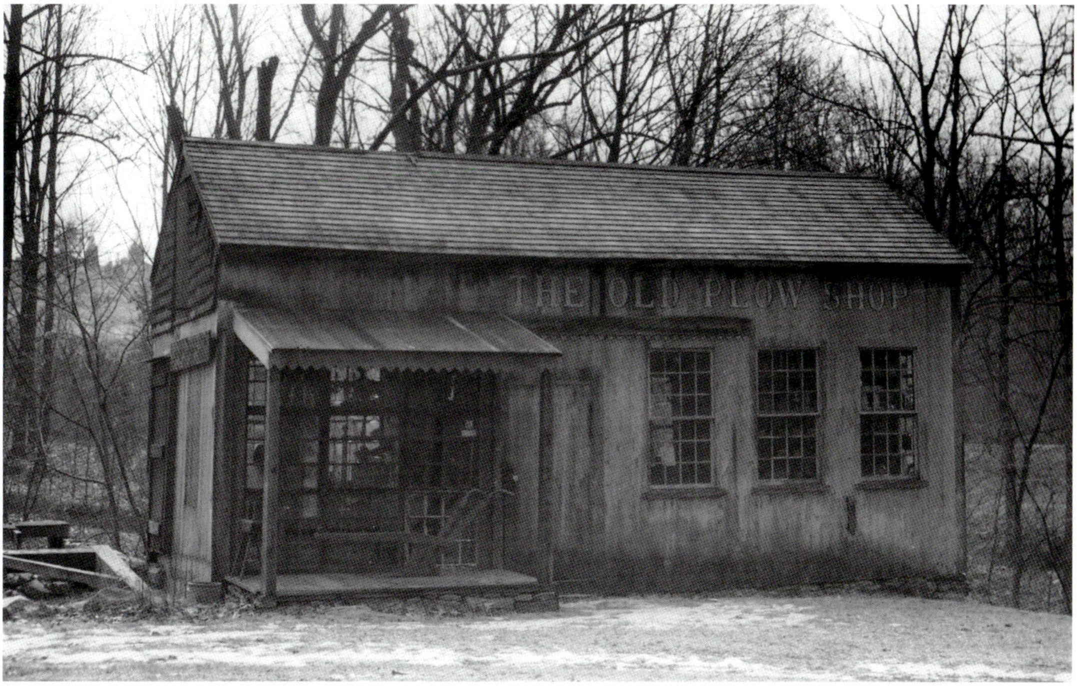

WAKELEE PLOW SHOP: Where ever you could find running water in Southbury, you were sure to find a mill nearby. The area between Community House Road and Route 67 was no exception. Over the years, the south branch of the Bullet Hill Brook was dammed and used to power various mills. The first mill was a saw mill built in 1740. Much later, Charles Wakelee built a plow shop about 1858, which he sold to Charles Hine about 1893. Hine ran a lumber mill and shingle shop. The mill, with its large iconic water wheel, fell apart in 1926 due to an ice jam, and eventually the whole building collapsed. The old plow shop still remains.

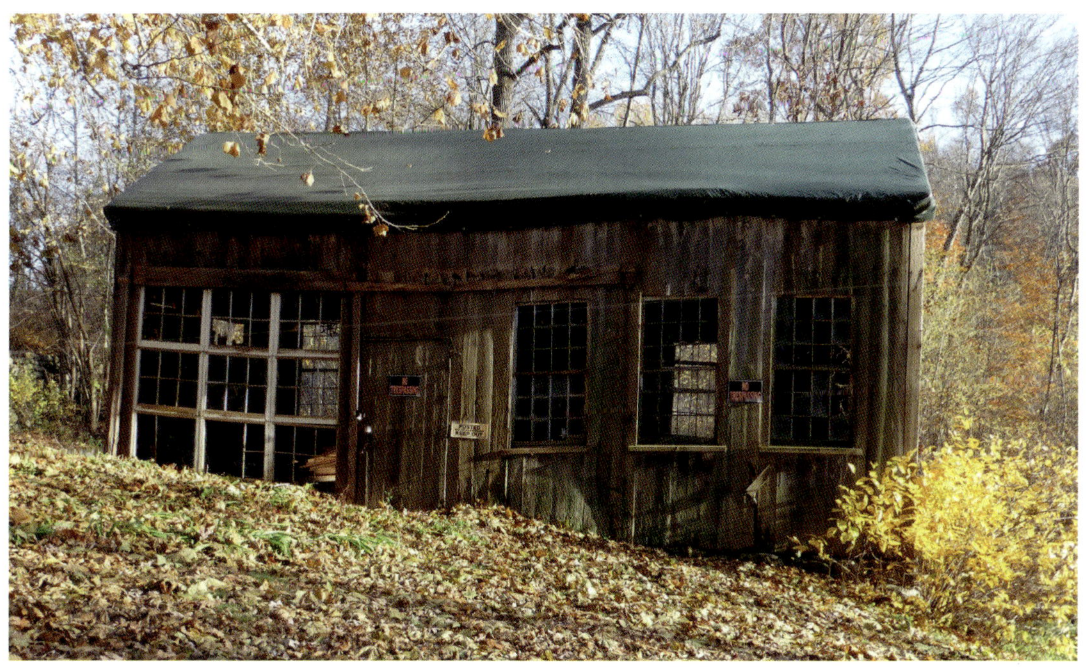

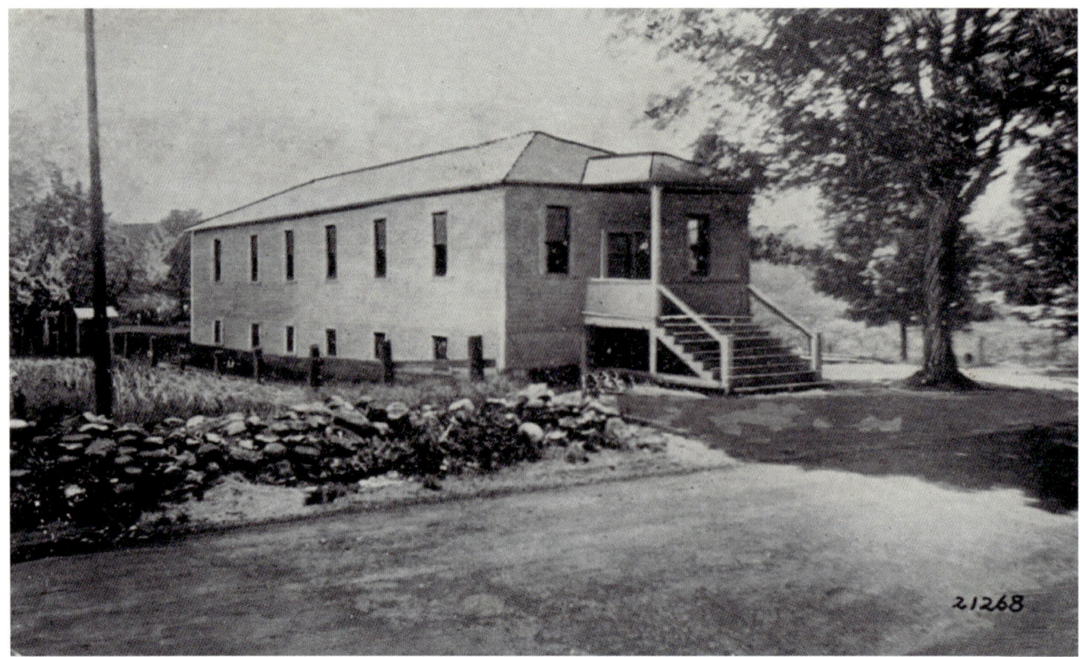

COMMUNITY HOUSE: On land donated by Howard A. Hicock, Sr., the Community House was constructed when Harry H. Stone rallied the local men to collect lumber from the buildings that were scheduled to be demolished in the flooding of Lake Zoar. It was used for grange meetings, receptions, dances, and community theater. In 1937, an important town meeting was held here to discuss the details of the new zoning code that had just been developed. Within the same month was the trial of the two German American Bund members who were arrested while working on a Sunday. The town uses the building for storage.

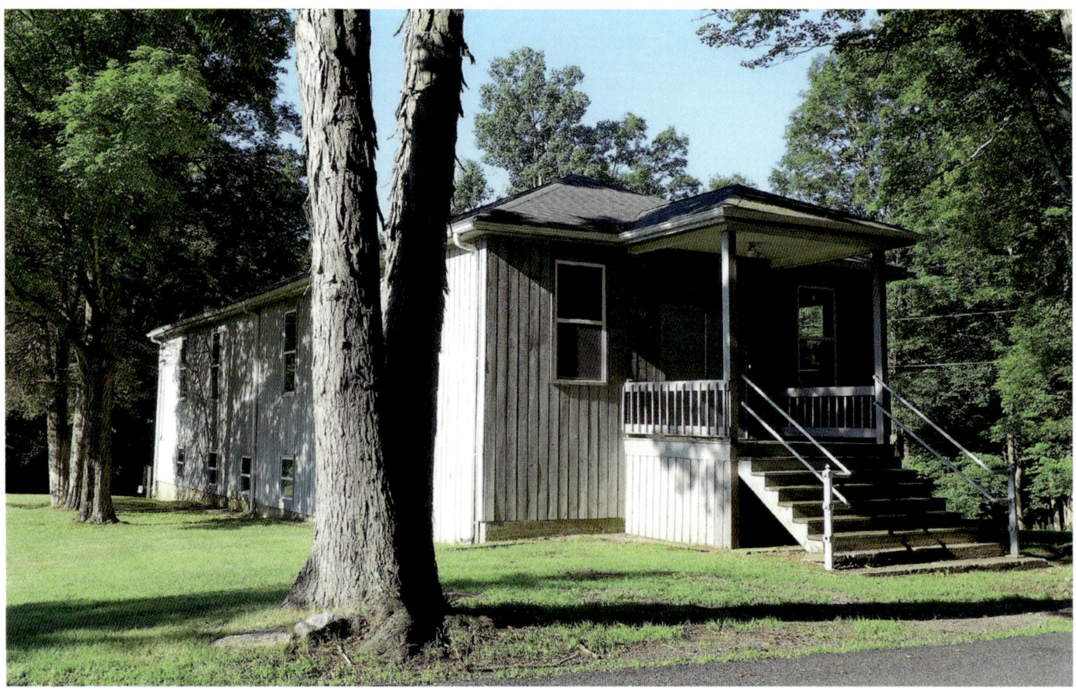

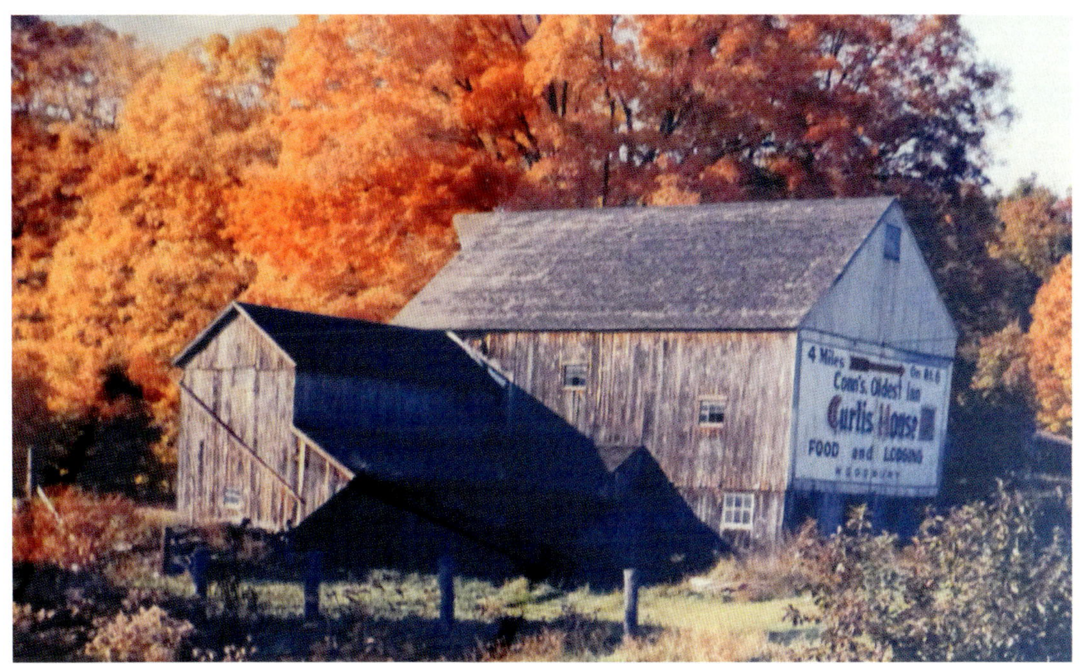

ADVERTISEMENT ON BARN: The Hicock Barn was a landmark along the Oxford Turnpike, which is now Route 67. On the side of the barn was an advertisement for the Curtis House, "Conn's Oldest Inn," located in Woodbury. Howard Hicock was a wheelwright who changed with the times and opened a gas station on his land. Hicock contributed a large amount of property to the town for the recreation fields, tennis courts, and basketball courts for the Community House Park. (Top photograph courtesy of Curtis House Inn.)

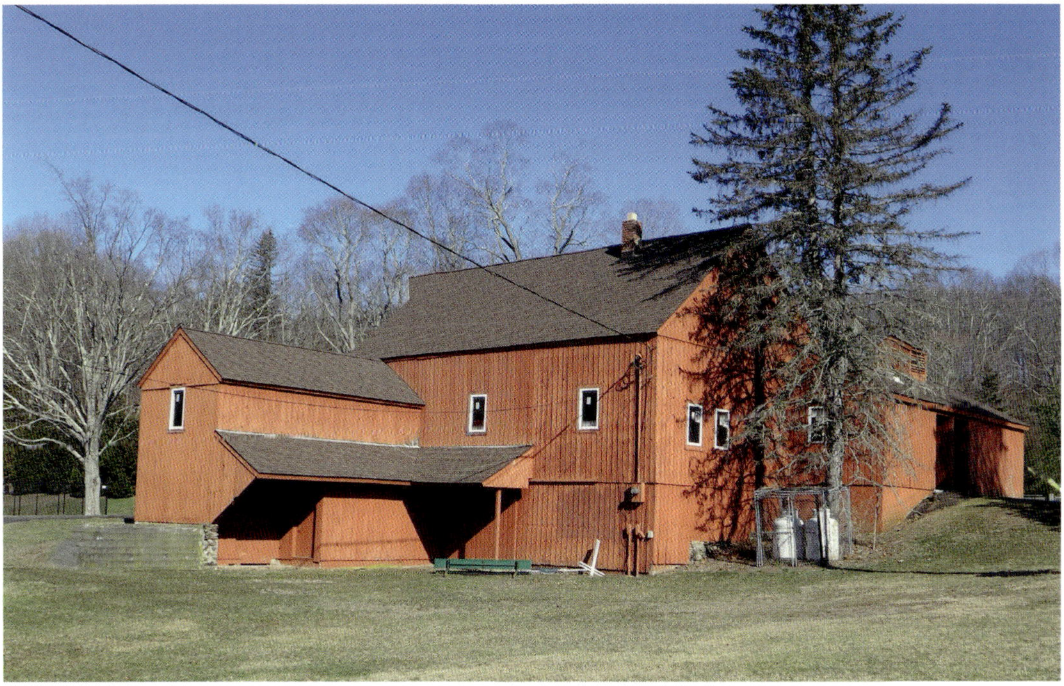

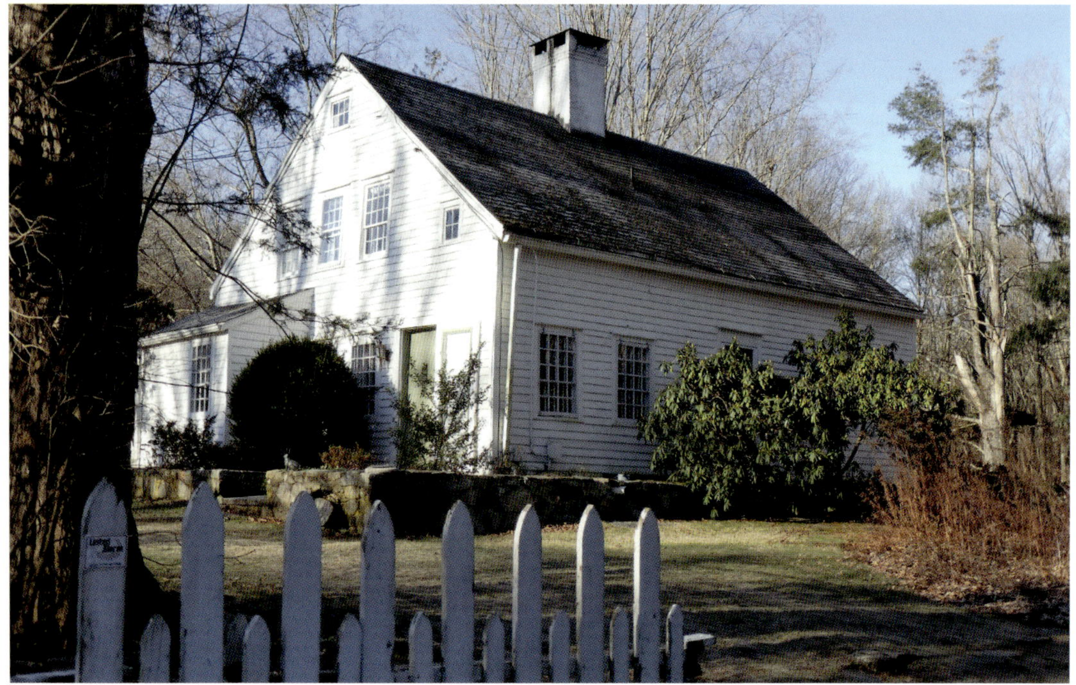

GLADYS TABOR'S FARM: Stillmeadow Farm was the home of Gladys Taber, a well-known writer who contributed articles to ladies' magazines and authored numerous books. On a trip to Boston, Gladys was stuck in a traffic jam in Southbury, and on a whim, stopped by a local real estate office. She immediately fell in love with the old farmhouse and the surrounding acres. Her tales of life at her peaceful farm off Jeremy Swamp Road tugged at the hearts of people across the country. Tabor left Stillmeadow in 1960. The organization, Friends of Gladys Taber, comes to Southbury every other year to visit Tabor's beloved home.

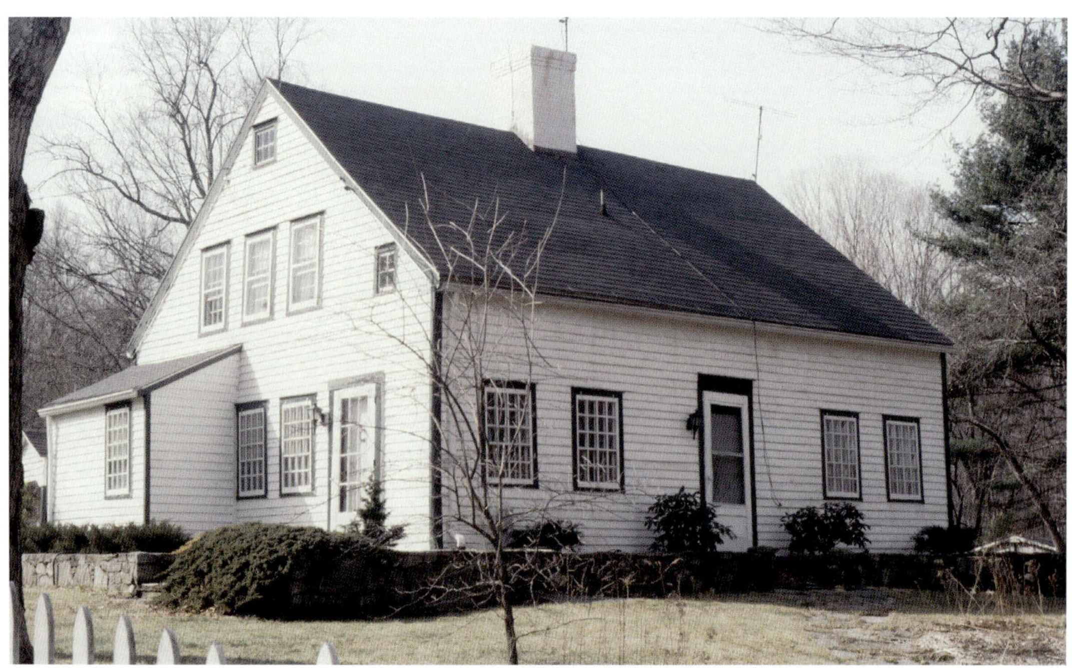

4
Southford

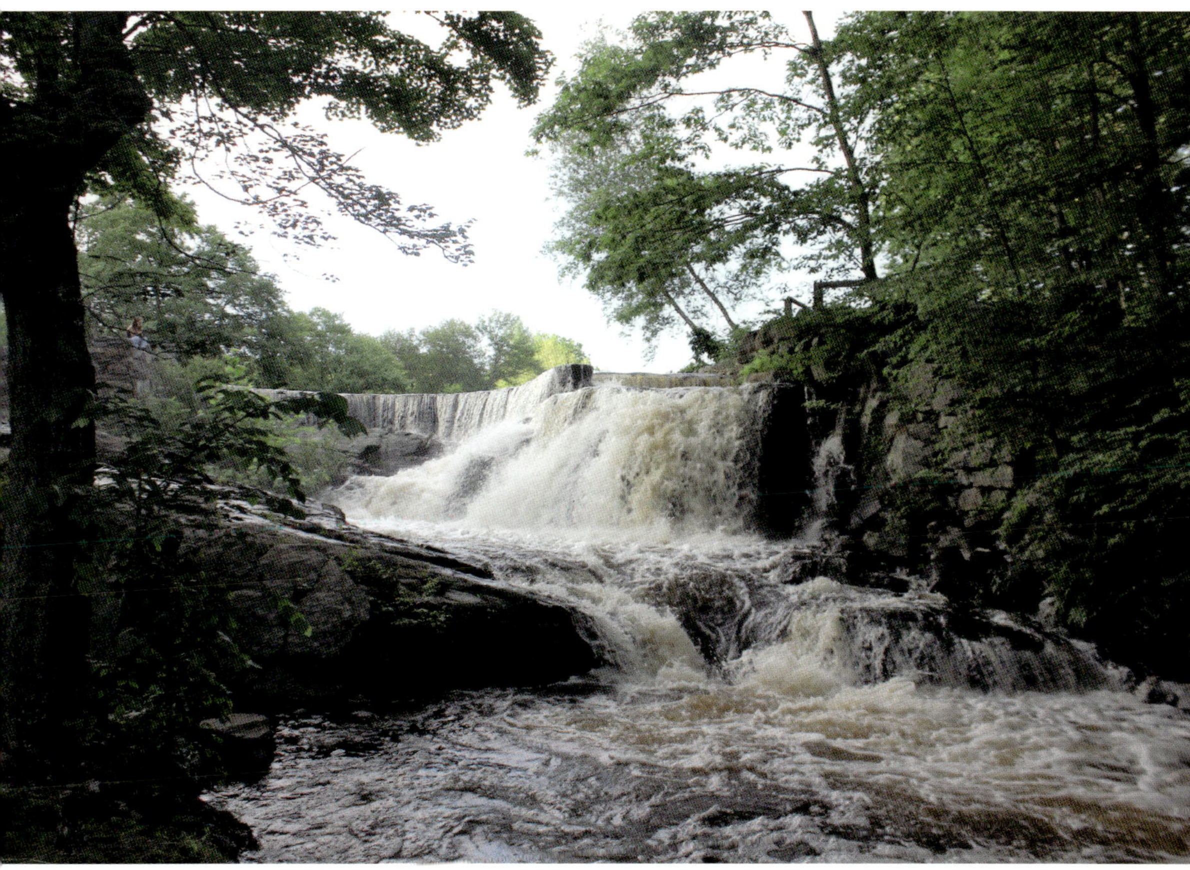

Southford was the ideal setting for a village due to the mills and factories along the Eight Mill Brook, and the fact it was the halfway point between New Haven and Litchfield. With the railroad depot placed a short distance away, factories could receive supplies and ship out the finished products. The Oxford turnpike followed the current route 67 and the ancient Woodbury Path went along Jeremy Swamp. Southford was a busy economic center with a chapel, three hotels, a blacksmith shop, store, and post office.

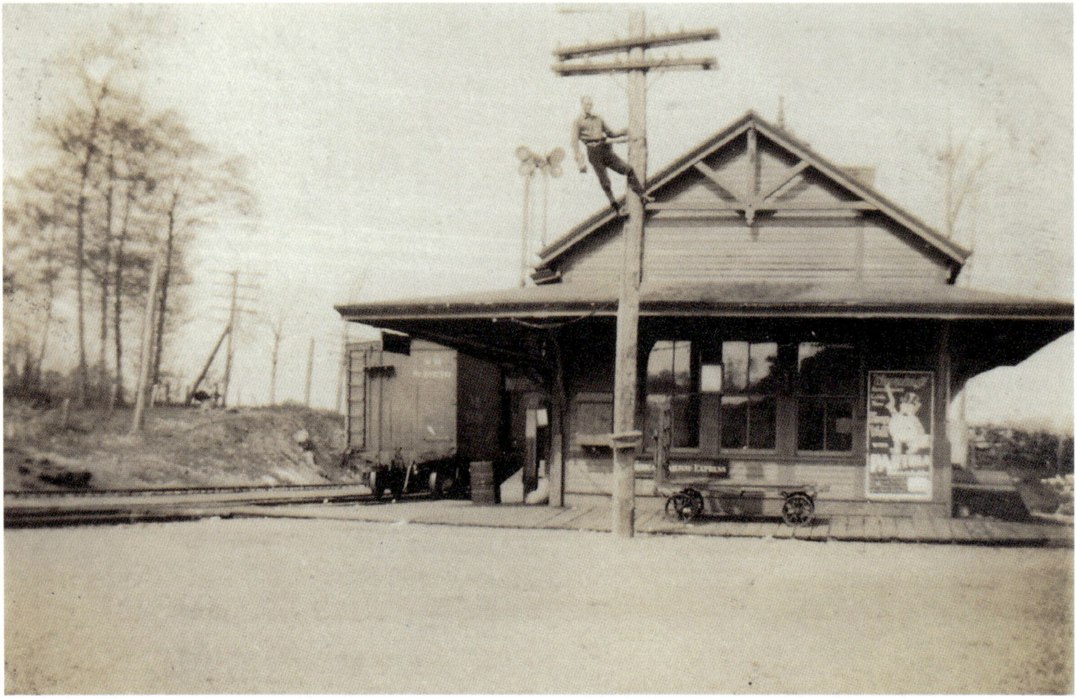

SOUTHFORD DEPOT: The Southford train station was north of the center of Southford. The building was constructed in 1881 by local resident Leman Oatman, and contained separate waiting rooms for men and women, a telegraph office, and a freight office. The building was painted olive green with red trim. The station closed in the 1940s and was used for storage until it burned down in 1987. The street view below is a scene from Southford, looking north. The building on the left was the Stone's feed store, with the train station off to the right of the railroad crossing sign. The Southford Schoolhouse was to the right at the white post.

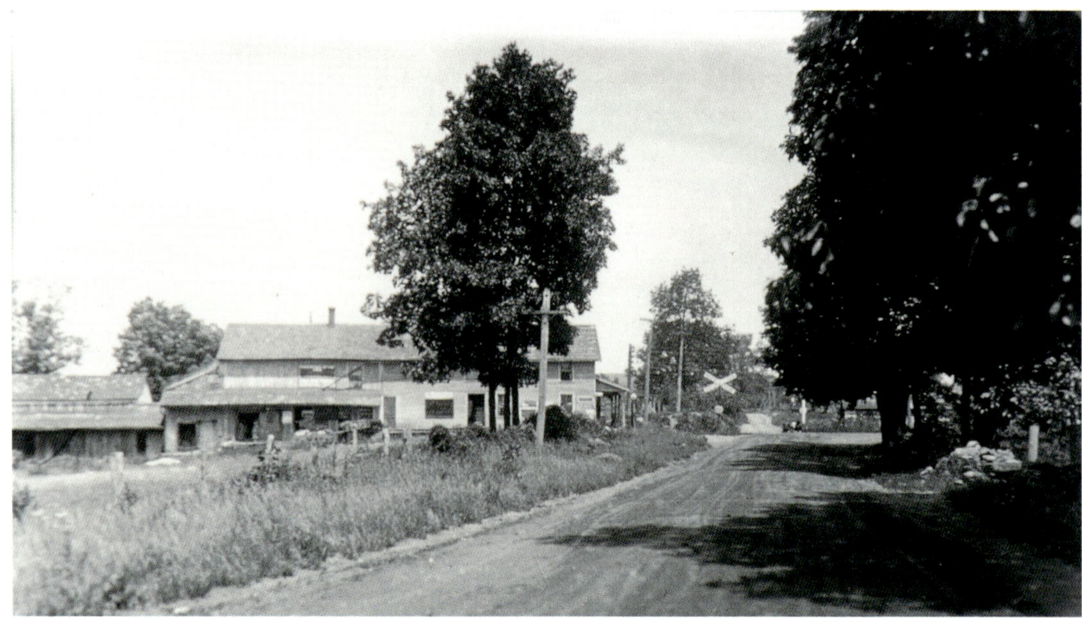

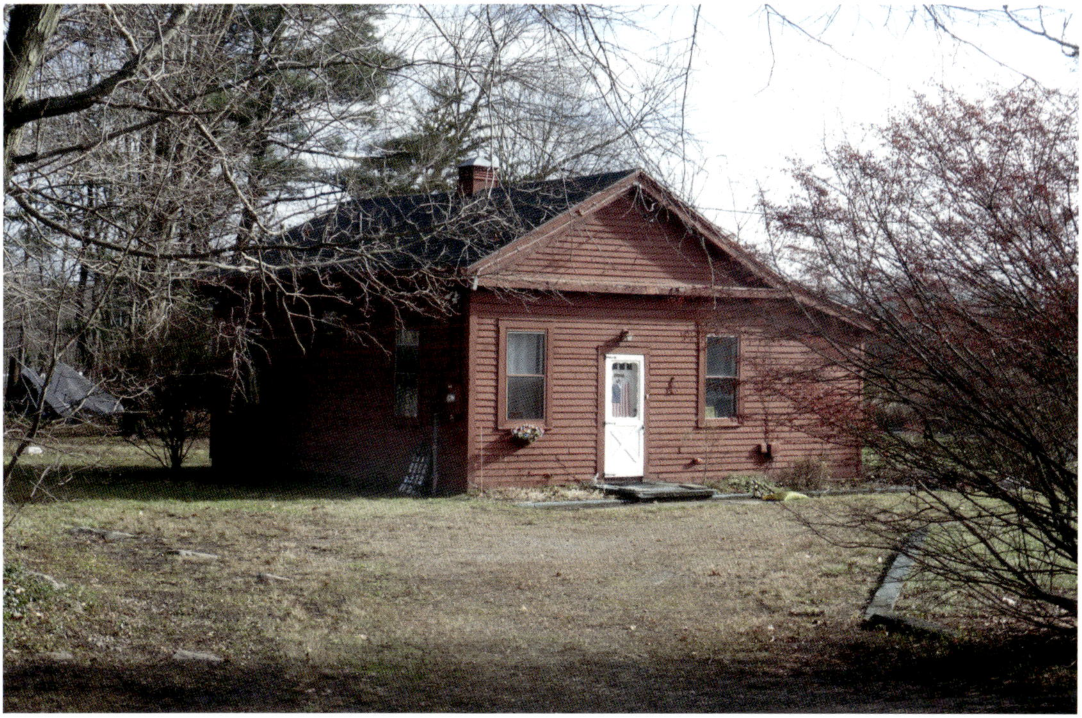

SCHOOLHOUSE: Just south of the train station, on adjoining property, sat the little one-room school. Likely built around 1840, the Southford School was one of the eleven district schools operating at that time in Southbury. At first the school sat close to the road, but was moved back 50 feet in 1905 because of the numerous heavy factory carts passing by on the way to the train. The teacher must have had a difficult time teaching the children with the constant distraction of the trains and other traffic.

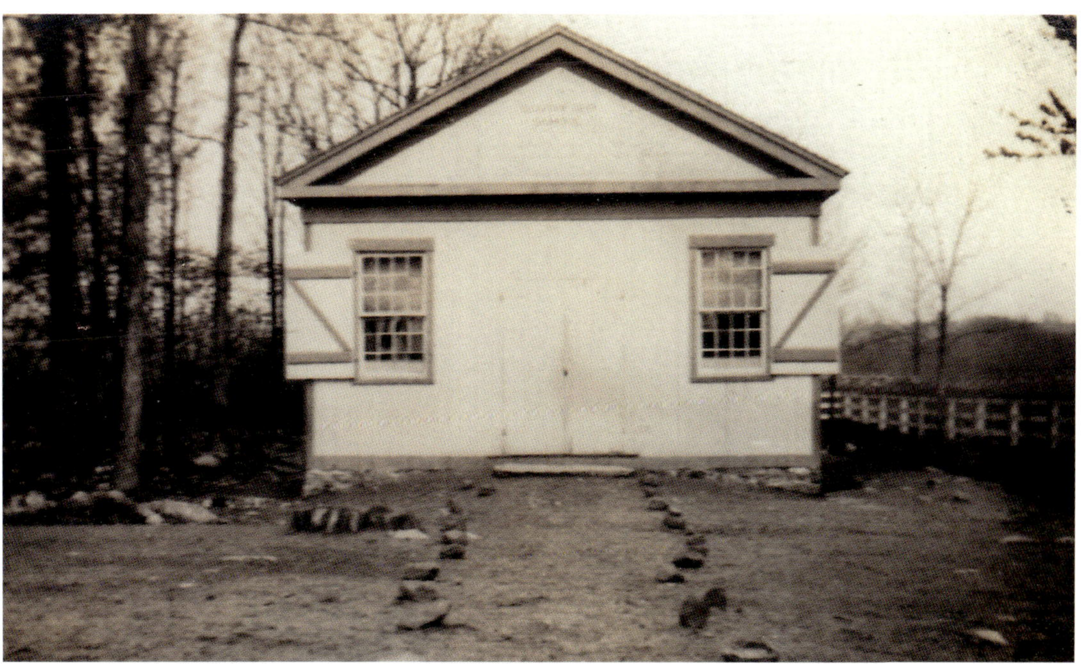

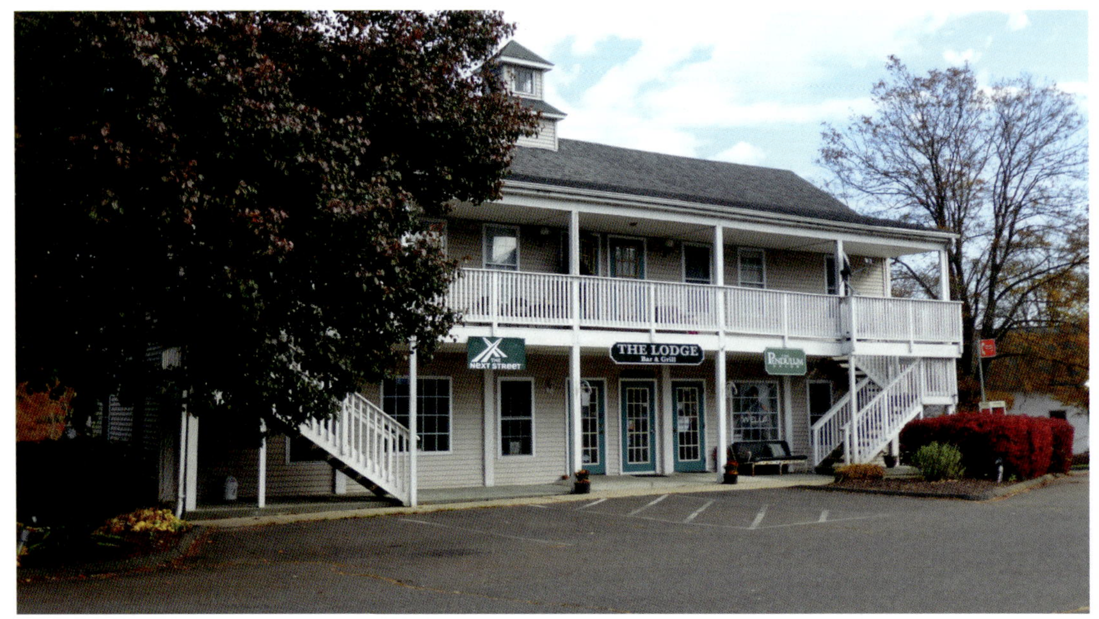

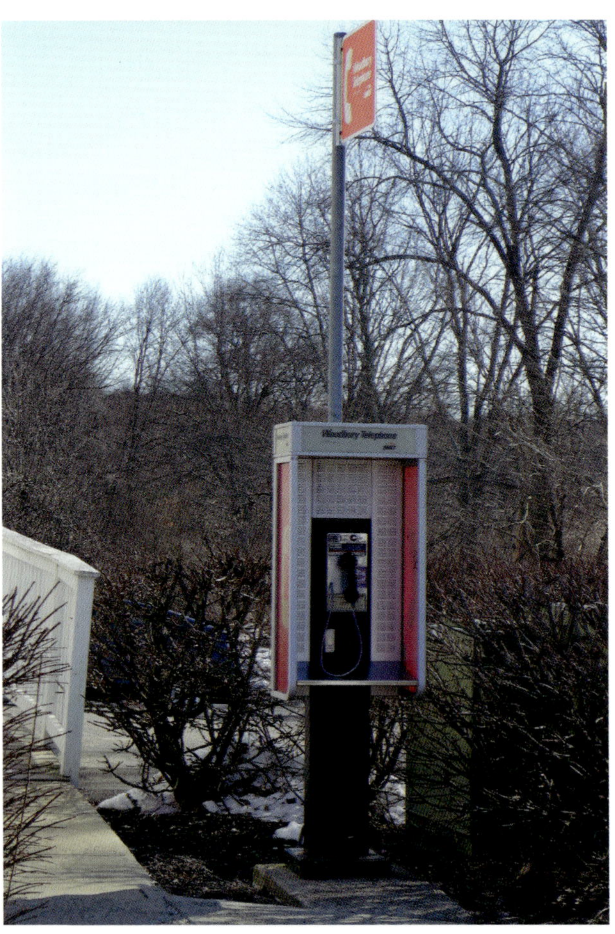

SOUTHFORD LODGE: The Old Southford Lodge began in the 1800s when the first portions of it were built. It sat close to the road with various other structures on the property, including a blacksmith shop. The lodge was one of several places for accommodations in Southford, especially for people coming off the train in 1881. In 1991, a fire destroyed part of the building. Within a few years, it was rebuilt and opened for apartments and businesses. Along the side of the lodge is a rare sight in Southbury: a telephone kiosk from long-gone Woodbury Telephone Company still stands with the telephone intact.

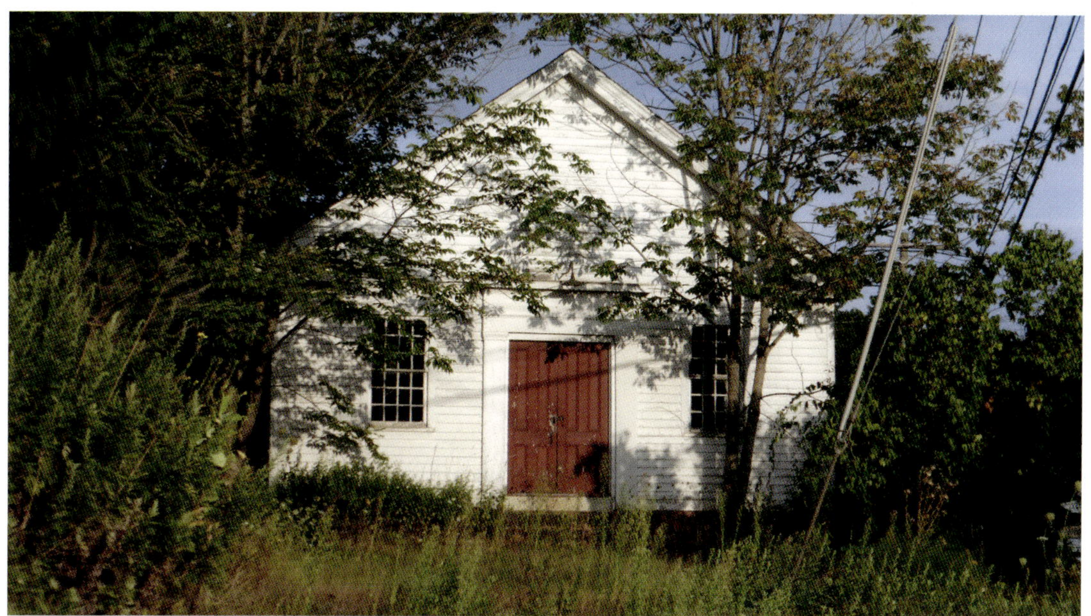

SOUTHFORD CHAPEL: As Southford was growing due to the numerous factories, there was need of a church in the area. The Union Chapel was built in 1830 as a non-denominational church in the heart of the village. The chapel was well-used for worship services, weddings, and community activities, and renovations took place in 1863. By the 1930s, it no longer served as a church, and in World War II, it was designated as an air raid shelter. In the 1950s, a garage door was added to the bottom floor to store a fire truck to serve as the first Southford fire house. The building is now in a deteriorating condition, sitting close to the intersection of Routes 67 and 188.

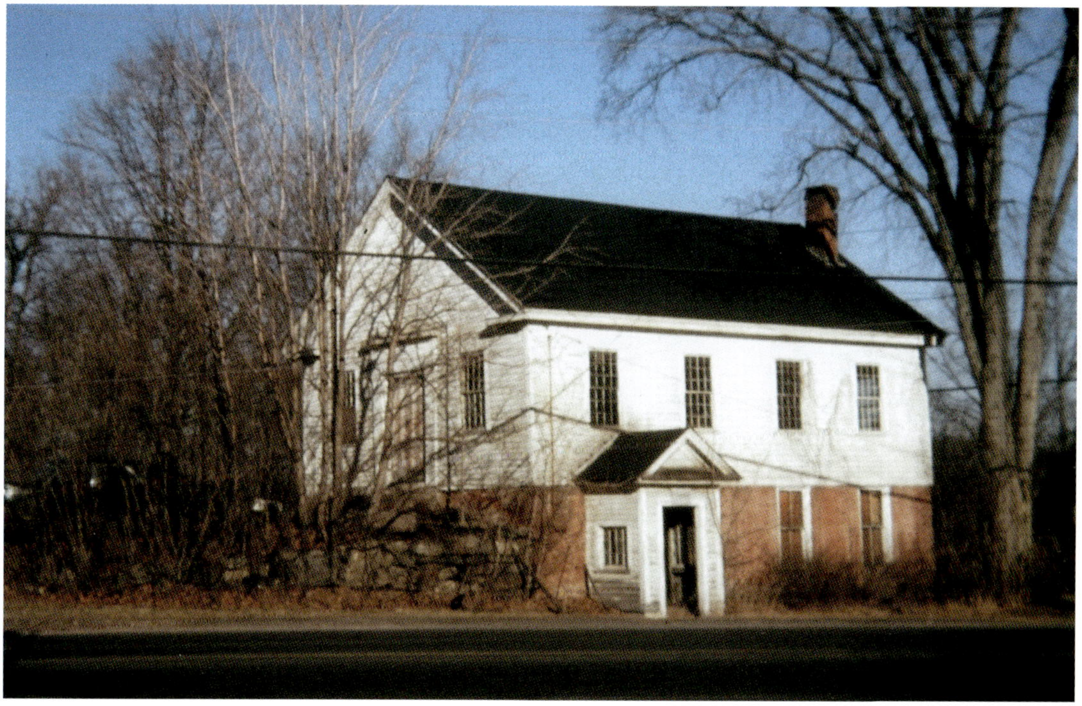

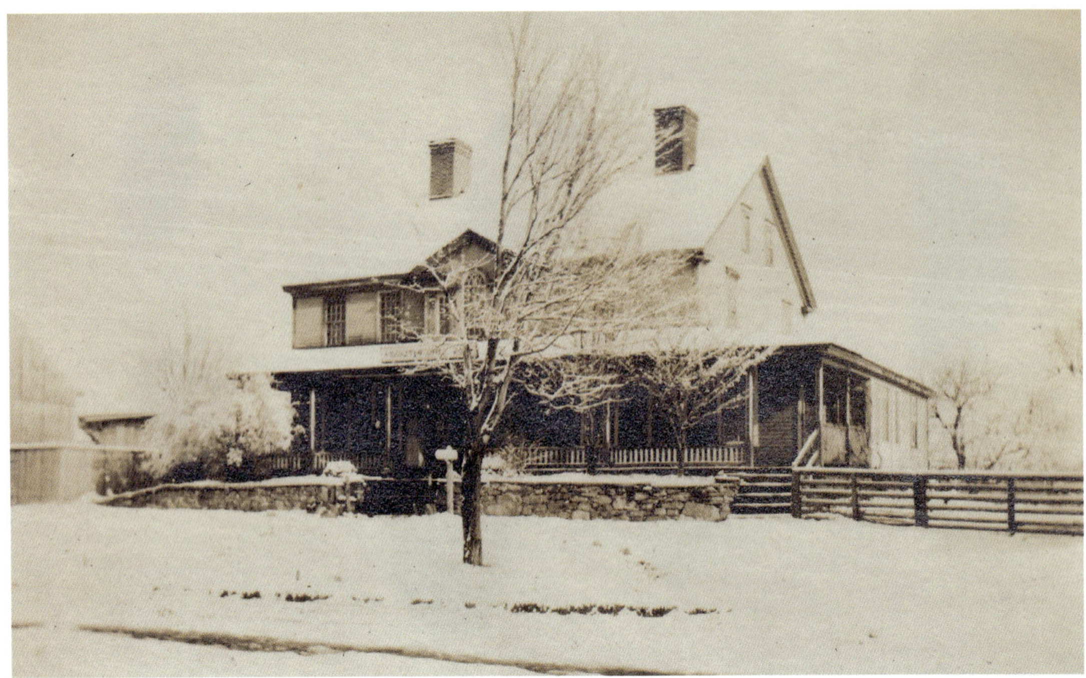

OATMAN HOUSE: The Oatman House looks very much like it did when it was built in 1802 by George Thompson. From the beginning, it was used as a hotel on the stage route because it was a stop halfway between New Haven and Litchfield. Of the three hotels in the area in the late 1800s, Oatman house was the first choice of travelers and had the best reputation. At one time, there was a porch that extended the length of the house, and several out buildings. A couple of the old barns remain. The bottom photograph was found in a photo album that belonged to the Merwin family, owners of the house after the Oatmans.

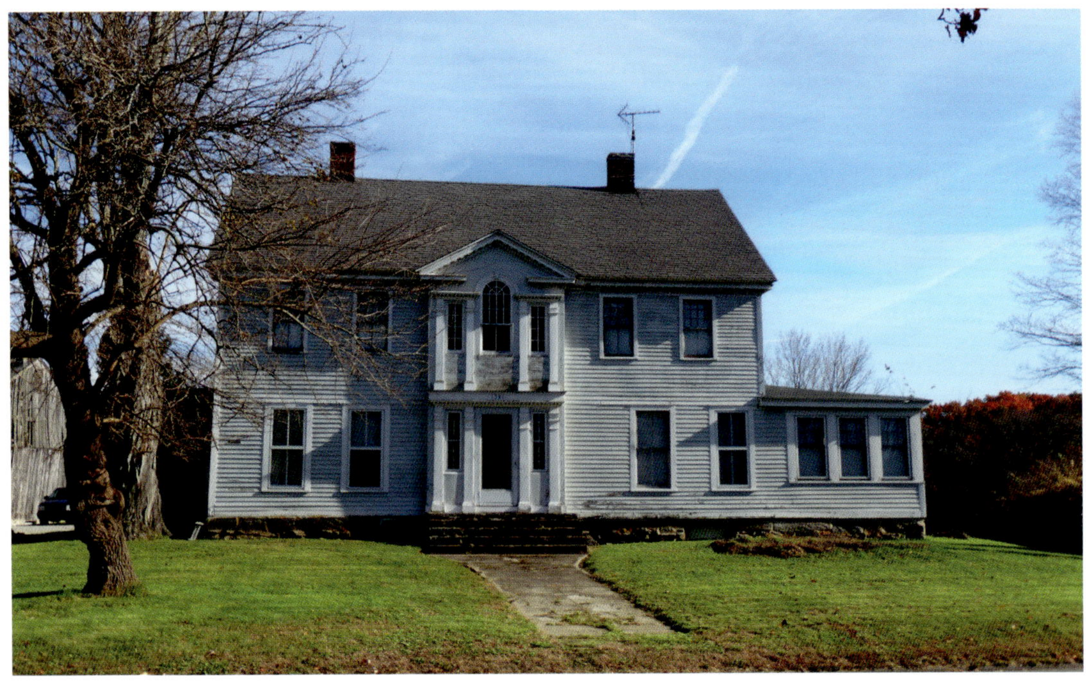

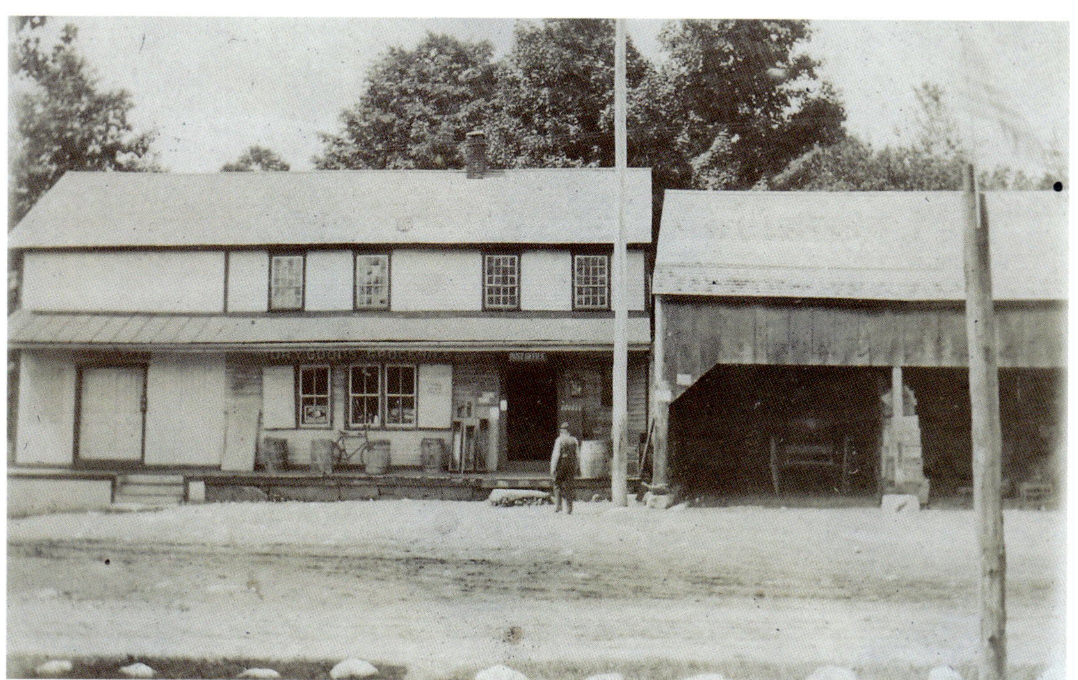

GENERAL STORE: The Southford Store, fondly remembered as the Davis Store, has been a fixture in Southford since at least 1810, possibly earlier. The store began under the direction of George Thompson. After being purchased by Horace Oatman in 1853, who owned the hotel across the street, the store was operated over 100 years by only two families, the Oatman and the Davis families. Mr. Davis updated and remodeled the store, borrowing architectural features from the Southford depot. The old photograph is from the Merwin photo album.

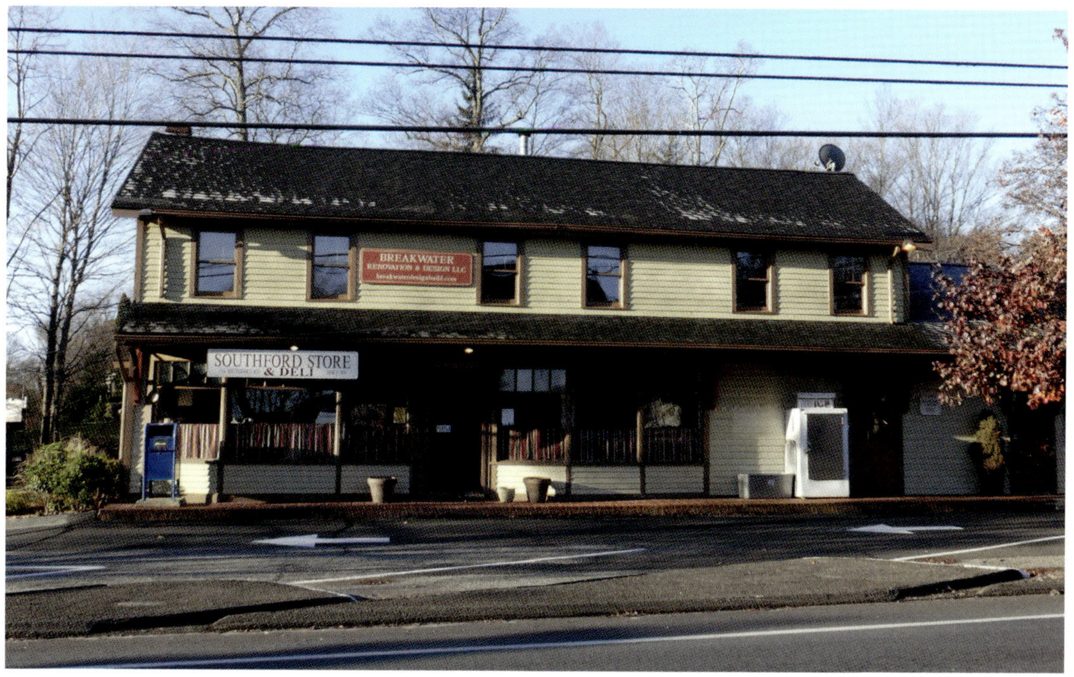

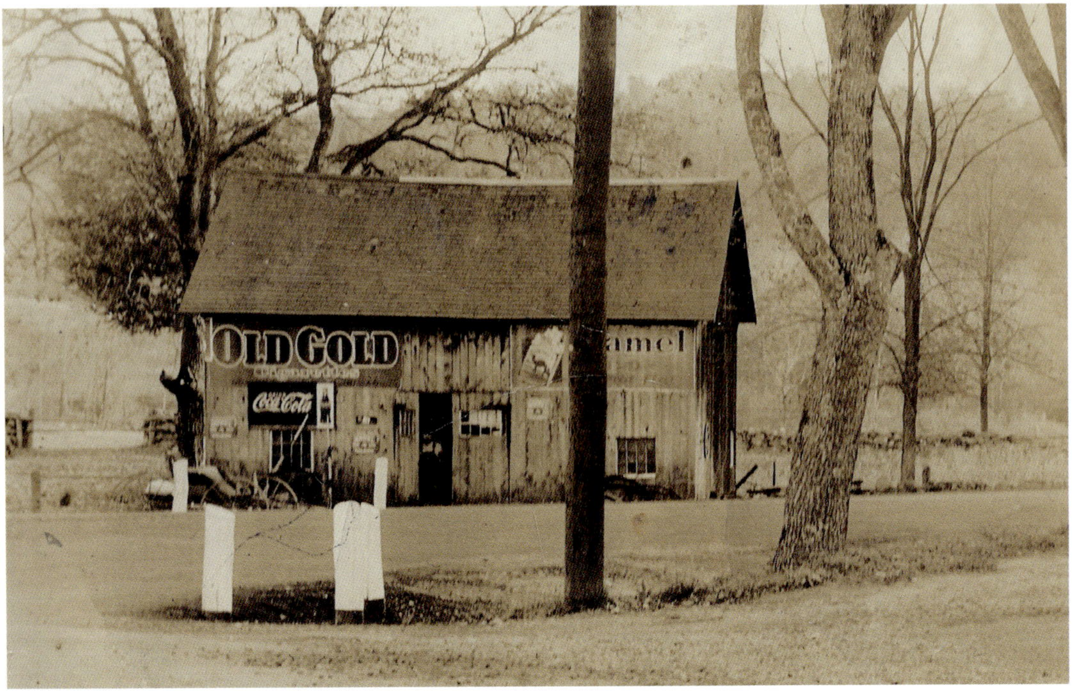

BLACKSMITH SHOP: The small building that sits at the corner of Routes 188 and 67 was once a nineteenth-century blacksmith shop. It was purchased in 1919 by Charles Saloks, who had emigrated from Lithuania and continued running the blacksmith shop for over twenty years. The building was sold in 1946 to Frank and Marguerite Gantert, who used it as a shop. When the land was purchased by the Liberty Bank, it was agreed that the old blacksmith shop would be saved as a remnant of old Southford. (Above photo courtesy of Marguerite Gantert.)

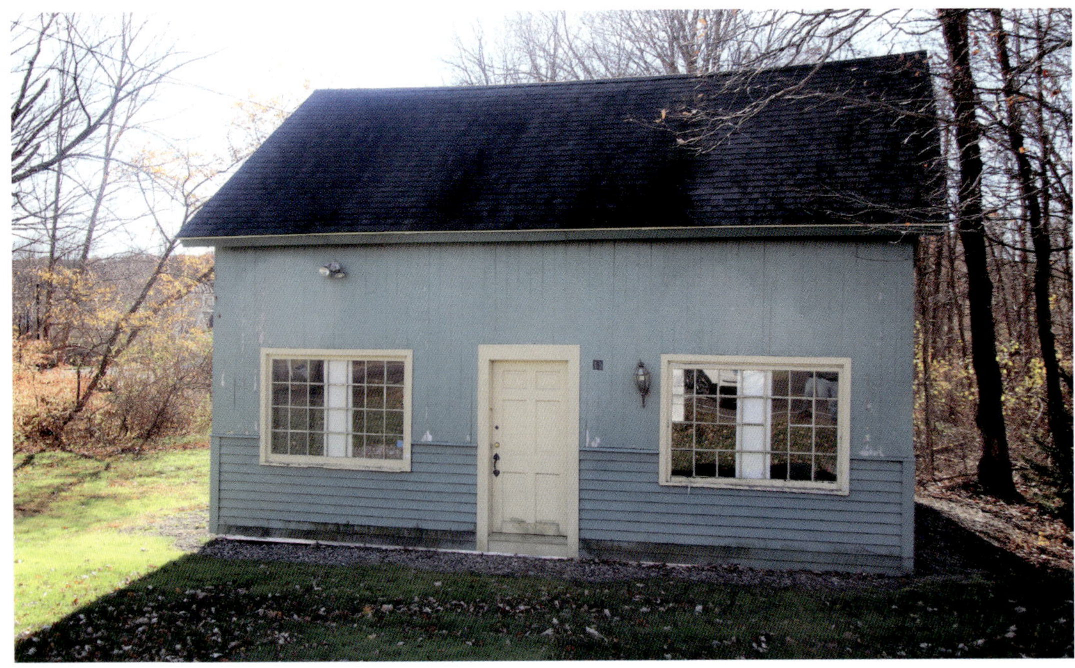

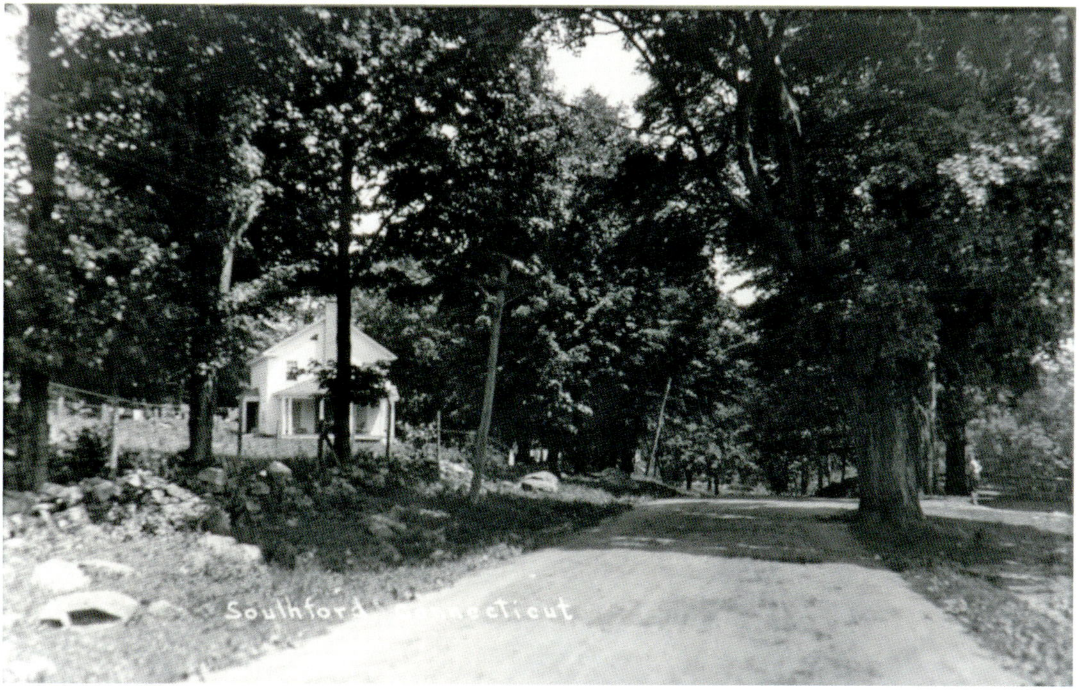

QUAKER FARMS ROAD VIEWS: In this old view looking toward the Southford Store and the blacksmith shop, the Davis residence is visible on the left side. The building is now part of the Southford Medical Center. The bottom photo is facing the opposite direction where the road is leading toward Quaker Farms and the Diamond Match Company. The top of the factory building is barely visible to left, with its sign peaking over the top. The road went past the factories and down to Quaker Farms, following what is now Route 188.

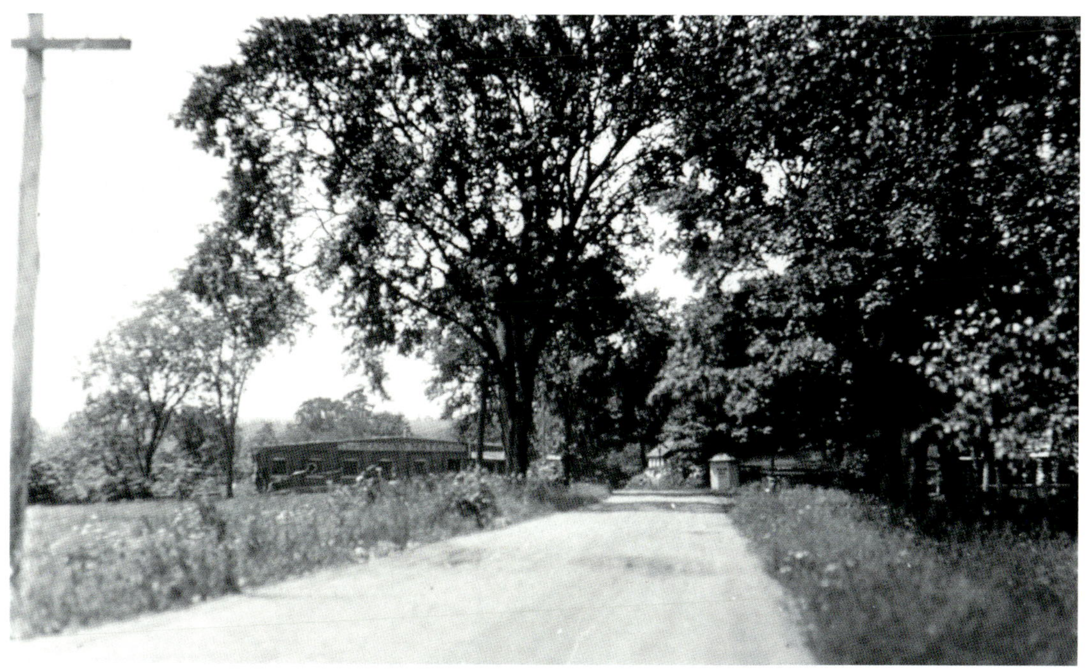

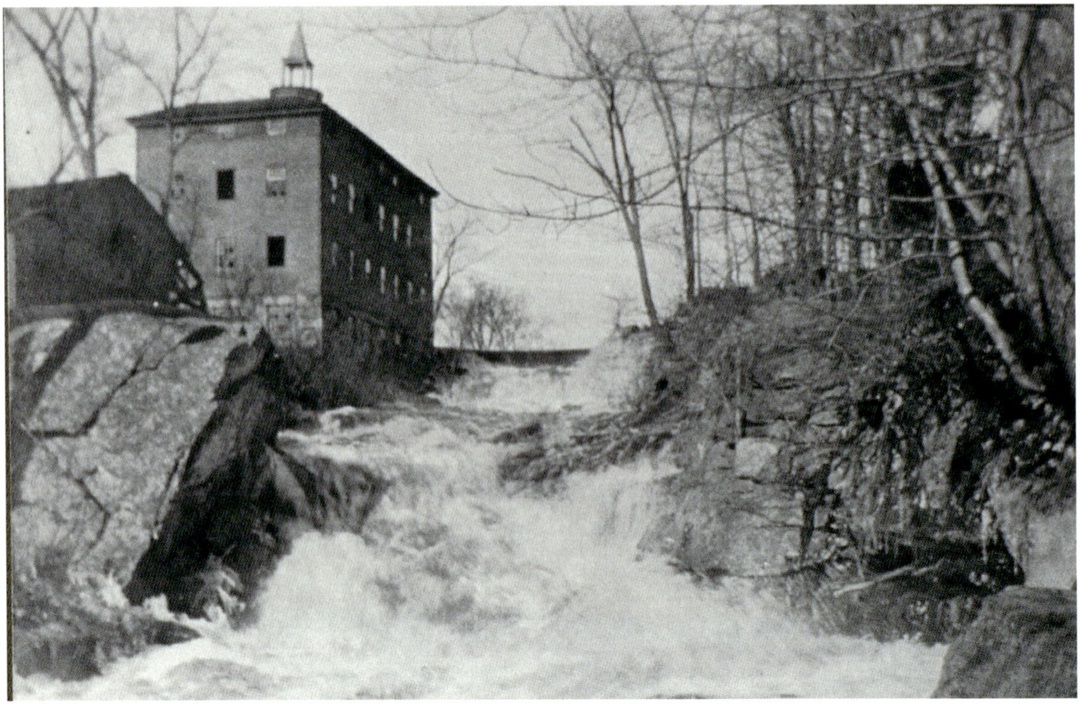

SOUTHFORD FALLS: The ravine along Southford Falls and the drop in elevation has made this home to many small factories through Southbury's history. As early as 1805, there was a fulling mill at falls along the Eight Mile Brook. By the 1868, there were dozens of small factories, which depended every day on the water power. Southford Paper Company was formed after 1881, and built a large brick factory.

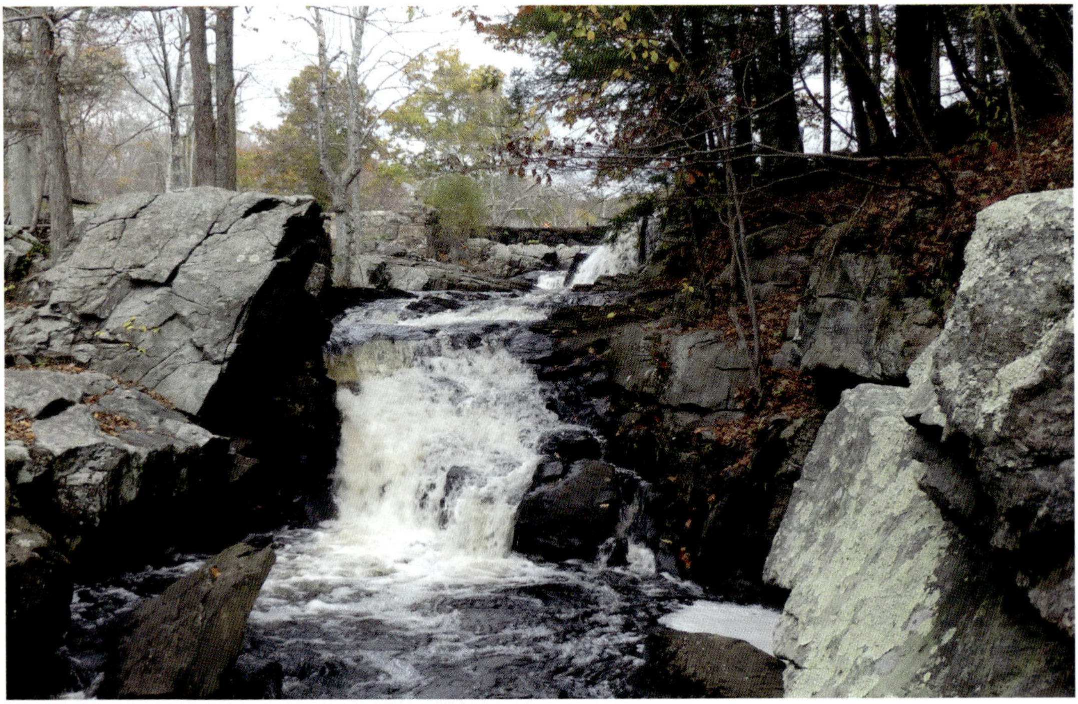

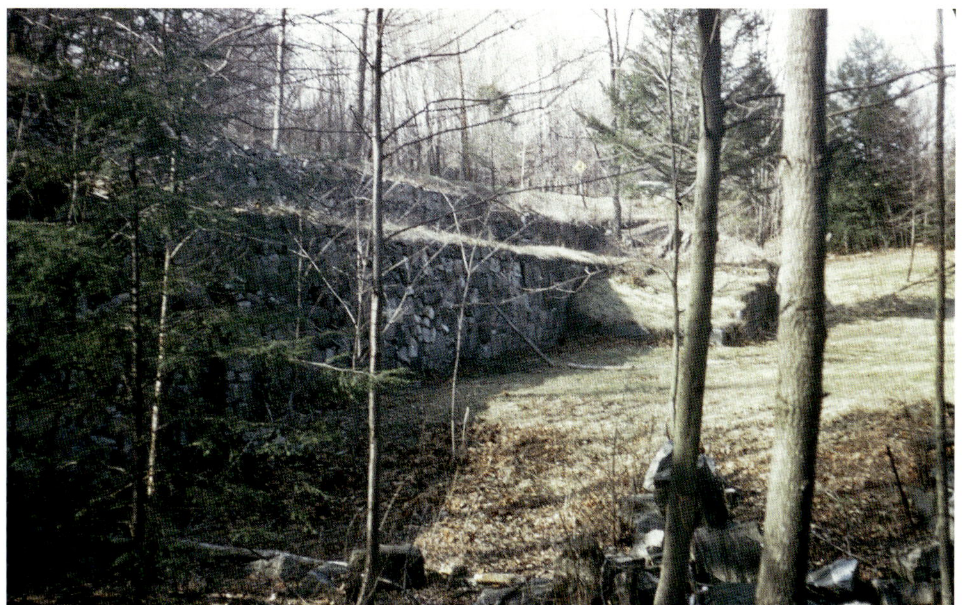

FACTORY TO STATE PARK: The Diamond Match Company purchased the property of Southford Paper Company in 1901. The Diamond Match Company did not make matches, but the match boxes, using straw from local farms and beyond. The complex of buildings took over all the space between the Eight Mile Brook and the Quaker Farms Road. A devastating fire destroyed three of the buildings in 1923, and the factory closed. In 1932, the land became state property and the cleanup began to establish Southford Falls State Park. Foundations of the previous buildings can still be found in several places, but especially near the covered bridge.

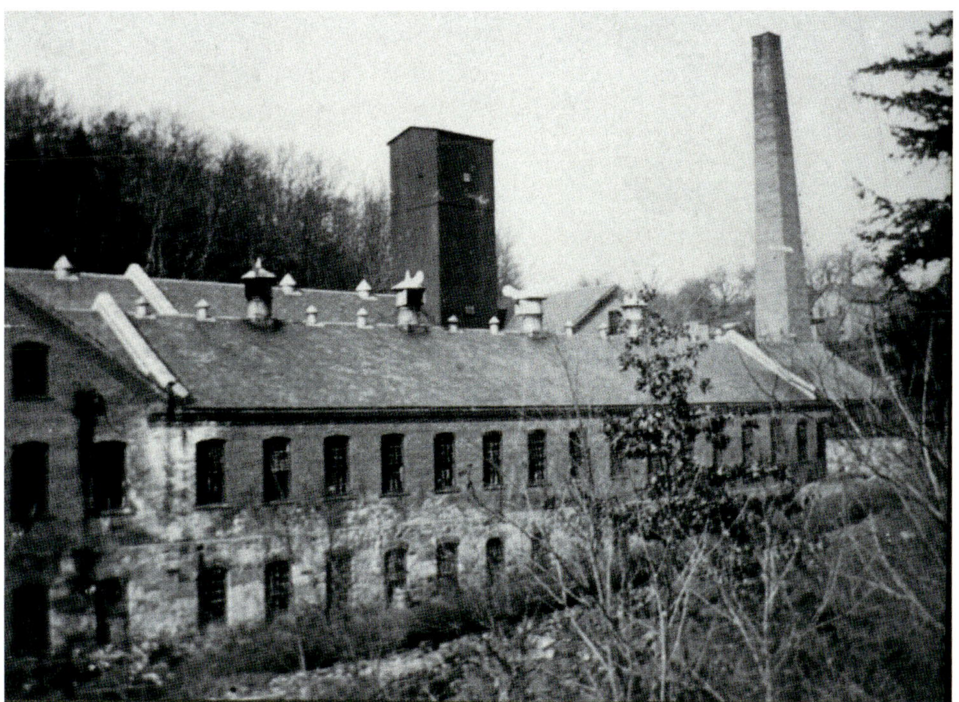

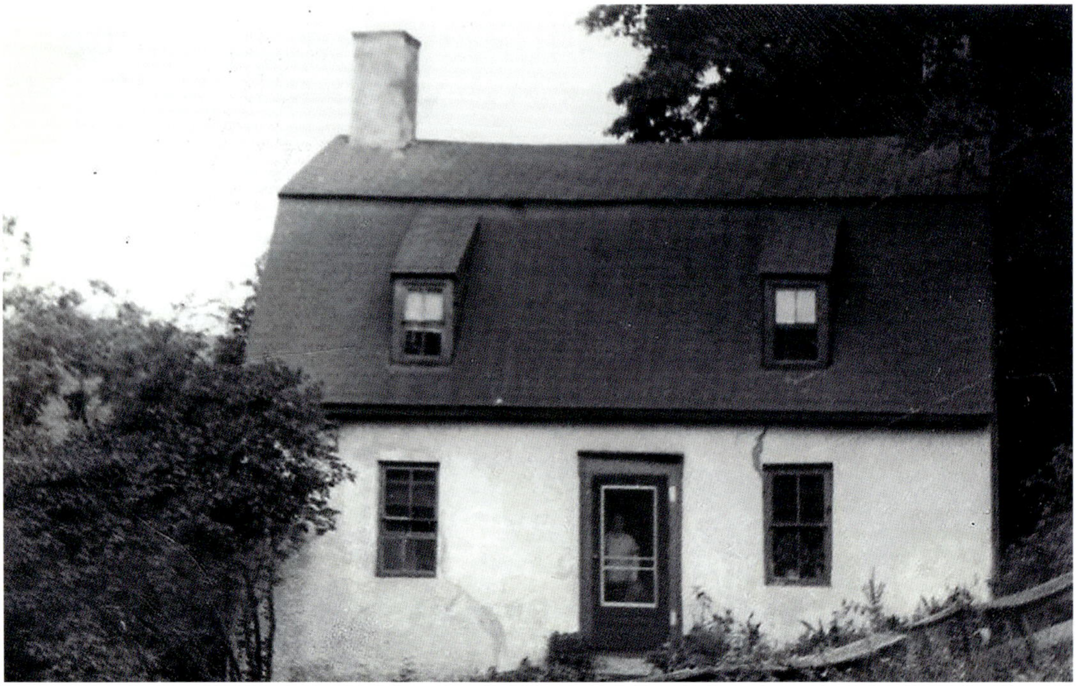

MILL HOUSE: At the end of Plaster House Road sits the small white house known as the Plaster House. The house was made of stone and covered with plaster and may have started as a mill house or a shop for the Hinman family. A paper mill was made on adjoining property by Hurd and Bartlett in the mid-1800s. To one side of the house is an old stone arch bridge and on the other side was the old Woodbury Path.

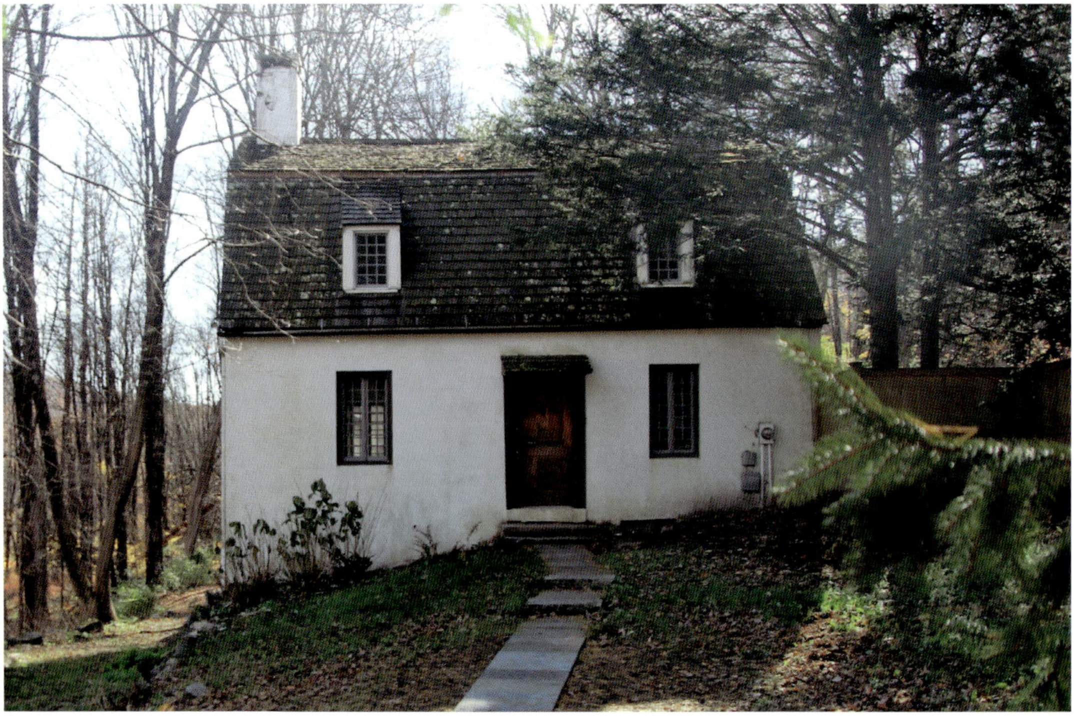

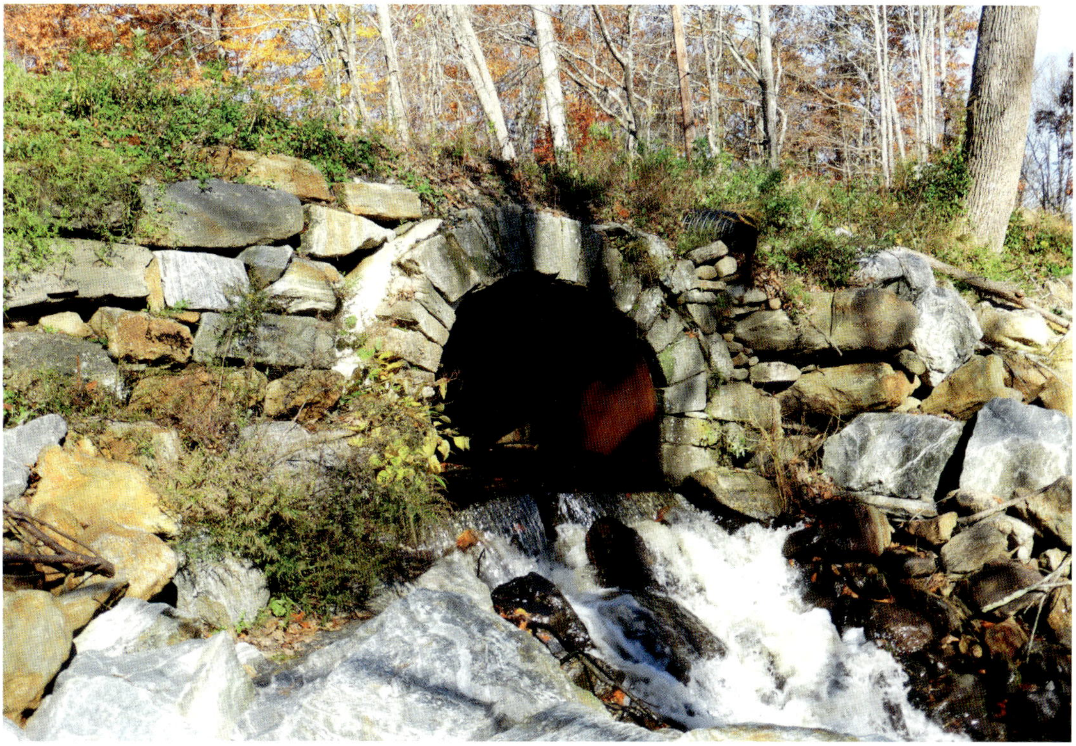

ARCH BRIDGE: A truly hidden gem in Southford is the Stone Arch Bridge built in the nineteenth century, near the end of Plaster House Road, where the road passes over the Jeremy Brook. On the north side, the Jeremy Brook meanders through a dried-up mill pond before it runs into a metal culvert and through the old ten-foot-wide granite bridge. In the photograph below, you can see a structure of wood timber, with stones in between to help with the stability of the sides of the stone bridge. The upper photograph shows additional large granite stones, protecting the whole structure.

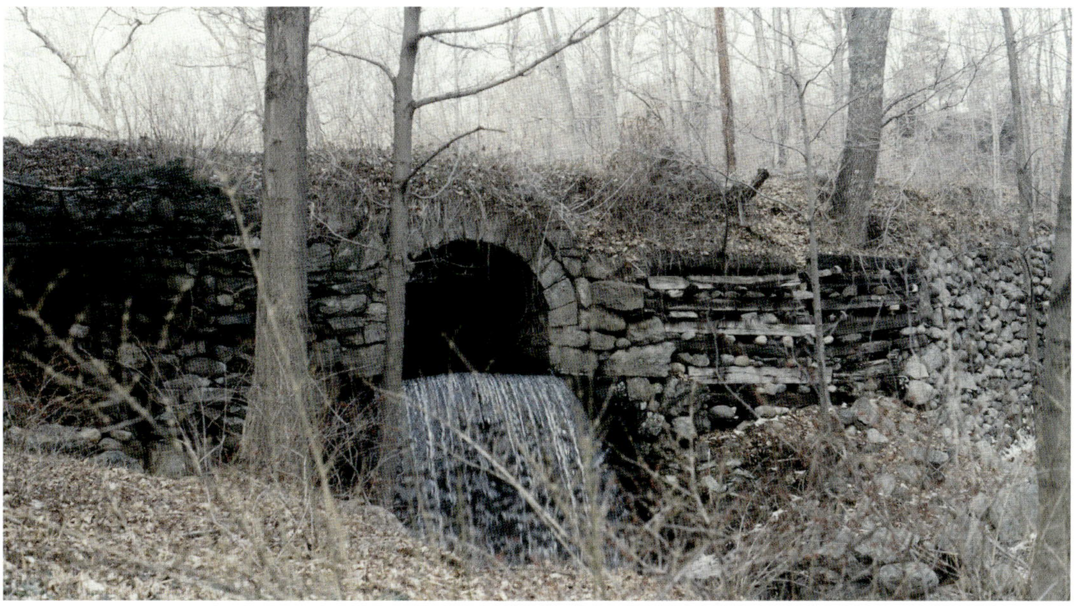

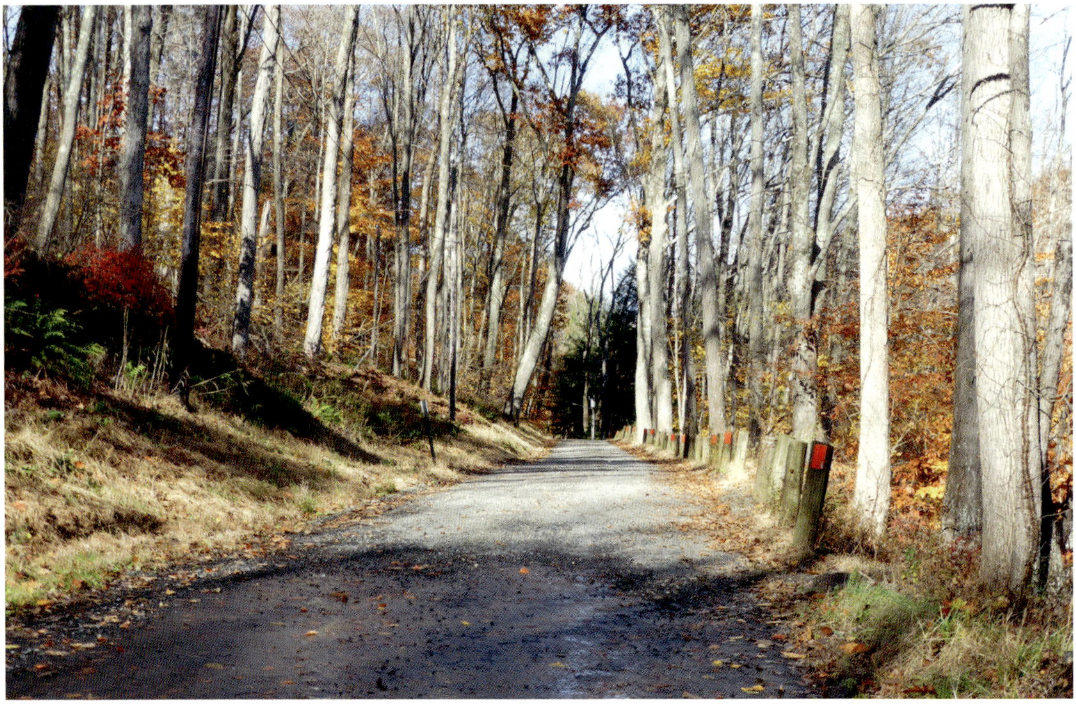

WOODBURY PATH: In 1675, the General Court directed that a road be made between Woodbury and East Derby, where there was a seaport. The route would allow trade by taking excess products to Derby, and purchasing needed supplies. Early road builders basically followed the trails of the local Natives. The path through Southbury included the Mansion House Road in the north, to Jeremy Swamp Road in the south. The last part of Jeremy Swamp is an untouched, unimproved road that takes you a step back into the past.

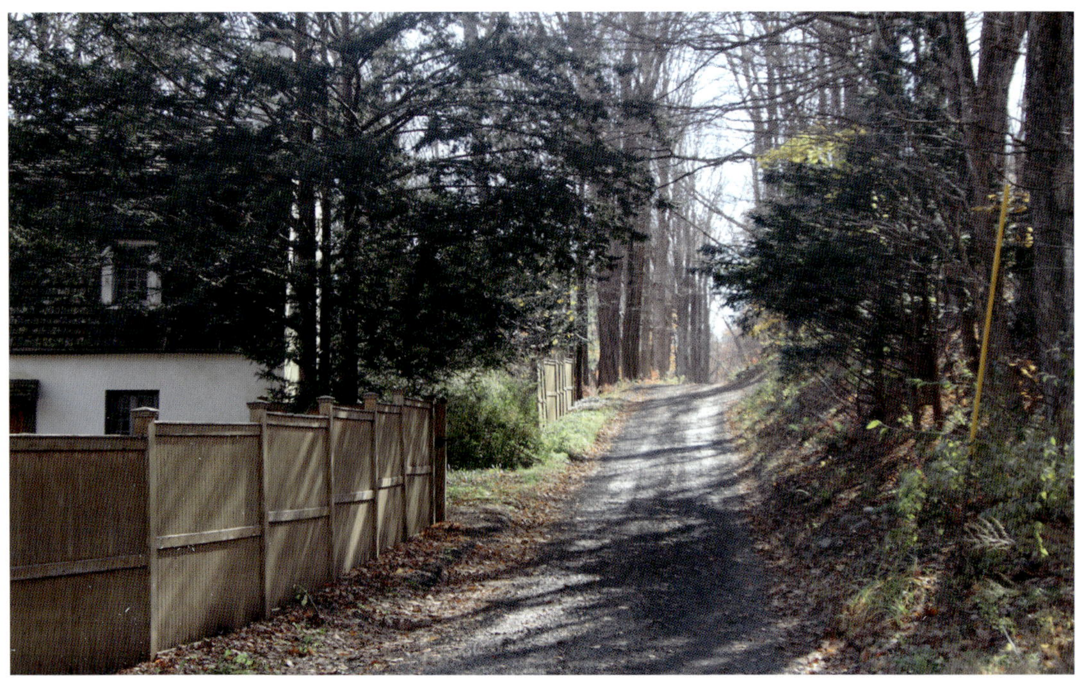

5

Going, Going, Gone

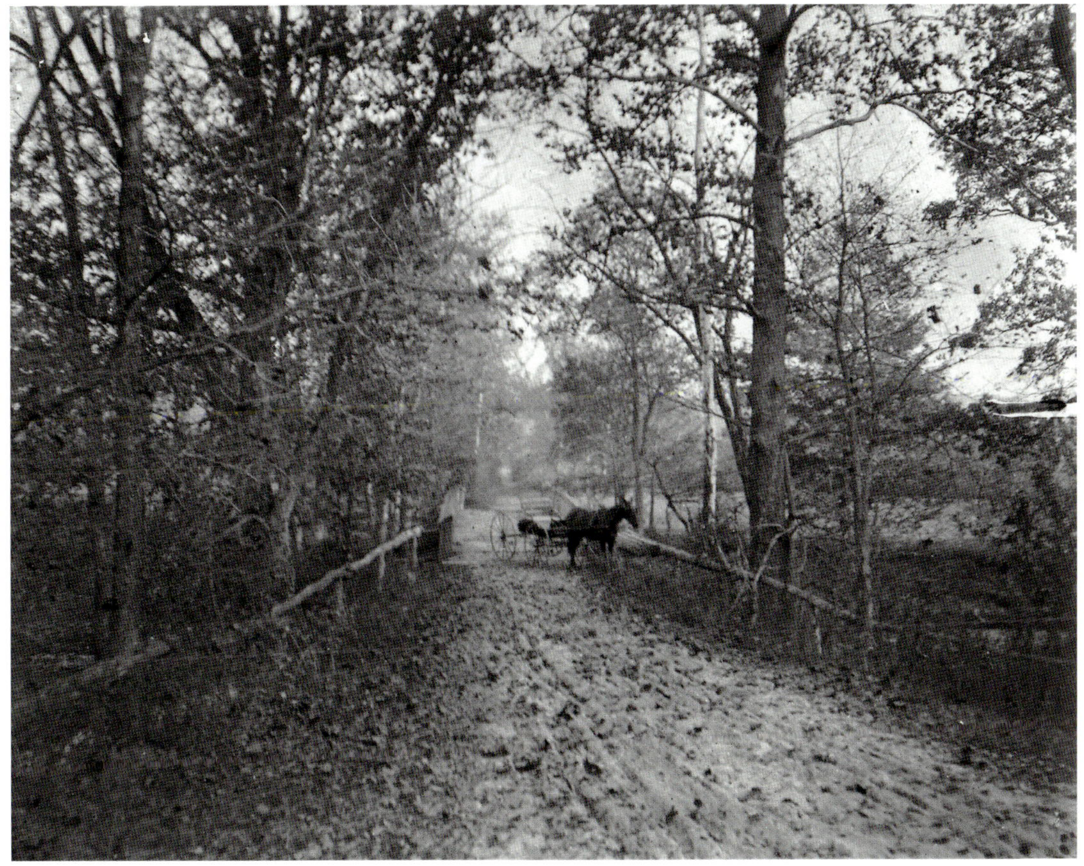

Sometimes the price of progress is the removal of the remnants of our past, but sometimes, they simply fall apart because of age and lack of funds or interest. Here is a group of photographs that depict remnants that have already disappeared or in the process of disappearing.

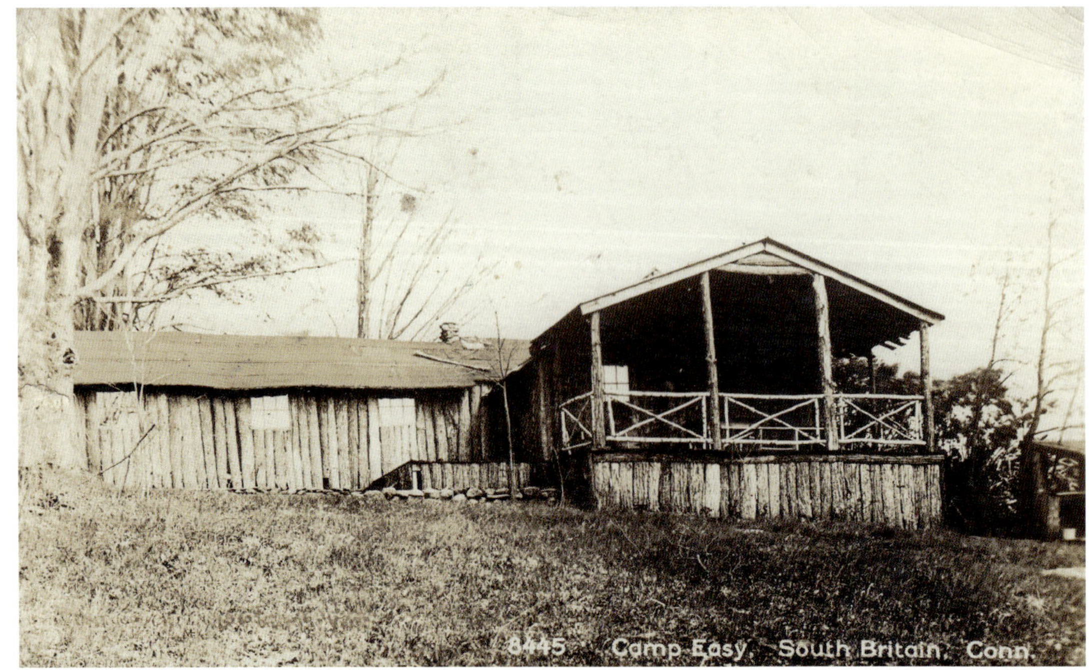

SUMMER CAMPS: After Lake Zoar was created in 1919, several summer communities were started including Riverside, Lakeside, and Cedarland. Some tiny lots were given away to bring people to the area. To keep the children occupied, summer camps popped up in the town. Two popular camps were Camp Easy (above) and Camp Rest-a-While. There was a Boy Scout camp called Camp Pomperaug along the lake.

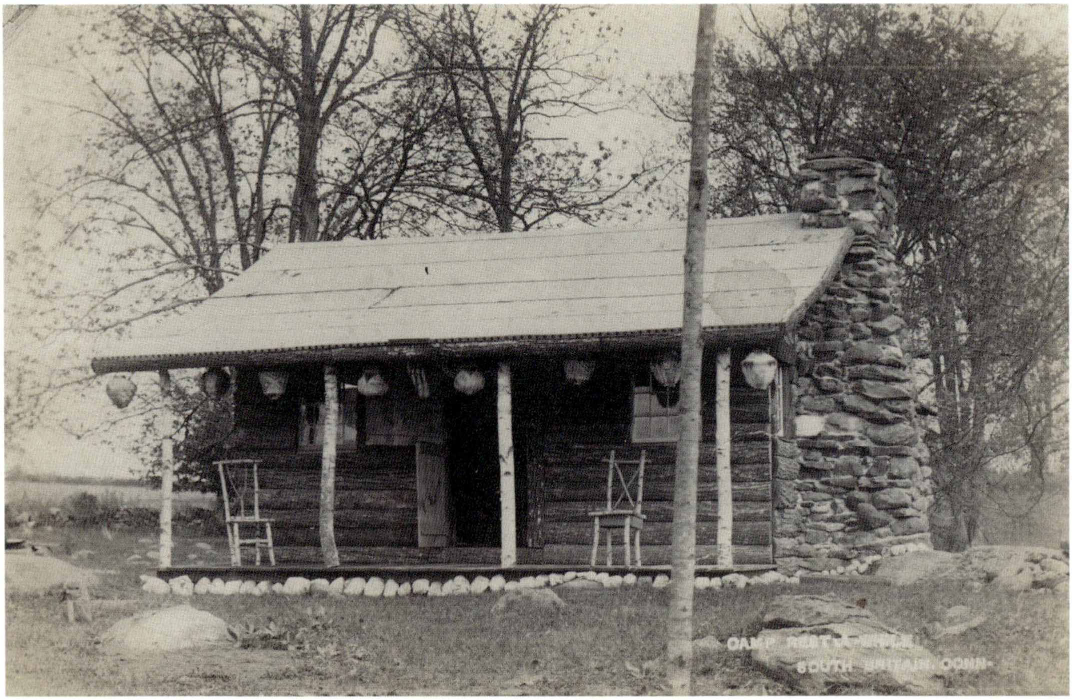

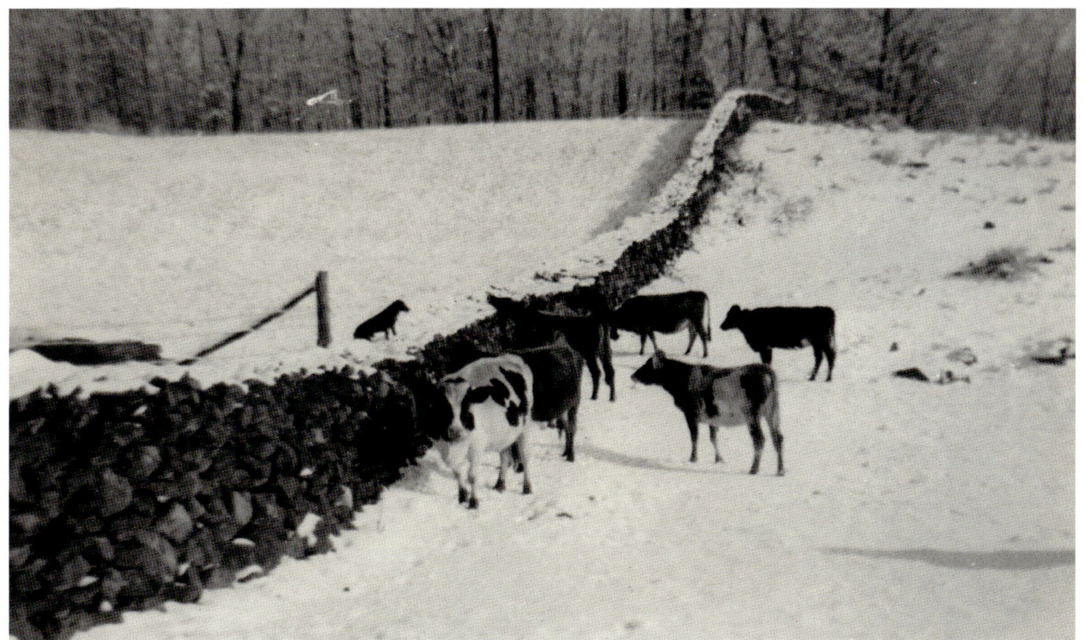

STONE FENCES: The early settlers found out right away that Southbury had a lot of rocks. In order to clear the fields of rocks, ditches were dug up to three feet deep and the stones were piled into it. When the base was stable, additional stones were placed in a taper formation until the required height was reached. The fences were used to keep the farm animals secure, or to protect crops from other animals. The upper photograph was an old picture taken at the Ludorf Farm. The bottom photograph is along the old roadway near the intersection of Heritage Road and Main Street North. (Upper photograph courtesy of Marty Ludorf.)

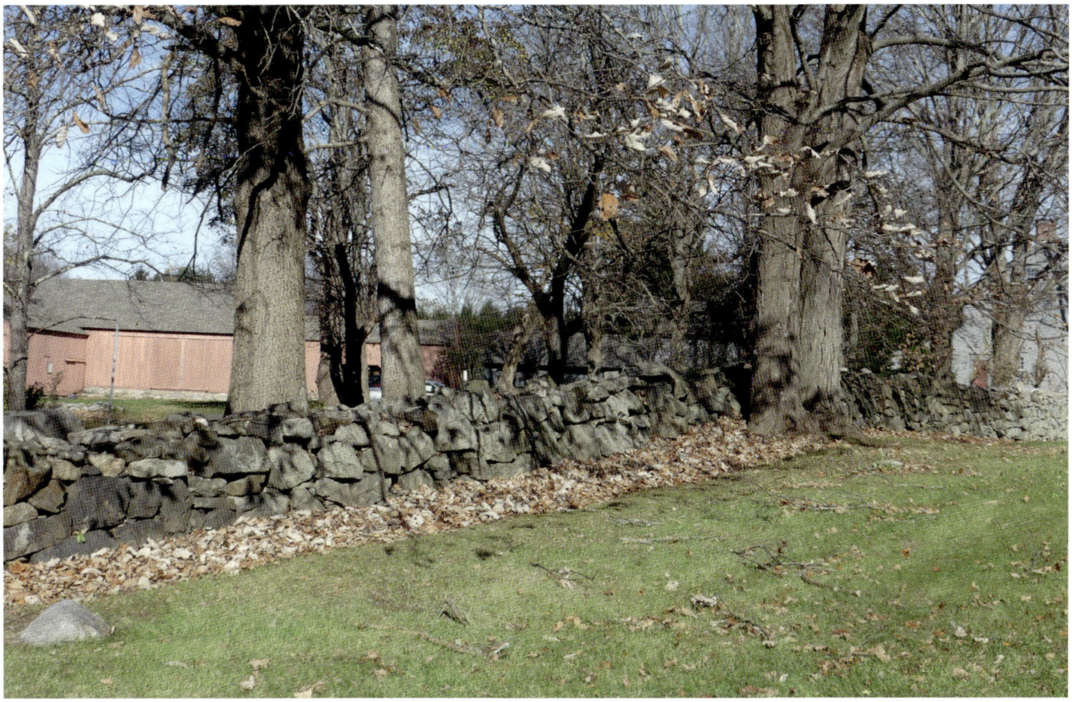

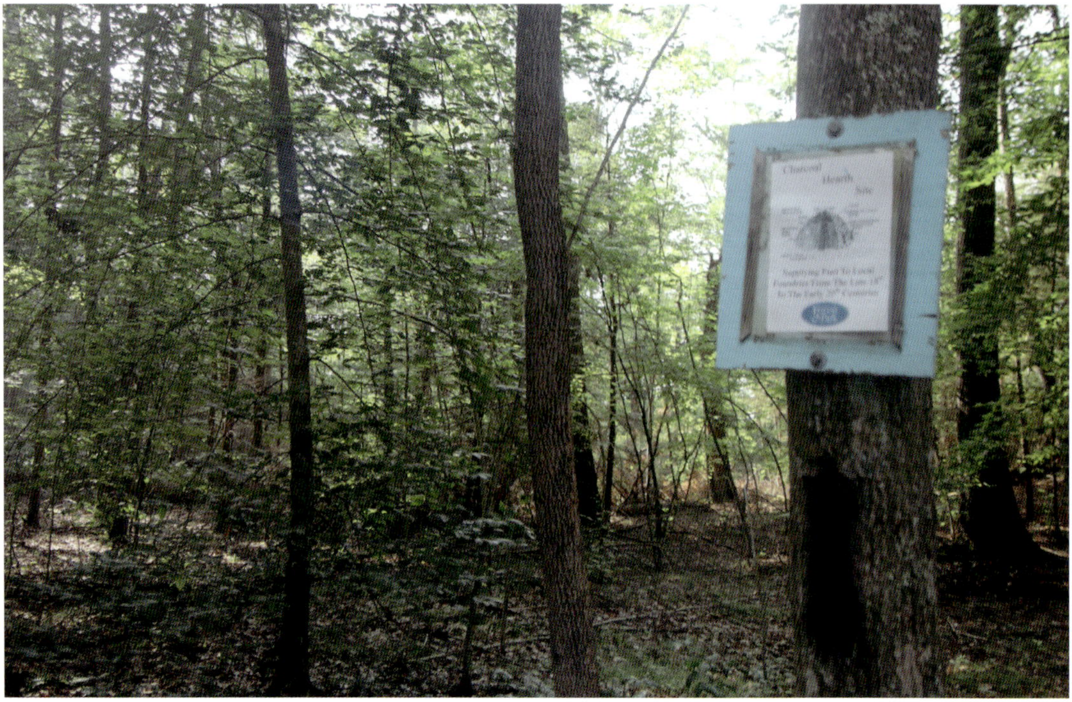

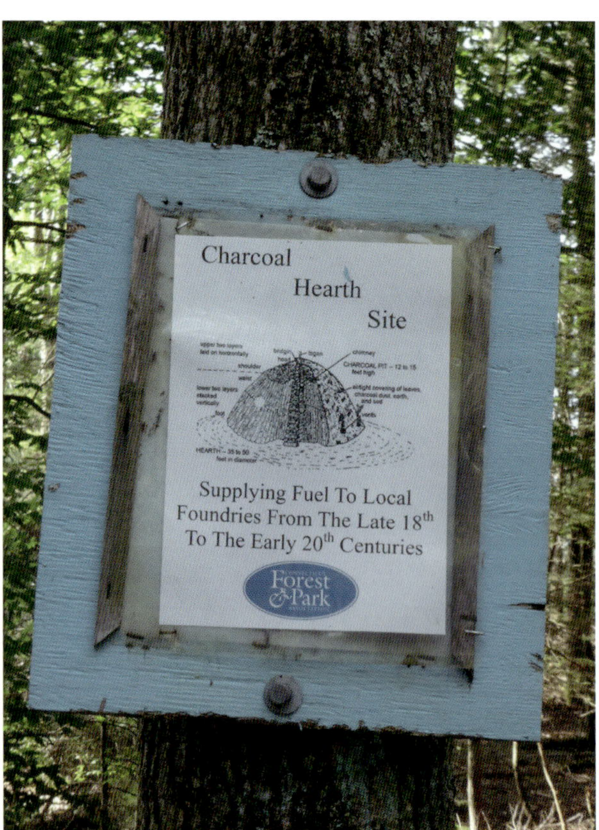

CHARCOAL HEARTH: An important item needed by eighteenth- to early-twentieth-century iron foundries and blacksmith forges was charcoal to burn as fuel. At one point, there were at least twenty charcoal hearths in Southbury, with half a dozen in what is now Kettletown State Park. Charcoal hearths were set up in a large flat area where trees were easily available. The logs were piled into a pyramid shape and covered with soil. A fire burned slowly in the hearth for several days before the charcoal was ready. The Crest Trail in the state park leads to the well-mark Charcoal Hearth Site.

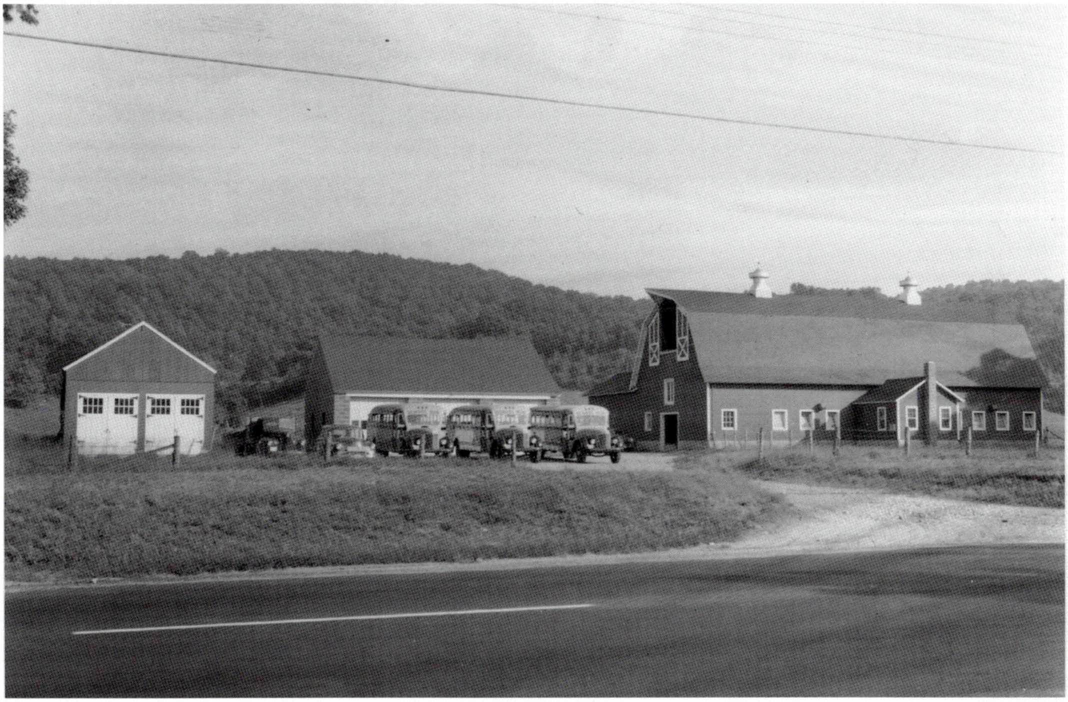

Brinley Farm Pumpkin Patch: The Brinley dairy farm was located on Main Street South not far from the current post office. Mr. Brinley had a fleet of busses for the students of Southbury and the vehicles were parked on the farm. The barn burned down in a spectacular fire, but the building to the far left survived and is still used as a vegetable stand in the summer. Of course, the farm will always be remembered for their pumpkin patch.

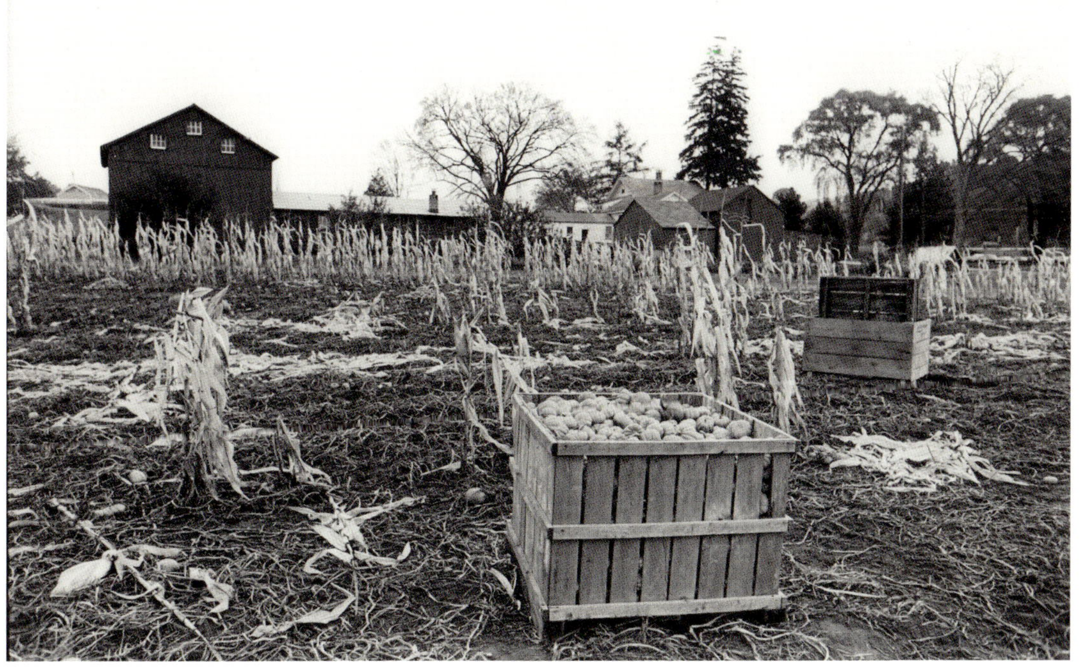

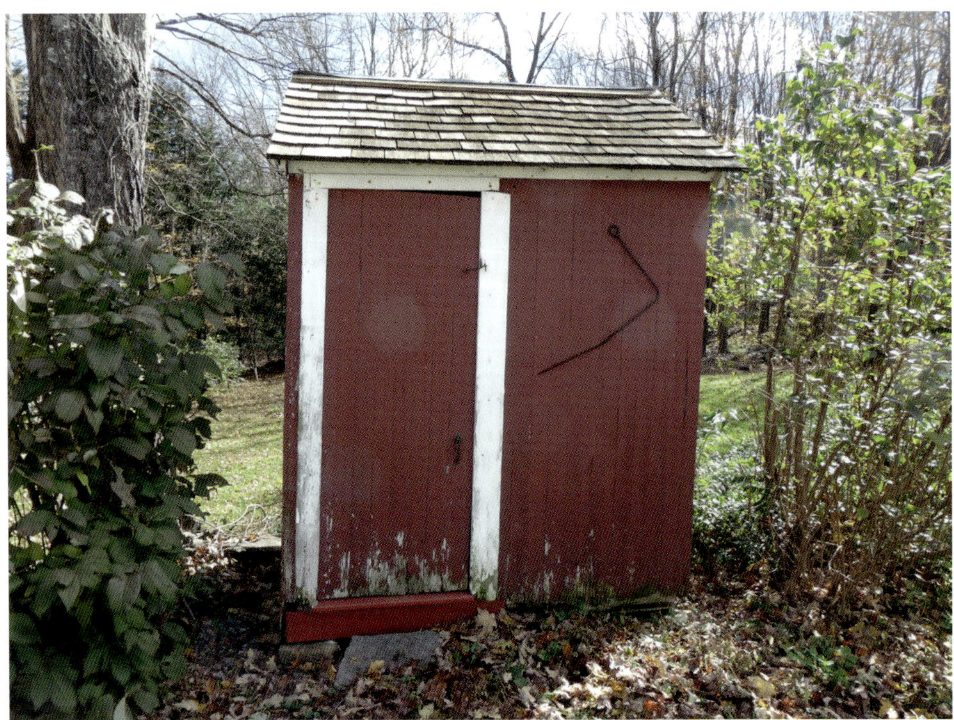

THE GREAT OUTHOUSE ROUNDUP: In the 1920s, many summer cottages were built near Lake Zoar with most land lots smaller than an eighth acre and each had an outhouse. In the 1960s, the health department declared the numerous outhouses a health hazard and picked up most of the buildings for destruction. One record claims that only ten outhouses remained in Southbury in 1970. The above outhouse has stood for generations. The bottom outhouse is at the Bullet Hill School where it has stood since the 1930s.

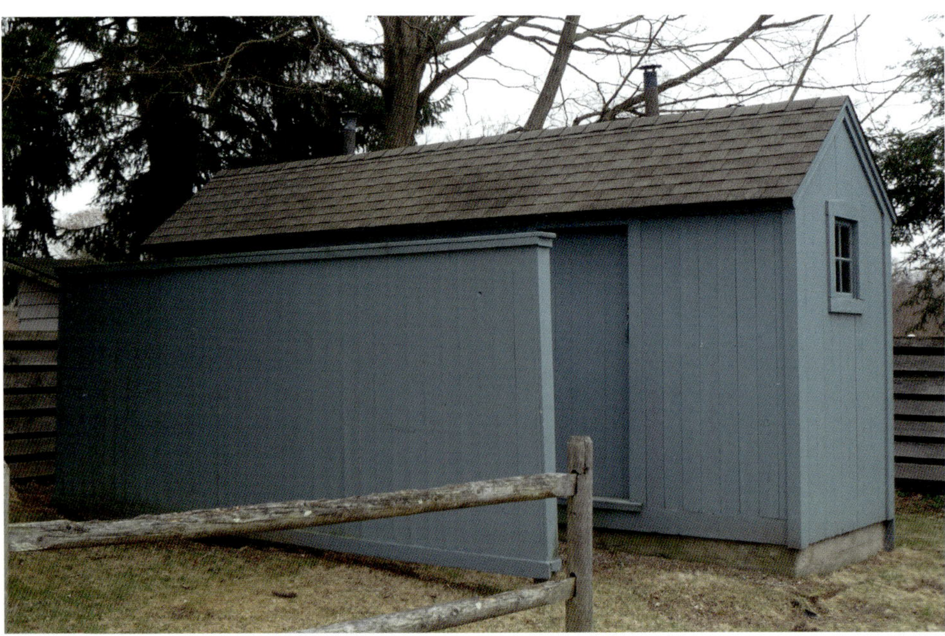

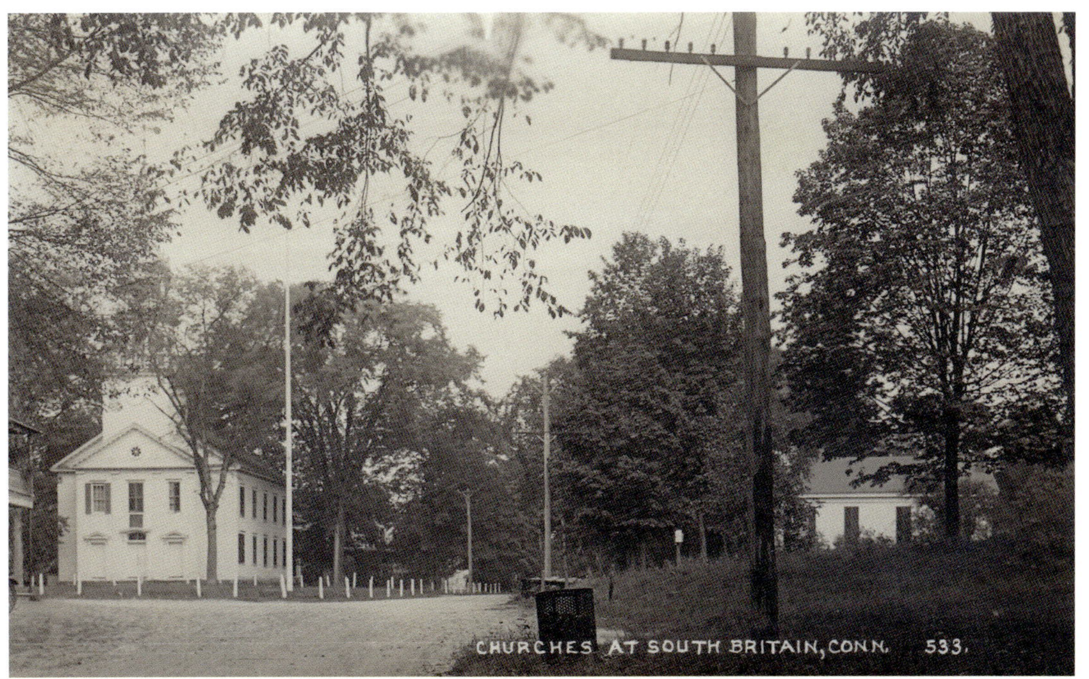

INFORMATION DISTRIBUTION:

The message post was a vital way of distributing information in Colonial Southbury, continuing on through the mid-1900s. Any important announcements were posted, giving warning of town meetings or other local information. The three Southbury message posts were placed near local churches in South Britain, Southbury, and Southford. In the above photo, the message post is the white box on the post near the South Britain Methodist Church. The bottom photo shows the up-rooted message post in front of the Old Town Hall. The inset is the South Britain message post. (WB)

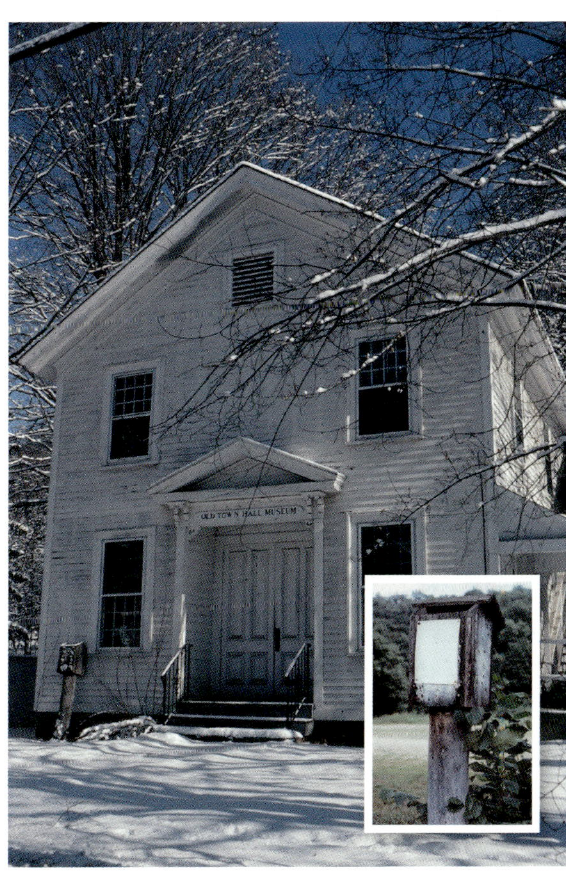

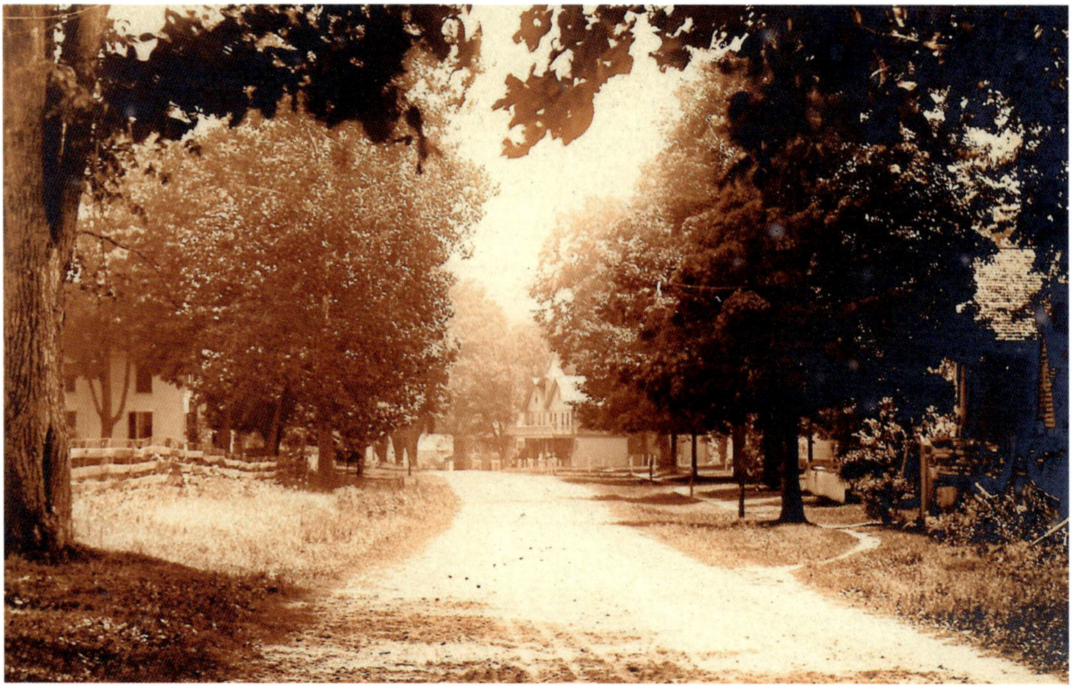

MORE SOUTH BRITAIN VIEWS: The above tree-lined South Britain Road view is taken from the north, looking south toward Mitchell Store. The photograph below is an old view of the northern intersection of Library Road and South Britain Road. The diagonal route forms a triangle piece of land, with the first South Britain post office directly in front, and the Moses Downs House to the left. The triangle piece of land was said to have been the location of the village stocks, used for punishment.

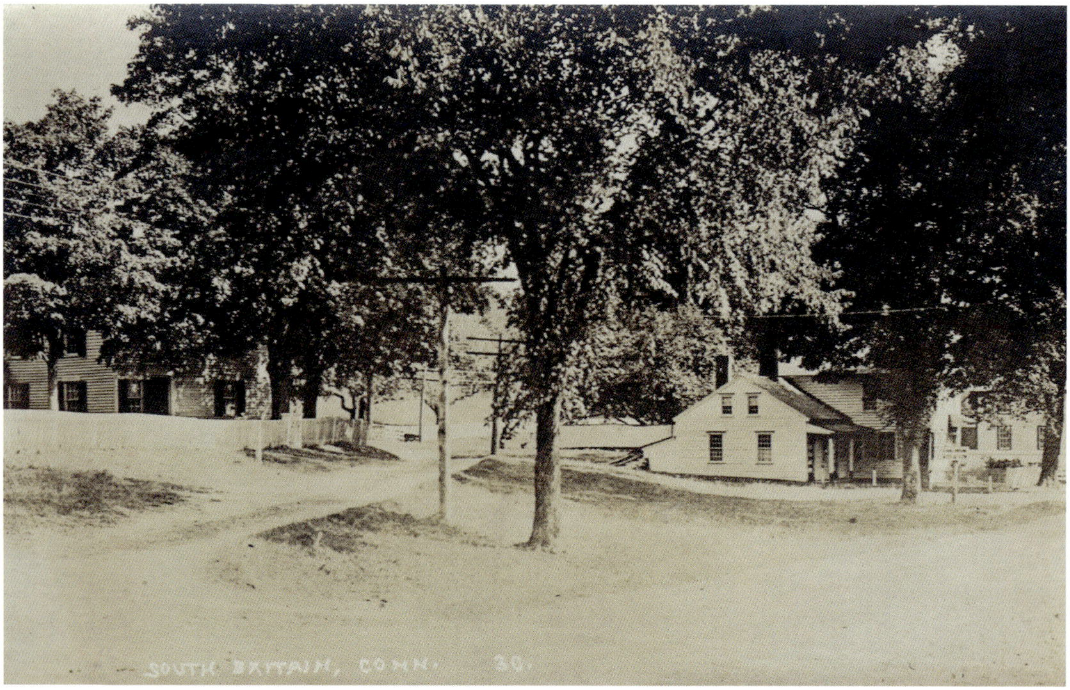

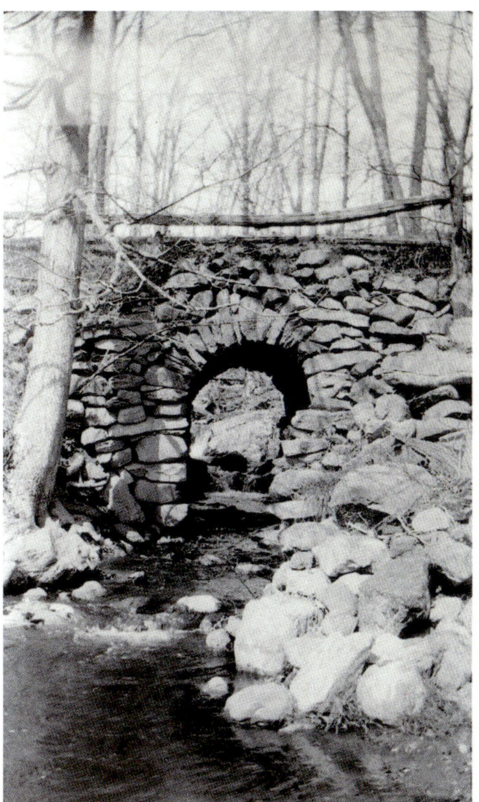

KETTLETOWN ARCH BRIDGE: The stone bridge over a tributary of the Kettletown Brook was once located on Kettletown Road, just south of Burr Road. The Happy Hollow Farm, owned by one-time First Selectman J. Edward Coer, was located next to the bridge. In 1930, each town was allowed state funds to widen and improve their roads, and the beautiful stone bridge was sacrificed during this process in 1940. (EC)

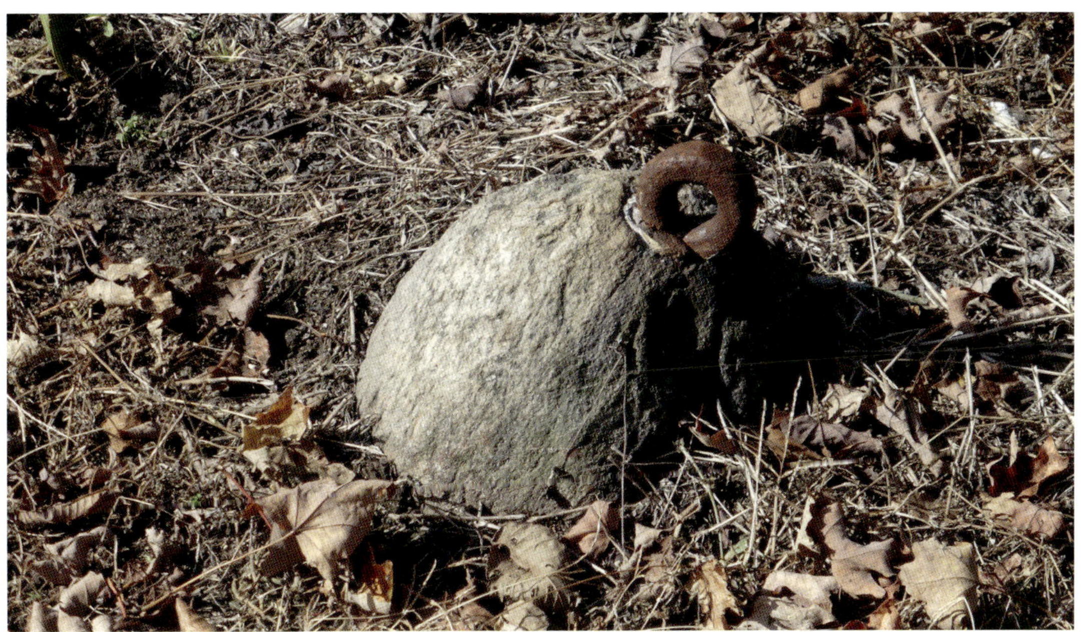

HITCHING RING: The Granite Hitching Ring was saved from road widening by a family who had the foresight to realize that this was a rare artifact in town. An iron ring is attached to a strong granite stone, giving a secure place to leave a horse.

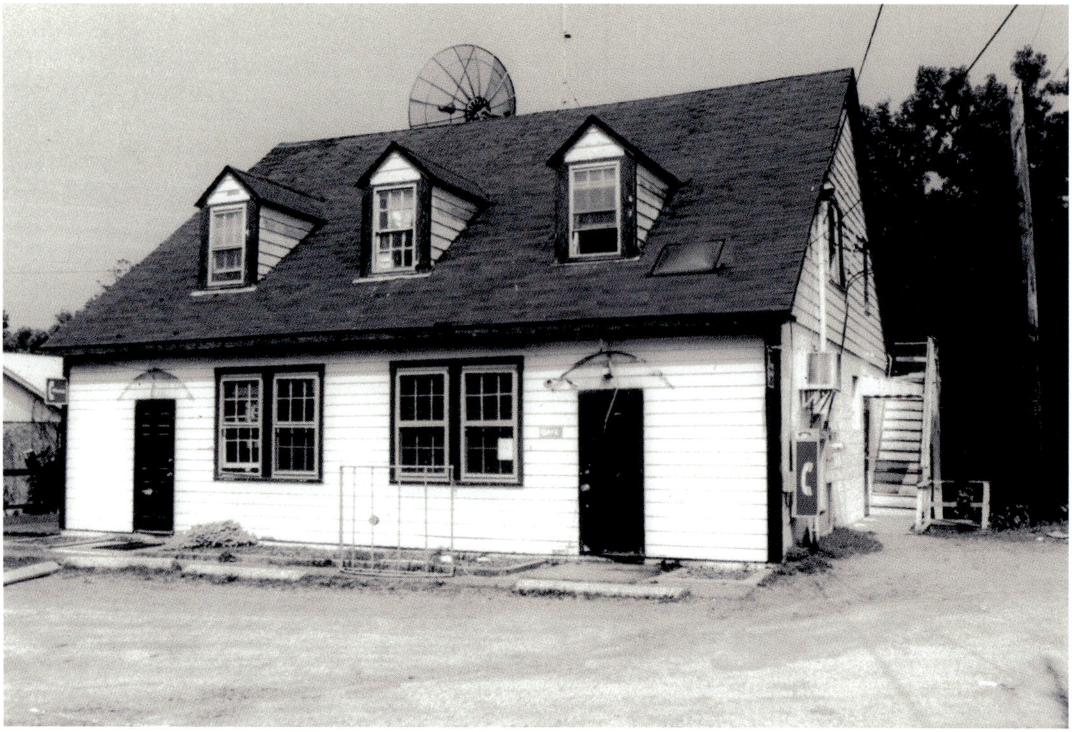

THE INN: The Southbury Inn was a local hangout that once was located on Main Street South. It was well-known for its telephone pole in an awkward position in the parking lot, which was often nudged by cars.

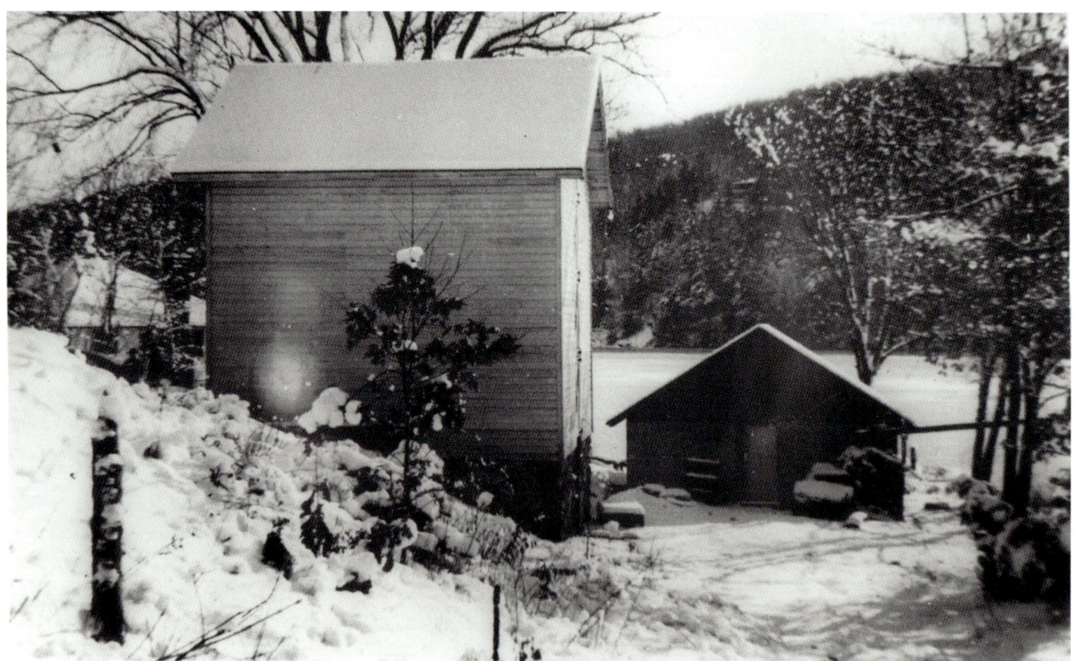

ICE HOUSE: This Ice House was located on Lake Zoar in Lakeside. During the winter, ice was cut from the frozen lake and stored in layers of hay to be delivered to ice boxes at a later date.

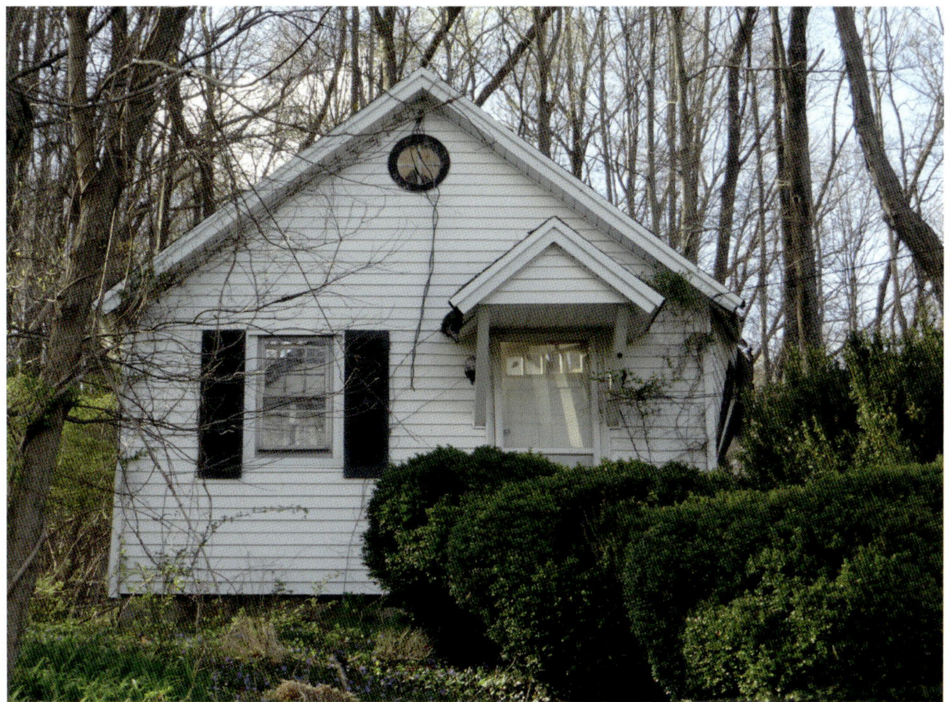

SCHOOLHOUSE GONE: The small Kettletown Schoolhouse sat on a hill overlooking Georges Hill Road for at least 100 years. Even though it was closed in 1939, the building survived much longer as a small house. The building collapsed several years ago in a winter storm.

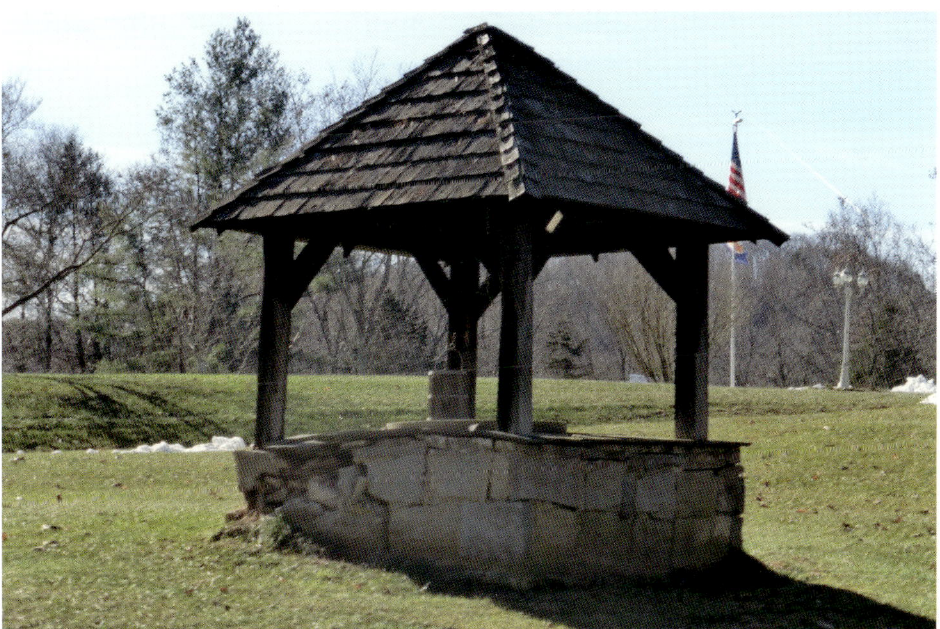

FEW WELLS: The major source of water for homes was from wells that had to be dug by hand. Now all of the old wells have been safely capped and very few well houses are still standing. This one can be found on South Britain Road.

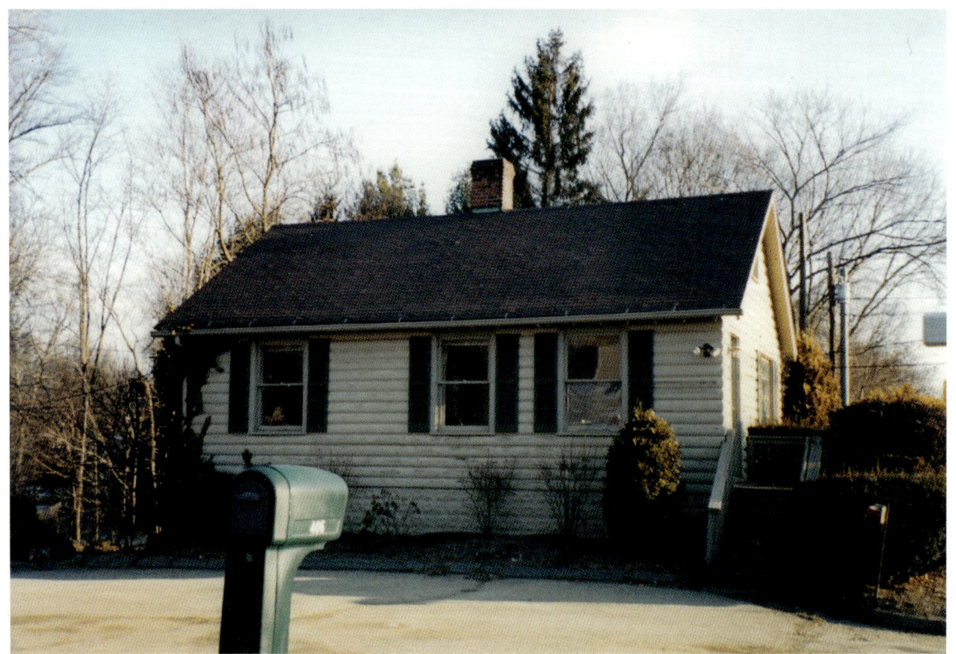

LOG CABIN BUSINESS: This log cabin sat at the corner of Main Street South and Old Field Road for several decades. It was once the sales office for the Cedarland development and later it was the home of the Shur-Moore Studio, a local artisan gift shop. Before the building was torn down, it was a real estate office. There is now a Union Savings Bank on the same location.

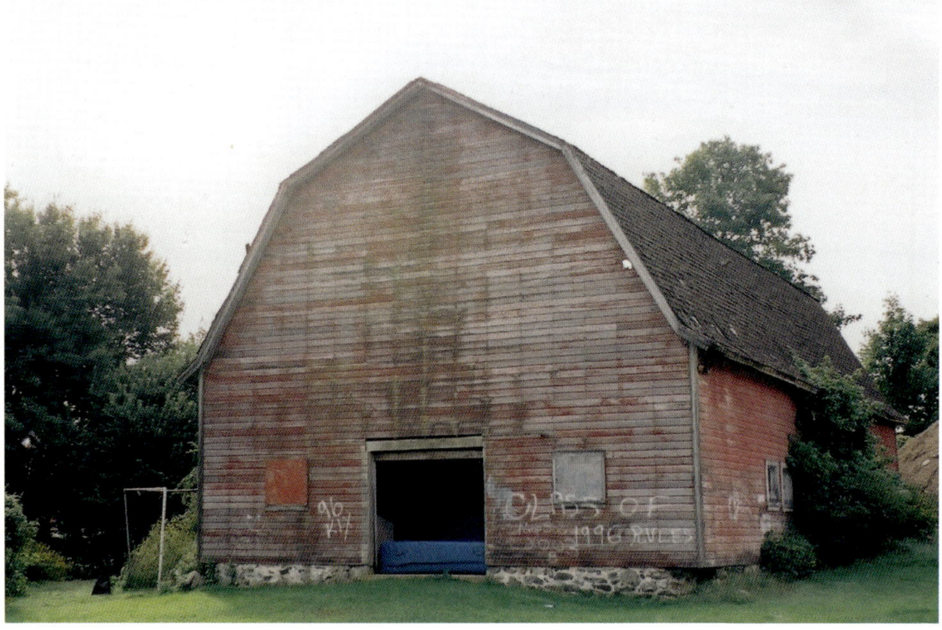

O'NEILL BARN: The barn at the corner of Judd Road and Route 188 was taken down at least ten years ago. It was on the O'Neill family farm, and had a matching Dutch gambrel architecture with the house. The Pomperaug students would paint their graduation year on the side of the barn.

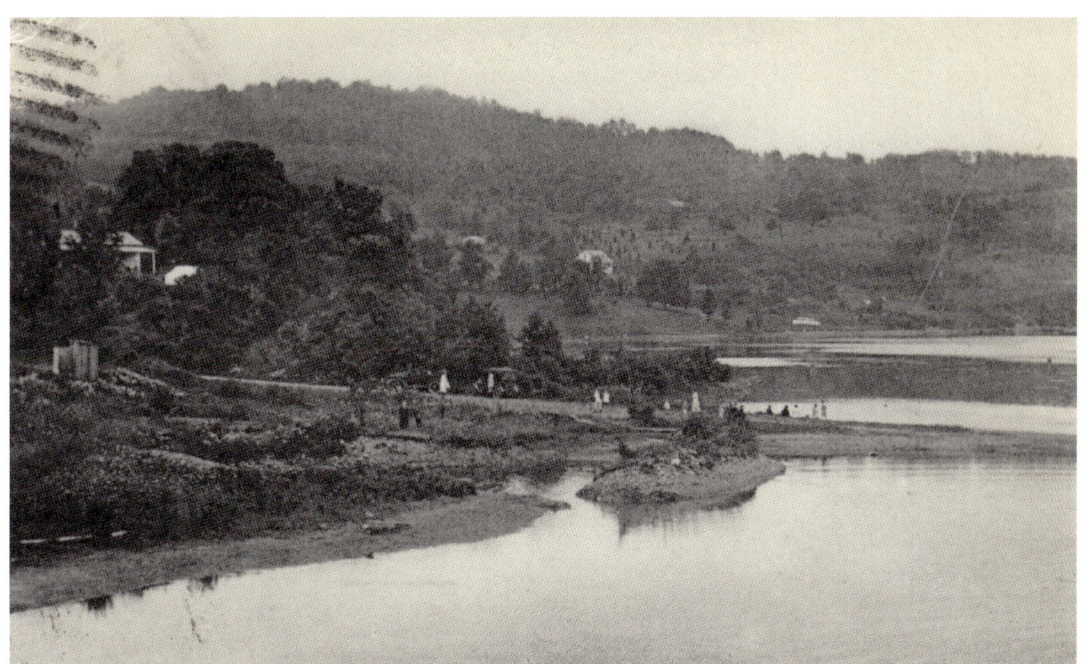

SIGHTSEEING: Before Stevenson Dam was completed in 1919, Bennett's Bridge was removed and the Housatonic River was scheduled to flood this area to become Lake Zoar. Before the deep waters arrived, the river was a curiosity that brought people from all around to view the changes.

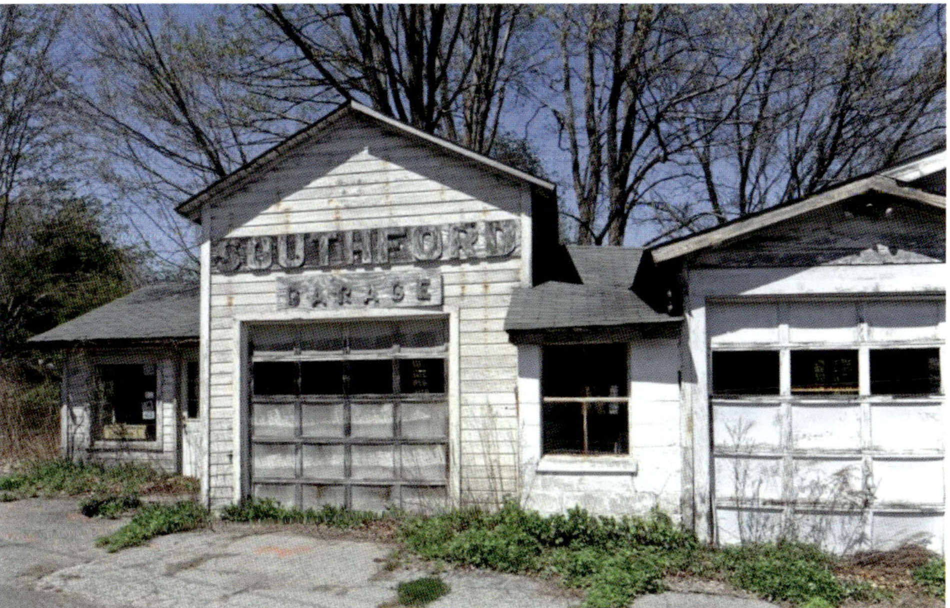

SOUTHFORD GARAGE: Until recently, this building was located in the heart of Southford north of Routes 188 and 67. The old Southford Garage was built by the McBaths in the 1930s as a gas station and garage. Later, the Baldwin family purchased the property, which included the Southford Chapel. The garage was once known as Mel's Garage, operated by Mel Tomlinson, who also sold used cars. It was recently torn down to make way for a new, modern gas station.

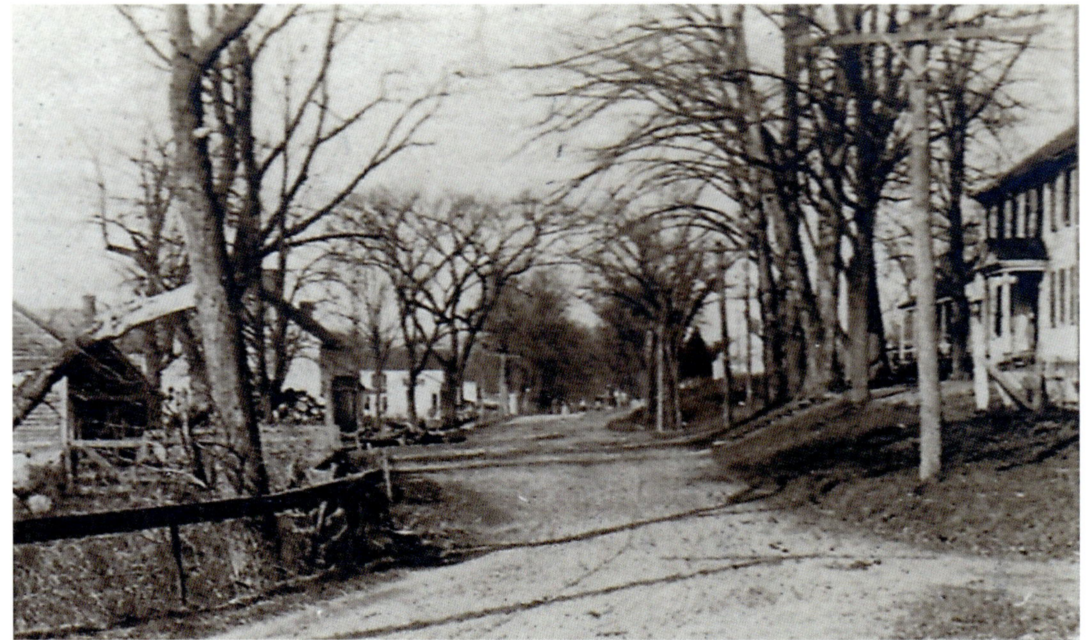

ROAD VIEW: The road view is in South Britain, taken near the Pomperaug River bridge and looking north. The old house on the right is still standing. According to a WPA survey, the house was likely built in 1780.

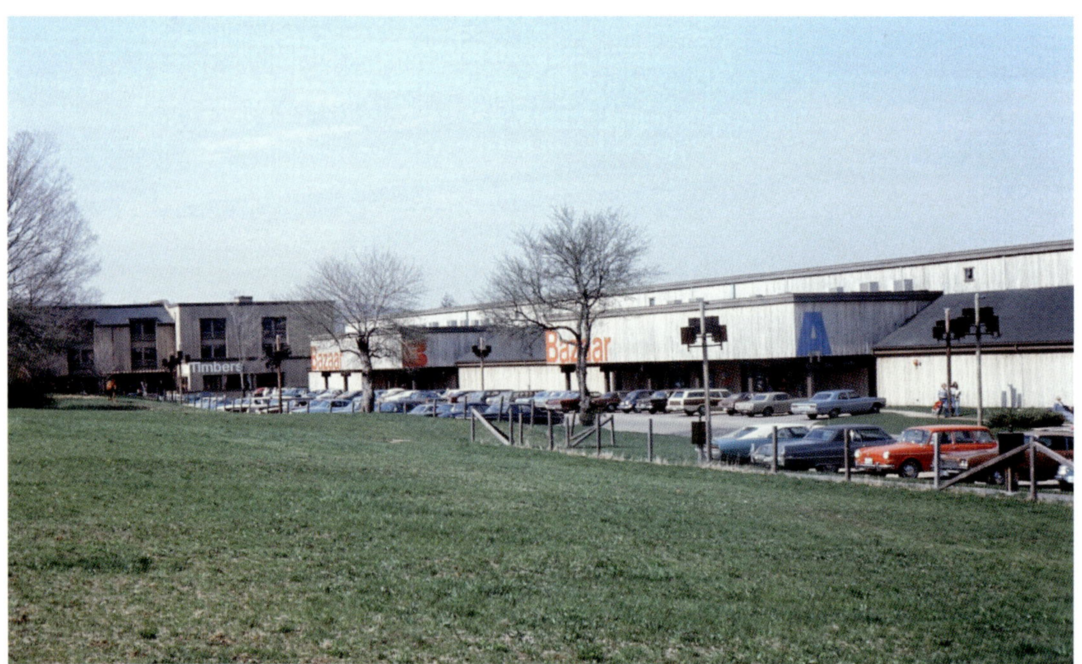

BAZAAR: Shortly after the condos of Heritage Village were built in 1967, a shopping plaza opened near the green. The Bazaar's interior was an open floor plan, multi-level shopping experience made of pine. Each shop blended into the next shop or restaurant. The nooks and crannies in the building were fun to explore, along with visiting the shops. It was torn down to make room for new condos.

Population of Southbury Through Time

Year	Population	Year	Population
1790	1,738	1910	1,233
1800	1,757	1920	1,093
1810	1,413	1930	1,134
1820	1,662	1940	1,532
1830	1,557	1950	3,828
1840	1,542	1960	5,186
1850	1,484	1970	7,852
1860	1,346	1980	14,156
1870	1,318	1990	15,818
1880	1,740	2000	18,567
1890	1,080	2010	19,904
1900	1,238		

Southbury Timeline

1673 Settlers from Stratford spend the night at white oak tree on their way to Pomperaug Plantation.

1674 Pomperaug Plantation officially becomes Woodbury.

1675 King Philip's War. Settlers return to Stratford for a short time for safety.

1690 Benjamin Stiles builds a barn.

1704 Stone house built as a fortification.

1708 White Oak Cemetery established.

1731 Southbury becomes the Second Ecclesiastical Society of Ancient Woodbury.

1733 First Meeting House built in Southbury in White Oak section.

1750 Pierce Hollow Burial Grounds open in South Britain.

1759 Pootatucks sold their land and moved away with other tribes.

1766 South Britain becomes its own Ecclesiastical Society.

1768 Replacement Meeting House constructed at Main Street and Old Field Hill Road.

1770 First South Britain church was built.

1775 Southbury provided supplies and men for Revolutionary War.

1778 Shadrach Osbourne hides pork barrels after Danbury raid.

1781 General Count de Rochambeau marches his troops through Southbury.

1787 Southbury Incorporated as a town.

1789 Bullet Hill School.

1790 Methodist meetings begin with circuit pastor.

1795 Oxford Turnpike began; basically following Route 67.

1796 School societies and districts organized.

1800 Charcoal Hearths above Housatonic River.

1803 Methodist Church meets in an old school house on Georges Hill.

1806 Oatman House in Southford built as hotel.

1808 Historic white oak tree falls in storm.

1812 Judson Manville builds a hat factory in South Britain.

1820 First mills on Bullet Hill Brook at Community House area.

1825 South Britain Congregational Church built; still standing.

1830 Union Church in Southford constructed.

1832 South Britain Methodist Church built.

1840 White Oak Schoolhouse erected.

1843 Episcopal Church organized in Bullet Hill School.

1844 Third Meeting House built; now known as the United Church of Christ.

1847 Methodist Church built in Southbury.

1849 Large mills established at Southford Falls.

1851 Bradley Mill in South Britain.

1863 Resident Henry Monroe appointed U.S. Counsel to Greece by President Lincoln.

1867 Church of Epiphany was built.

1873 Town Hall built in South Britain.

1876 First telephone in town.

1881 Railroad service begins.

1882 Southford Lodge attracts train passengers.

1884 Sacred Heart church is built in White Oak.

1885 Oil well drilled by Southbury Company in area now Heritage Village.

1901 Diamond Match factory.

1902 Constitutional Convention pin oak seedling planted.

1904 First Public Library Building in South Britain.

1906 Wallace Nutting makes hand-colored photographs.

1919 Stevenson Dam completed, forming Lake Zoar.

1920 Summer communities boom.

1923 Southbury Federated Church.

1926 C. L. Adams stops grinding grains.

1937 German American Bund comes to Southbury.

1938 Railroad picks up tracks between Southbury and Waterbury.

1940 Opening of Southbury Training School.

1942 Consolidated school begins on January 5, 1942.

1948 Railroad service stopped.

1955 Shepaug Dam finished.

1955 Devastating flood.

1955 Methodist Church building attached to United Church of Christ.

1963 Interstate 84 is opened from Housatonic River to Waterbury.

1964 New Town Hall opened; now the Police Station.

1967 Heritage Village opens.

1973 Tercentennial Celebration.

1979 Opening of Southbury Plaza.

1988 IBM arrives in town.

1997 Southbury Green replaces pumpkin patch.

2017 Riverview Cinema opens in time for Christmas.

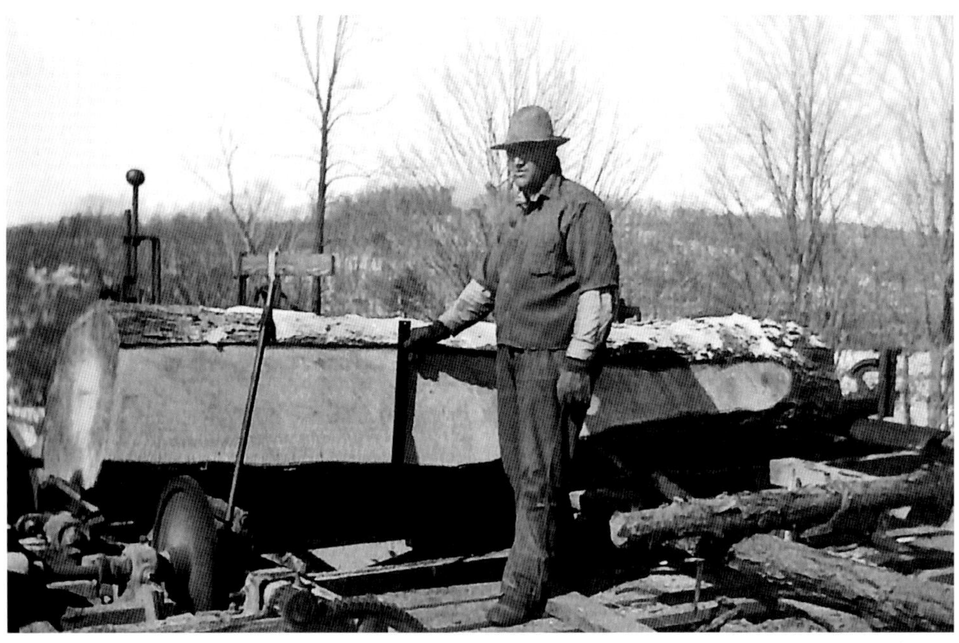

Saw mill at Happy Hollow Farm. (EC)

Index

Old Town Hall Museum Resources Mentioned in the Book

Constitutional Oak Marker
Constitutional Oak Slice
George Grebentschikoff's typewriter
Gladys Taber Books
Hand-drawn Russian Village Map
Hawkins Traps
Historical & Architectural Survey of Southbury
Ludorf Barn Lithograph
Mitchell & Williams Store Sign
Native Arrowheads
Old Photographs
Peter Parley Books
Petrified Wood log
Primary Source Documents
Railroad Lantern
Red Sandstone (foundation)
Remnant of the White Oak Tree, saved by Shadrach Osborn in 1808
Russian Books
Southbury Playhouse Playbills and show photographs
Traps from the Hawkins Factory
Victorian Privy
Wakelee Plow
World War II Civil Air Patrol Map with Wardens

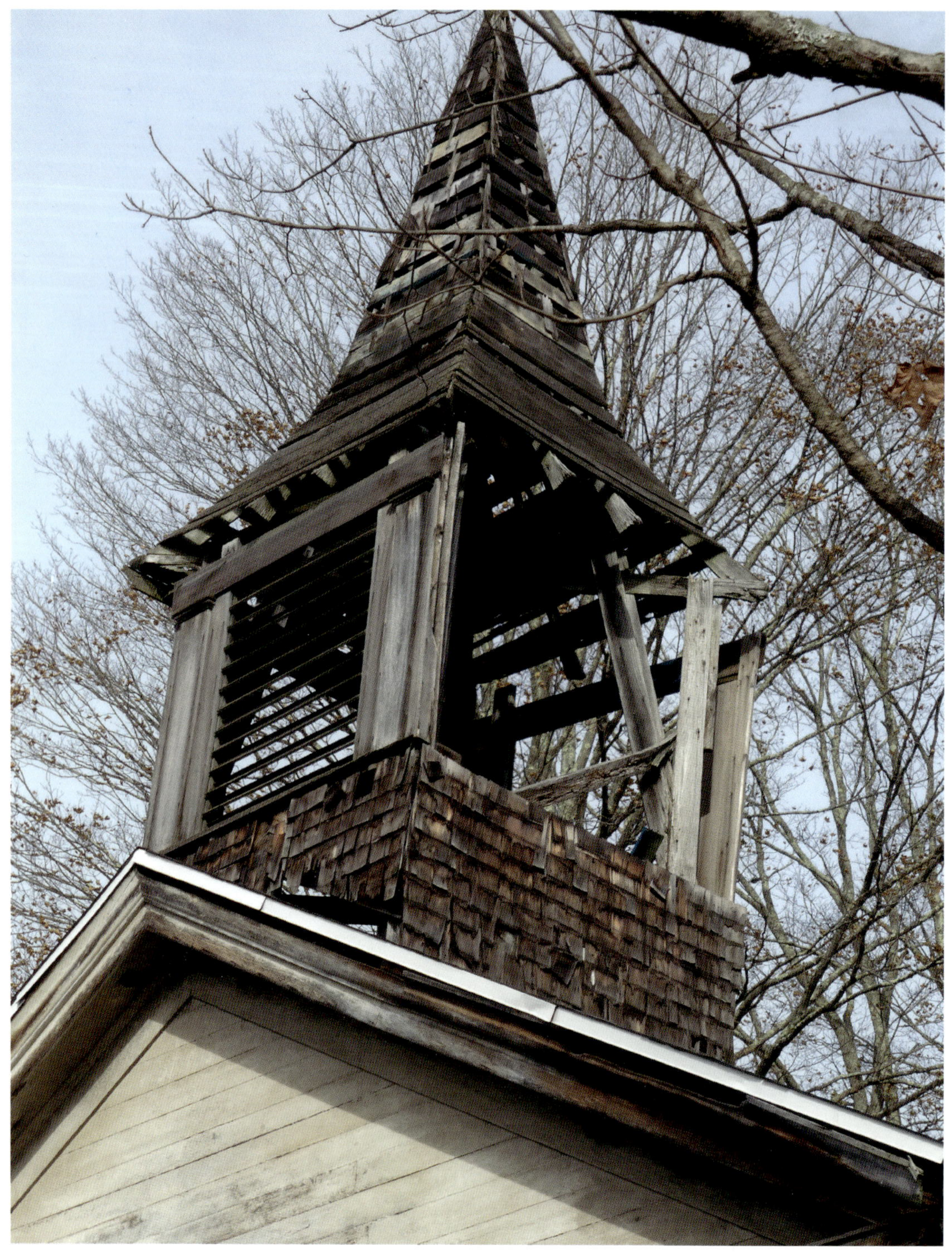

Although it is impossible to save every remnant of our past physically, we can keep detailed records and photographs, so our past will never be forgotten.